OWNERSHIP

OWNERSHIP
Reinventing Companies, Capitalism, and Who Owns What

Corey Rosen and John Case

Berrett–Koehler Publishers, Inc.

Berrett-Koehler Publishers, Inc.
1333 Broadway, Suite 1000
Oakland, CA 94612-1921
Tel: (510) 817-2277
Fax: (510) 817-2278
www.bkconnection.com

ORDERING INFORMATION

Quantity sales. Special discounts are available on quantity purchases by corporations, associations, and others. For details, contact the "Special Sales Department" at the Berrett-Koehler address above.

Individual sales. Berrett-Koehler publications are available through most bookstores. They can also be ordered directly from Berrett-Koehler: Tel: (800) 929-2929; Fax: (802) 864-7626; www.bkconnection.com.

Orders for college textbook / course adoption use. Please contact Berrett-Koehler: Tel: (800) 929-2929; Fax: (802) 864-7626.

Distributed to the U.S. trade and internationally by Penguin Random House Publisher Services.

Berrett-Koehler and the BK logo are registered trademarks of Berrett-Koehler Publishers, Inc.

Printed in the United States of America

Berrett-Koehler books are printed on long-lasting acid-free paper. When it is available, we choose paper that has been manufactured by environmentally responsible processes. These may include using trees grown in sustainable forests, incorporating recycled paper, minimizing chlorine in bleaching, or recycling the energy produced at the paper mill.

Library of Congress Cataloging-in-Publication Data
Names: Rosen, Corey M., author. | Case, John, 1944- author.
Title: Ownership : reinventing companies, capitalism, and who owns what / Corey Rosen and John Case.
Description: First Edition. | Oakland, CA : Berrett-Koehler Publishers, [2022] | Includes bibliographical references and index.
Identifiers: LCCN 2022006157 (print) | LCCN 2022006158 (ebook) | ISBN 9781523000821 (paperback) | ISBN 9781523000838 (pdf) | ISBN 9781523000845 (epub) | ISBN 9781523000852
Subjects: LCSH: Employee ownership—Case studies. | Management—Employee Participation—Case studies. | Capitalism—Case studies.
Classification: LCC HD5650 .R7347 2022 (print) | LCC HD5650 (ebook) | DDC 658.3/152—dc23/eng/20220520
LC record available at https://lccn.loc.gov/2022006157
LC ebook record available at https://lccn.loc.gov/2022006158

First Edition
28 27 26 25 24 23 22   10 9 8 7 6 5 4 3 2 1

Book producer and text designer : Happenstance Type-O-Rama
Cover designer: Alvaro Villanueva
Photo of John Case by Ross Harris

This book is dedicated to the millions of employee owners in the United States and worldwide. Their stories and their accomplishments have taught us, inspired us, and sustained us in our decades of work to help create an economy that is both more equitable and more productive.

CONTENTS

Preface ix

Introduction: Ownership Matters 1

PART I: What's Wrong with What We Have?
1. The Ownership Crazy Quilt 13
2. Wall Street: Faceless Ownership 23
3. Private Equity: Concentrated Ownership 39

PART II: How Can We Change Things?
4. The Limits of (Conventional) Reform 55
5. Ownership in Today's Economy 67

PART III: Reinventing Capitalism for the 21st Century
6. A Different Kind of Company 79
7. Why Isn't There More Employee Ownership? 95
8. Opportunity #1: Employee Ownership on Wall Street 111
9. Opportunity #2: Private Equity and Impact Investing 125
10. Opportunity #3: Trusts, Co-ops, and the Gig Economy 139
11. Opportunity #4: Policies and Programs for Spreading
    Employee Ownership 157
12. Tomorrow the World 169

Conclusion: How You Can Make a Difference 189

Afterword by Michael Quarrey, Web Industries 199
Discussion Guide 203
Notes 207
Acknowledgments 225
Index 229
About the Authors 239

PREFACE

What ails the American economy? Why does it leave so many people behind, living paycheck to uncertain paycheck, while so many others grow rich? For that matter, what ails the world's other capitalist economies, which suffer from a similar malady?

There's no shortage of diagnoses and prescriptions. Liberals and conservatives argue endlessly about minimum wages, about tax rates and entitlement programs, about business regulations and labor unions.

But one element has repeatedly and inexplicably been left out of the discussion: who owns the companies that drive our economy. It's a frustrating omission, because ownership is what gives people a claim on the fruits of free enterprise. Broaden ownership and you automatically broaden people's abilities to build wealth and plan for a secure future.

So this book aims to put ownership squarely on the agendas of the United States and every other country that is struggling with the inequities of free enterprise. It demonstrates the limitations and flaws—indeed, the absurdities—of our current structures of ownership. It describes a powerful alternative, employee ownership, *that is already in place*, and that has demonstrated its worth in the marketplace. For reasons that we'll explore, employee ownership is not nearly as common as it could be or should be. So we'll also show how the employee-owned sector can be greatly expanded, thereby extending the benefits of ownership and wealth-building to millions of wage earners.

Our goal in writing this book isn't to abolish capitalism. Capitalism has been a remarkable engine for growth and innovation. The goal is to extend ownership, to help create a capitalist economy that works for the many rather than just for the few. You might say that the goal is to create more capitalists, people who have a greater stake in the system and more money in the bank than they do now. We think that's an objective that Americans—and other countries' citizens as well—can agree on regardless of their political leanings. In fact, most already do: multiple polls show that Americans overwhelmingly like the idea of employee ownership.[1] As with the public, so with politicians. Employee ownership has had almost unanimous support from both parties in Congress since the 1970s.

Extending ownership to employees has another virtue as well. It makes for a more effective economy. Decades' worth of research shows that employee-owned companies outperform their conventionally owned counterparts. They improve a country's productivity and international competitiveness. That, too, is an outcome that few would object to.

Who should read this book? If you're a political leader, a professor, or an activist looking for fresh ideas, you need it. If you're a business owner or investor, we think it will open your eyes to an alternative future. And if you're a citizen who worries about the health of your country's economy and the economic security of your friends and neighbors, well, we have written the book most of all for you. It's an easy read. It requires no special expertise. It tells stories that will, we hope, spawn both outrage about the current system and hope for the future.

The United States can build a better, fairer economy than it has yet done. So can other countries. The key is ownership. Let's put it on the table.

INTRODUCTION
Ownership Matters

*People who own property feel a sense of ownership
in their future and their society. They study, save,
work, strive and vote.*

—HENRY LOUIS GATES
Professor, Harvard University

*I am a single mother of two beautiful girls, and being
an owner at Recology has given me the tools I need to
make them successful in life.*

—AYANNA BANKS
Sorter, Recology (a 100 percent employee-owned company)

This book rests on a simple premise: ownership matters. It makes a big difference who owns a nation's businesses, both to families and to the whole economy.

Think about it. If you own even a modest stock portfolio, or if you have a stake in a profitable business, your life changes. You may have a second source of income to supplement your family's earnings. You'll almost certainly have a nest egg you can draw on to meet an emergency or (eventually) to help finance a comfortable retirement. Meanwhile, many of your wage-earning fellow citizens don't have these advantages. They live from one paycheck to the next, often struggling to make ends meet and worrying about the security of their job. A Federal Reserve study a few years ago found that nearly half of Americans couldn't come up with $400 to meet an unexpected bill. About half of all employees approaching retirement have no assets in a retirement plan.[1]

Ownership is also a prime path to real wealth. Owners profit enormously from a successful business, while most of that business's employees get nothing but their wage or salary. Imagine a prosperous midsized company—a restaurant chain, say, or a construction company with $200 million in annual revenue and $10 million to $20 million in net profit. If it is owned by one person or a small group, as is often the case, these owners may pay themselves hundreds of thousands of dollars every year in salary and dividends, and they own an asset that is worth tens of millions. For their employees it's a different story. According to US government figures, the average annual wage of restaurant workers is less than $30,000. The average for construction workers varies considerably by trade and region, but it's typically between $40,000 and $55,000.[2] Today, less than 60 percent of Americans' overall income comes from working. The rest comes from owning capital.[3]

These disparities might not matter much if ownership were widely distributed. It isn't. In 2021, the Federal Reserve reported that 89 percent of stocks held by households were owned by the richest tenth of the US population, and just 11 percent by everyone else (Figure 1).

FIGURE 1: Ownership Inequality in America

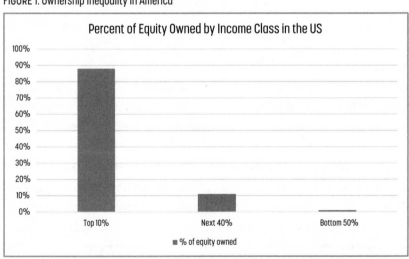

Source: Authors, from Federal Reserve data

THE same group owned 85 percent of the wealth held in private businesses.[4] There's a racial gap, too: families of color are less likely to own stocks than white families.[5] Nearly half of American households own no stock at all.

The gap between owners and wage earners has widened enormously in recent decades. Between 1979 and 2018, the typical worker's wages grew about 0.27 percent a year after correcting for inflation.[6] Real returns on stock ownership grew about 8 percent per year, or nearly 30 times as much.[7] So people who depend on working for a living have seen their incomes stagnate, while people with significant ownership income have done very well indeed. Of course, any reputable economist will point out that comparing wages—a stream of income—with the returns to ownership is comparing apples and pomegranates: though they may look similar, they're conceptually different. But we're making a simple point here, which is that both wage levels and asset ownership affect people's economic security and view of the future. By those measures, owners have fared much better than wage earners.

Ownership matters in another way as well. It sets the constraints and incentives that affect how businesses operate.

Many Americans grow up with a benign view of business ownership. The owners of local companies in this view are community residents, neighbors. They expect to own their businesses for many years. They value good relations with their employees, their customers, their suppliers, and the communities where they operate. They are accountable for what their companies do.

And indeed, plenty of companies operate in just this way.

But larger companies, those with hundreds or thousands of employees, often have a different kind of ownership. They're owned by stock-market investors, by other corporations, or by financial firms. These owners aren't on site. They typically care little about their companies' employees or communities or any other stakeholders. What they do care about, very much, is the companies' share price or financial performance. If the financial results don't come up to expectations, the owners are likely to sell their stock (or sell the whole company) and move on.

Alternatively—and if the owners are in a position to do so—they may take drastic action to improve those results, often including layoffs, consolidations, and shutdowns.

Capitalism for (More) People

Two conclusions seem to follow logically from these observations.

First: if ownership is so important to the well-being of individuals and families, wouldn't most of us want an economic system that spreads business ownership as widely as possible—that enables people to become owners and build a nest egg even if they don't have the spare cash to buy stock or the skills to start their own company? You can imagine such a system as a kind of capitalism for people.

Right now we seem to have pretty much the opposite, which is capitalism for the already rich. The Americans who own no stock have little chance of obtaining any because they don't make enough money. Some of their fellow citizens, meanwhile, come into ownership the easy way, by choosing their parents wisely. Estimates suggest that 35 to 40 percent of the nation's privately held wealth is inherited.[8] Is it any wonder that so many people feel that the economy is fundamentally unfair? A 2020 Pew Research poll found that a whopping 70 percent of respondents thought the "economy unfairly favors the powerful interests."[9]

Second: if ownership is so important to how businesses operate, this capitalism for people would want to foster *responsible* ownership—the kind of ownership that encourages company executives to take the long view and to balance the interests of a company's financial backers with those of employees, customers, and communities.

Again, we have pretty much the opposite right now. Setting family-owned companies aside for the moment—we'll discuss them in Chapter 1—most of the biggest businesses in our country are owned by those faceless Wall Street shareholders. Thousands of other substantial companies are owned by larger corporations or by private equity firms. These businesses can be milked for cash, burdened with debt, merged, or sold off as their owners' short-term interests dictate. This is not a recipe for an effective economy, let alone for one that people feel is fair. Again, little wonder that so many citizens—wage earners in particular— feel misused, ignored, or shunted aside.

So how can we get from where we are now to that kind of capitalism for people, a capitalism with widespread ownership? We need a solution that goes to the root of the problem. We also need a solution that both sides of the political aisle can agree on so that change can actually happen. That's what this book is about.

Ownership: A Road Map

Like a play, the book's argument comes in three parts—three acts, so to speak.

Part I. The first part of the book asks the key question: What's wrong with what we have now? It doesn't make sense to talk about alternatives without understanding how we got in the mess we're in today.

Chapter 1 sets the stage, and a convoluted stage it is. Companies can be owned by individuals or families, by active partners or small groups of financial backers. They can be owned by Wall Street shareholders (sometimes with different classes of stock for insiders and everybody else), by investment firms, by other corporations, or by their employees. They can be bought, sold, or carved up into pieces and the pieces sold off. The result is a kind of crazy-quilt ownership landscape. It got that way because our laws assume that anyone should be able to buy shares or buy a company; all they need is the money.

The dominant features of this ownership landscape are—not to put too fine a point on it—absurd institutions that exist primarily to serve the affluent.

One of these institutions is ownership by Wall Street shareholders, discussed in Chapter 2. For many of these owners, Wall Street is little more than a casino, a way of gambling on stock prices (and many other things). For businesses, Wall Street ownership is a kind of Faustian bargain that lets executives reward themselves handsomely while dictating much about how they must run their companies.

The other main feature of the landscape is the big and still-growing world of private equity, which some have termed Wall Street's misbegotten child. Private equity—and if you don't know about it, you should—is the subject of Chapter 3. You'll learn about financial-engineering tactics such as the dividend recap, a handy tool that essentially lets private equity firms play with the house's money.

The absurdity in all this? In both cases, as we'll show, the ownership structures mean that the rich grow richer. They mean that the nation's most important companies pretty much have to concentrate on the short-term moves and financial manipulations that make them more valuable to investors. The people who actually do the work—the managers and specialists and front-line employees who make up the real company as opposed to the financial one—get short shrift. It's the exact opposite of long-term responsible ownership, and the economy suffers for it.

Part II. The chapters in this section ask how we can change things.

Reformers have been trying to soften the rough edges of capitalism for centuries. They have had some success—the economies of the developed world these days aren't nearly as brutal as they once were—but most advocates of reform have never really addressed the issue of ownership. Chapter 4 shows the limitations of traditional approaches. Chapter 5 looks squarely at ownership, describing how the current system emerged and what sorts of ownership fit with today's economy. It outlines what the complexity scientist Stuart Kauffman has called the *adjacent possible*—an alternative that is significantly different from today's reality but still realistic and practical.

Part III. The third section of the book introduces an alternative, employee ownership, that has not only worked well but thrived. It's very much adjacent to the current system—no babies get thrown out with capitalism's dirty bathwater. And it's very much possible, because it already exists.

Employee ownership in the US is a story of one man with a compelling idea, one powerful senator who wrote the idea into law, and then, over time, the creation of thousands of employee-owned companies. In most of these, the employees own a majority of the stock. Without much difficulty, you could drive to work on roads and bridges and work in buildings designed and built by employee-owned companies. On the way home you could stop at an employee-owned supermarket to pick up employee-owned craft beers or pancake mixes and then relax in the home you have financed through an employee-owned mortgage company. Ownership of this sort has enabled millions of people to share in the wealth they help create. It has enabled CEOs to run companies that really do act responsibly. In Chapter 6 we'll describe this world and the people who have benefited from it.

But we also want to ask some hard questions about employee ownership. Chapter 7 poses the obvious one: Given the idea's success, why has it not yet spread further? What are the obstacles, and where are the opportunities? Chapters 8 through 11 examine those opportunities in detail: on Wall Street, in private equity, in co-ops and trusts, in the platform companies such as Uber that dominate the so-called gig economy, and in government programs. Obstacles there are—but the opportunities beckon, both in the US and elsewhere. We Americans really do have a chance to reshape ownership. So do the citizens of other countries; Chapter 12 looks at the wide variety of experiments taking place elsewhere. The conclusion winds things up with some thoughts about how all of us can push this practical idea forward.

This book, in short, will take you on a journey. It will show exactly what's wrong with the way ownership is organized today. It will clear up misconceptions about ownership and describe the elements of a better system. And it will uncover an often overlooked but dynamic part of the economy where everyday people, people who are citizens of Main Street rather than Wall Street, the 99 percent rather than the 1 percent, share in ownership—a system that awaits only the political will to become a model for a new kind of capitalism.

PART I

WHAT'S WRONG WITH WHAT WE HAVE?

"WHO OWNS THE BUSINESSES?" is a critical question to ask about any economy. Ownership determines who profits from companies' operations. Ownership sets the constraints and incentives that govern how boards and chief executives run those companies. Ownership is how the rich stay rich; lack of ownership is why so many others toil on an economic treadmill. If we want to spread the wealth that ownership represents—and if we want to change how companies operate—we need to change the structures of ownership.

But the first step toward change is understanding the failures and follies of the current system. That's the goal of this part of the book.

Right now, most of our largest and most important companies are owned—if that's the right word—by people who buy their stock on Wall Street. The shares that represent ownership are bought and sold by the millions every day. Meanwhile, many midsized businesses, bedrocks of their local communities, have been sold off by their founders, and then maybe resold by whoever bought them. They are now owned by big corporations or by financial firms that hope to sell them again in a few years.

We have grown accustomed to all this buying and selling. But we shouldn't assume that it's either inevitable or desirable.

Wall Street ownership, discussed in Chapter 2, isn't really ownership as most of us think of it. Shareholders don't have the usual rights and responsibilities of owners. They aren't accountable for "their" company's actions. What they care about isn't the business, it's the share price. Not surprisingly, companies have learned how to boost share prices in the short term. The system rewards financial manipulation even while it penalizes long-term thinking and investment.

Private equity firms, the subject of Chapter 3, typically hope to resell the companies they acquire in anywhere from three to seven years. Their focus, naturally enough, is on generating maximum return for their investors. But that single-minded focus often jeopardizes the long-term health of the businesses they acquire. Again, it's a system that often rewards financial manipulation.

If a company is owned by Wall Street investors, by private equity, or even by a large corporation, its owners are most often financial owners. Those owners probably won't evaluate it by how good an employer it is or how much it contributes to a community's economic well-being. They will evaluate it primarily by the monetary returns it can deliver. And they will operate it accordingly.

This relentless focus on profits—usually short-to-medium-term profits—makes for a skewed economy. The financial owners get richer as their companies grow and as they make astute decisions about buying and selling. Everyone else continues to work for a wage. So the system tends to worsen inequality. Businesses—organizations that employ millions upon millions of people, that support the economies of communities and cities and whole regions, that provide the goods and services that their customers need—wind up being treated *only* as revenue-producing entities for their shareholders.

To change the way those systems work, we'll need a different kind of ownership.

THE OWNERSHIP CRAZY QUILT

*[Someone] who uses an imaginary map
thinking that it is a true one, is likely to be worse
off than someone with no map at all.*

—E. F. SCHUMACHER
Small Is Beautiful: Economics as if People Mattered

CONSIDER THE SUPERMARKET.

The grocery business is probably the single most familiar industry in the world. Nearly everyone in developed countries shops in a supermarket. In the US alone, groceries account for $758 billion in annual sales and employ about 2.9 million people.[1]

But who owns your local supermarket? If you shop at a Walmart, the answer is obvious. Conversely, if you shop at one of the many small local chains that dot the grocery marketplace, you may even know the family that owns those stores.

Some family-owned grocers have grown large and are loved by both customers and employees. Wegmans has become a name to conjure with among supermarket shoppers in New York State and elsewhere in the eastern United States. A new Wegmans in a community is a cause for celebration. H-E-B, named after the founding Butt family, is a Texas icon, a valued part of many neighborhoods. "H-E-B is a grocery store chain," declared a recent article in the *New York Times*. "But it is also more than that. People buy T-shirts that say 'H-E-B for President,' and they post videos to TikTok declaring their love, like the woman clutching a small bouquet of flowers handed to her by an employee: 'I wish I had a boyfriend like H-E-B. Always there. Gives me flowers. Feeds me.'"[2] The idea of the friendly, family-owned grocery store is deeply embedded in the nation's psyche.

Several US supermarket chains are owned not by families but by their employees. By far the largest is Publix Super Markets, based in Florida, with a payroll of over 225,000. Others include fast-growing WinCo Foods (Idaho), Brookshire Brothers (Texas), Homeland Food Stores (Oklahoma), and Harps Food Stores (Arkansas).[3] These companies, too, emphasize their local ownership. "Who Owns WinCo Foods?" asks the website of the Boise-based chain. "WinCo is employee owned. WinCo is owned and operated by people in your community, and when the company does well, those hard-working people see the reward."

But this is the 21st century. The full ownership landscape is complicated—and global.

Would it surprise you to learn that Stop & Shop, the popular New England chain, is owned by Ahold Delhaize, a company based in the Netherlands? Or that the same Ahold Delhaize also owns Hannaford, Food Lion, Giant, and several other supermarket brands? Safeway, a chain that was once one of the nation's largest, was acquired by Albertsons in 2015; the principal owner of Albertsons at the time was Cerberus Capital Management, a private equity firm. Albertsons (whose stock is now traded on the New York Stock Exchange) owns about twenty other chains, including Acme, Vons, and Tom Thumb, as well as its eponymous stores. The quirky Trader Joe's, the choice of many budget-minded food mavens, is owned by Aldi Nord, a German multinational—not to be confused with Aldi Süd, which owns the US stores of the Aldi chain. (The Aldi family fell out and split their business into two companies.) Tesco and Sainsbury's, the big British supermarket chains, are publicly traded on the London Stock Exchange; the largest shareholder in Sainsbury's in 2021 was the sovereign wealth fund of Qatar. Monoprix, in France, is owned by an international retail conglomerate called Groupe Casino, whose shares trade on the Paris stock exchange.

Whew. If you don't know who owns your favorite store, don't worry; the owner is likely to be different the next time you turn around. Individual stores and whole chains in this business are being bought up and sold off all the time. While we were writing this chapter, a private equity firm called Clayton, Dubilier & Rice topped other would-be buyers in a "frenzied" bidding war to acquire the British supermarket chain Morrisons.

And it isn't just supermarkets where the ownership landscape gets complex and global. The manufacturer of MINI automobiles, which typically come decked out in the Union Jack and other Britishisms, is a division of BMW, a German company. Volvo, for decades a flagship of Sweden's economy, was sold in 1999 to Ford, which later sold it to China's Geely Holding. Budweiser, once the main product of the fabled US brewer Anheuser-Busch, is now part of an international brewing giant known as AB InBev, created by the Brazilian-American investment firm 3G Capital. 3G was also instrumental in buying out Kraft Foods and later merging Kraft with Heinz. Other food operations, including Keurig Dr Pepper, Krispy Kreme, Panera, and Peet's Coffee, are owned by a German company called JAB Holding Company, itself mostly owned by Germany's billionaire Reimann family.

Fortune magazine, once the prime chronicler of US corporations and the flagship business publication of Time Inc., is itself a symbol of this new crazy-quilt world. Here's what the magazine's 2020 statement of ownership says (full mailing addresses are omitted, but the various companies' headquarters are indicated in brackets):

> Owner: Fortune Media (USA) Corporation [New York City], which is a wholly owned subsidiary of Fortune Media Group Holdings, Limited [Macau], which is a direct wholly owned subsidiary of True Cosmic Bliss Media Holdings, Limited [Grand Cayman], which is wholly owned by Chatchaval Jiaravanon [Thailand].

You can't help wondering how many lawyers Mr. Jiaravanon employs to keep the ownership straight.

Why the Crazy Quilt? Tradeable Shares

In principle, business ownership seems so simple.

An entrepreneur starts a company. Of course she should own and control it. It's her idea, it's her time that she's spending trying to make the venture a success, and it's her money that is at stake.

If the founder then wants to bring in other financial partners, active or passive, isn't it natural that she should give them—or sell them—part ownership in the business? Like her, they're risking their money. And if one of the new partners then loses interest in the enterprise, shouldn't he be able to sell his share to someone else? A share of a company, after all, is a piece of property, worth whatever someone will pay for it. We don't put restrictions on the buying and selling of a house or a horse, as long as there's no fraud involved.

But this idea of portable, transferable ownership—tradeable shares— is nothing more than a convention, determined by a particular combination of laws and business practices developed over the last couple of centuries.

You can see that it is a convention because it applies only to certain kinds of enterprises. If someone starts a community center, a school, or a charitable organization, it will likely be structured as a nonprofit. Nonprofits—including large ones such as the American Red Cross or Harvard University—are not owned in the conventional sense by anyone. They are governed by a board and run by an appointed chief executive, just like business corporations. But there are no shares to be sold, so nobody can buy them.

Alternatively, imagine that our entrepreneur starts a law firm or an accounting firm. In this case the company will almost certainly be structured as a partnership. The founder may take on partners, who may be required to buy their partnership interest. But those partners normally can't sell their interest in the firm to a bystander on the street or an outside investor. They can only sell it back to the firm. Their ownership is a kind of property right, but it is attached to membership in the firm—being invited in by one's fellow partners—rather than to the investment of money. A somewhat similar principle applies to cooperatives, including consumer co-ops such as REI, the outdoor equipment company; producer co-ops such as Land O'Lakes; and worker co-ops such as Spain's remarkable Mondragon Corporation. These are for-profit businesses. But they are owned by their members, who are customers or suppliers or employees. The owners remain owners only as long as they remain members, and they can't sell their interest to an outsider.

Even in the case of a conventional business corporation, ownership isn't automatically attached to the provision of capital. Investors can provide money to a company by lending it money—by buying its bonds, for example. Bonds are portable and transferable, like stocks. In theory they could be structured to carry a variable rate of return so that an investor could profit handsomely if the company were to grow and make money. But bondholders have no right of ownership or control, only the rights of a creditor. So it's easy to imagine an entrepreneur or a group of partners starting a company and acquiring the necessary capital by borrowing it. In this case the "capitalists"—meaning the lenders who are putting up the money—would be entitled to a return on their investment but not to any ownership.

And yet, despite the exceptions and counterexamples, tradeable shares have long dominated the free-enterprise system. The legal owners of a company are the founders plus anyone who purchases stock—equity capital—either from the company itself or from another shareholder. Once you do own shares, you can usually sell them to any buyer at any price the buyer is willing to pay. It follows naturally that markets in shares would develop, and even that whole companies could be bought and sold—in some cases, again and again, as in the supermarket industry. Hence the crazy quilt.

Wait! What about keeping it in the family? Our company founder may have exactly that in mind. She might not want other owners, let alone the anonymous investors of Wall Street, mucking about in her business. She might hope to build a company that she can pass on to her children and her children's children. And indeed, the idea isn't implausible.

Wegmans, H-E-B, and other family-owned companies are key players in the supermarket business. Franklin Clarence Mars launched Mars, Inc., the candy company, back in 1920. His son Forrest Mars Sr. took it over and expanded it. Other Mars descendants continued the tradition. Today Mars is a worldwide operation with 130,000 employees and $40 billion in sales—and it is still owned and controlled by members of the Mars family, reportedly the third wealthiest family in the United States.[4] There are plenty of other big family-owned companies throughout the world. Some, such as Germany's JAB, are active acquirers of other companies, doing their part to maintain the crazy quilt.

But it's hard to maintain a family business over time, which is why there aren't more of them in the big-business landscape.

Think about the dynamics of most families. The sons and daughters of the founder grow up with the business. They are often interested in inheriting the company from their parents and running it themselves. If they have the skills to run it successfully—not a given—it may survive and prosper. But the third generation is less likely to be interested, just because it's a larger group and apt to be more diverse. Some of these young men and women may want to pursue other careers. Some may be more interested in enjoying the privileges of inherited wealth than in taking on the responsibilities of running a company. Nor are the traits required for managerial success necessarily passed on through genetics or upbringing. The "idiot third generation" is a trope you hear a lot from family-business consultants.

But let's say that the company does make it to the third or fourth generation of family ownership. The founding patriarch or matriarch has died. There are now dozens of shareholders, widely dispersed, all with their own interests. Those not in the business may be looking for other family members to buy them out. Those who need regular income may lobby the board to pay large dividends. Those who are still involved will argue that the company needs the money for long-term investments. It's a recipe for conflict and bad blood—and it is likely to be resolved through selling the company and distributing the cash.

The Inevitability of a Sale, and Its Effects

So what we are left with is a truism that everyone in the business world knows: *nearly every company that does not close its doors will eventually be sold.*

If you own a successful company of significant size, you will find prospective buyers lining up at the door, each one offering a big payday. Large corporations and private equity firms will come calling. So will competitors, though they may be more interested in your company's physical assets or customer lists than in your business as a going concern. If your company is big enough or enjoys significant growth prospects, investment bankers will also be knocking on the door, hoping to sponsor an initial public offering (IPO) or some other device for selling the company's shares to Wall Street investors.

Many companies, of course, are founded with a sale to Wall Street explicitly in mind. Start a growth-oriented business in computer hardware or biotech or electric cars and you are likely to bring in venture capitalists (VCs) as partners from the very beginning. The VCs will expect a share of the company's equity in return for their money; they will also expect some sort of sale, sometimes to Wall Street investors but more often to another company, within a period of five to ten years. (VCs refer to such a sale as a *liquidity event.*) The proceeds from these sales fund the VC firm itself and provide a return to the firm's investment partners. Again, the original owners get a big payday.

In all these ways, every company that is not still owned by its founders becomes part of those markets for shares or for whole businesses. Ownership almost inevitably passes on.

The metamorphosis. Once a company is sold to financial owners, it is no longer anybody's baby. It is no longer tied to the founder's values or to the communities where it operates. It may no longer put a priority on ensuring long-term jobs for its employees. It has been transformed into a financial asset, of value to its new owners only insofar as it fits with their business strategies and generates the expected levels of profits. It can be managed for maximum short-term gains, such as through layoffs and other cost cuts, or it can be managed for growth. It can be resold, merged, carved up into pieces and the pieces sold off, or milked until it winds up in bankruptcy and then—the antiseptic term of art—"reorganized." Whatever best suits the new owners' judgments of their financial interests.

It's hard to overstate the effects of this transformation. Way back in the 1970s, one of us (Corey Rosen) was working on Washington, DC's Capitol Hill and organized a hearing of the Senate Small Business Committee. Robert Reich, then on the Federal Trade Commission and later Secretary of Labor under Bill Clinton, told the committee that the United States was becoming a nation of paper entrepreneurs, with people focused on moving money around rather than actually producing anything. In 2002, the bestselling author Kevin Phillips (once a Republican strategist) made a similar argument in his book *Wealth and Democracy*.[5] As countries move from producing to financing, he wrote, they chart a path toward economic decline and rising inequality.

Their concerns were prescient. Decisions made by absentee owners purely on the basis of financial gain inevitably seem arbitrary, even capricious, to the millions of people who are affected. Communities— even cities—can find their economies decimated. Employees can be shunted about or left to fend for themselves while the owners move on to the next opportunity for profit. Before long, the entire economy comes to seem fundamentally unfair.

Ironically, it's the very fact of tradeable shares that opens up those opportunities for financial wheeling and dealing. No one would want to get in the way of the plumber, the graphic designer, or the shopkeeper who starts and runs a small business. And few would fault a system that gives successful entrepreneurs a substantial reward. But when businesses grow larger—when their operations affect significant numbers of people as customers, employees, or taxpayers—they will almost certainly be sold. At that point, society has an interest in encouraging some kinds of sales and discouraging others.

So let's take a hard look at the world this convention has created. We'll begin with the two huge industries that have devoted themselves to making money mainly from the buying and selling of stock and of companies. One is Wall Street, purveyor of shares in publicly traded enterprises. The other is private equity—buyers and sellers of businesses. Both industries have swelled in recent decades to the point of absurdity, a point where the owners and the operators of the nation's most important companies are two largely separate groups—and where these companies' day-to-day workings are ultimately governed by the needs of investors and the executives who serve them.

Takeaways

○ Ownership is more complex, and more open to change, than it first appears. Ownership by shareholders is just a convention, not a law of nature.

○ When a company is sold—and nearly every company that doesn't shut up shop will be sold—there's an opportunity to transform its ownership.

WHICH COMPANY WOULD YOU LIKE TO WORK FOR?

The largest grocer in the US is Walmart, with about a quarter of the market. In 1970, founder Sam Walton took Walmart public, selling shares on Wall Street. But he retained a large number of those shares, which he passed on to his descendants. Since then, those descendants have become the richest family in the world. Their company, however, has long had a poor reputation as an employer. Its wages lag those of competitors. Its benefits are meager. Annual turnover in the workforce is high. Few people think of working at Walmart as a great job.

George Jenkins, founder of the Publix Super Markets chain, took a different route, selling much of his stock over time to the company's employees. Today, Publix is the nation's largest employee-owned enterprise, and it's as different from Walmart as June from December. In 2016, *Fortune* magazine sent a reporter to Florida to work in a Publix supermarket for a week. The magazine wanted to learn the secrets of a company that had shown up on its list of "100 Best Companies to Work For" every year since the list began.

One such secret, reporter Christopher Tkaczyk found, was happy employees. "Or more accurately: pleased-as-punch, over-the-moon, ridiculously contented" employees. Voluntary turnover was far lower than the retail average. There had never been a layoff. After a year of employment, every worker who puts in at least 1,000 hours gets a stock allotment, which in the last several years has been worth 8.5 percent of an employee's pay. As owners, Publix employees who stay with the company for their careers can accumulate a nice nest egg. People told the *Fortune* reporter things like, "I love working for Publix!"[6]

George Jenkins's descendants aren't doing badly either—they're #39 on *Forbes*'s list of the richest US families, with an estimated fortune of $8.8 billion.

WALL STREET
Faceless Ownership

*Rather than a healthy marriage, the
investor-company relationship is now more
akin to anonymous sex.*

—ROGER L. MARTIN
Former dean, Rotman School of Management
University of Toronto

CLOSE TO 6,000 COMPANIES are listed on the two major stock exchanges in the United States. Other exchanges around the world list thousands more. The roster includes the Exxons and Walmarts and Apples that dominate much of the world's economy, along with many lesser lights. Anyone with the necessary cash can buy stock in these companies, so they are said to be publicly traded. Legally, the shareholders are the companies' owners.

Owners. Really?

It's certainly a peculiar kind of ownership. Shareholders of public companies can't help themselves to the goods or services their company delivers. They can't set foot on the company's premises unless invited.

They don't have any effective say over the operation of the business they supposedly own, and they rarely try to use the limited power they do have.

The only time shareholders enjoy a chance to be active owners is when they accumulate a large chunk of stock. Buy up more than 50 percent of the shares and it's your company—you can do what you want with it. Own a substantial minority stake, anywhere from 10 to 30 percent, and the company's management may offer you a seat or two on the board of directors. But how often does any of this happen? A few financial firms, as we'll see, make a specialty of accumulating stock and trying to bring about changes in a company's management or operations. And very occasionally, a conventional institution such as a pension fund will try to force a specific change—for example, voting "no" on excessive stock awards to top executives. (The awards have to be *very* excessive to provoke such a challenge.) But most shareholders, both institutions and individuals, are content just to be passive investors.

So for 99 percent of the people 99 percent of the time, shareholder control of a publicly traded company is a complete and utter fiction. What the shareholders do own and control is their stock. Each share entitles them to a portion of the profits if the company's management decides to pay a dividend. (Many companies don't.) It entitles them to vote for the board of directors, a vote that will almost certainly be meaningless. (Management's nominations for the board nearly always pass unchallenged, and there are almost never any other names on the proxy; elections are more like those in the old Soviet Union than like those of a democracy.) Shareholders also have the right to sell the stock any time they want, to sue the company for alleged malfeasance, and a few other minor rights. But that's it.

So imagine that you're a shareholder. Which is likely to engage your interest more, the long-term fate of "your" company, which you have no say over, or the price of your stock?

It's true that some shareholders try to act like real investors. They buy stock with the intention of holding it over a period of years and thereby sharing in the company's growth. Even though they aren't privy to the company's plans, they study reports of new developments in the business and in the company's markets. They may buy more shares if the long-term prospects look good even if—or especially if—the price has dropped.

But most people who play the market—the phrase is telling—have their eye squarely on something else, which is the price of shares right now and the likely price tomorrow or next quarter. That's where they hope to make their money, not through dividends or long-term appreciation but through short-term movements in the stock price. Day traders may buy and sell dozens of stocks every day. Some Wall Street investment funds employ program trading, with computers rapidly buying or selling millions of shares according to proprietary algorithms; the funds may hold shares for no more than a fraction of a second. Others are purely passive investors and blindly buy whatever stocks appear on some independently compiled index, such as the S&P 500. By 2019, program or algorithmic trading was accounting for more trades than those managed by humans. (Figure 2 shows the relevant numbers.)

FIGURE 2: Assets Managed by Type of Stock Trader

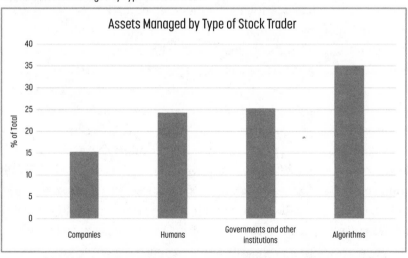

Source: Authors, with data from Katharina Buchholz, "Computers Manage More Stock Than Humans Do," Statista, December 9, 2019, https://www.statista.com/chart/20245/share-of-computerized-and-human-trading-in-us-equities/.

Even the managers of actively managed mutual funds and pension funds, who pick stocks on behalf of ordinary citizens, pay close attention to short-term stock movements, because they are rewarded on the basis of their quarterly performance. In all these cases, the individuals whose money these managers invest typically know or care little about the companies that they supposedly own.

It's a bizarre arrangement, this world of absentee and faceless owners, one in which the whole concept of business ownership virtually disappears. Let's look at what it means for how companies operate and for society as a whole.

Focus: The Share Price

In a privately held company, the owners have choices. They can invest in long-term growth. They can maximize short-term cash flow. They can create great places to work and pursue responsible environmental policies—or not. Executives of large private companies typically balance a variety of objectives in keeping with the owners' priorities and values.

Chief executives of publicly traded companies rarely have such broad choices, and the balancing act is far more difficult. Their "owners" are a disparate, anonymous bunch of shareholders who typically care about only one thing: a rising share price. CEOs have every incentive to concentrate on that goal to the exclusion of pretty much everything else.[1]

One incentive is the natural human desire for acclaim. The Street, after all, is a society unto itself. Stock analysts issue reports and assessments of major public companies. Business media dig up stories on managerial moves and developments likely to affect share prices. CEOs who outperform the Street's collective expectations are lauded. Their companies' share prices will almost certainly rise. Those who underperform may find their share prices dropping and their boards of directors unhappy. Underperform too often and you will be ushered out the door.

Of course, corporate boards are notorious for cutting chief executives a lot of slack. Most of the directors were probably nominated by the CEO. They may be personal friends. But even if a friendly board forgives a few quarters (or a few years!) of underperformance, Wall Street will not. The firms that have come to be known as activist investors—organizations often led by name-brand individuals such as Carl Icahn and Bill Ackman—keep a close eye on companies whose share prices are lagging. They study these companies, analyzing ways to cut costs or otherwise increase short-term profits. If the prospects look good, they begin accumulating stock, to the point where management has to listen to them.

The activists may then propose a series of profit-boosting actions. If management doesn't go along, they may buy still more shares and request a number of board seats. Ultimately they may try to replace the entire executive team. A CEO who is managing a troubled company—meaning one whose stock isn't doing well—is likely to have nightmares about that phone call from an Icahn or an Ackman. It's one more reason to keep the share price up.

CEO pay. There's another big incentive for CEOs to watch the share price closely: their compensation almost always depends on it.

Until the mid-1970s, public-company CEOs received their compensation mainly in the form of salary. The stock market was quieter back then, involving many fewer people. More shareholders tended to hold on to their stocks through thick and thin. (The average holding period on the New York Stock Exchange in 1970 was over five years; today it is less than six months.) The combination of the Great Depression, World War II, and union power put a damper on corporate salaries. It's hard to pay your CEO millions and then stonewall a union demand for a 3 percent raise.

But things began changing in the 1970s. Inflation was rife. Globalization reared its head. New technologies upended one industry after another. Unions were losing power. Chief executives who could steer a company through all this turbulence were highly valuable. So there were upward pressures—and fewer constraints—on their compensation.

Meanwhile, and serendipitously for CEOs, some business-school professors began worrying about what they saw as a misalignment between shareholders (a company's ostensible owners) and the executives who actually ran the business. They called it an example of the *principal-agent problem.* Shareholders were the principals. CEOs and other executives were their agents. Paid on salary, these executives had little direct incentive to worry about the owners' interest in a rising share price. The solution, as these critics saw it, was to pay CEOs less in cash and more in stock. Over the next several years, that logical-sounding argument percolated outward from the ivory tower to corporate boardrooms, where it found a highly receptive audience.[2] In 2020 stock-based compensation accounted for more than 80 percent of average CEO earnings. The more valuable the stock, the higher the top team's pay. The ratio of CEO pay to average worker pay was 21 to 1 in 1965. In 2019 it was 320 to 1.[3]

There is, not surprisingly, a trick here. Stock-based compensation has turned out to be such a gold mine for CEOs in part because they and their colleagues have their hands on the levers that can affect the share price.

Managing the Share Price

Running any large company is a tough job. Executives of private companies have to balance the objectives of the company's owners, some of which may be in conflict. Running a public company isn't any easier, especially since you have that one critical measurement of your performance staring you in the face day in and day out. Little wonder that CEOs and their colleagues have come to understand *how* to manage the share price.

One set of tools is pretty obvious: hold down costs. Keep a lid on wages. Send production overseas when you can. Avoid taxes wherever possible—for example by setting up nominal entities in low-tax countries and funneling much of your profit through them. Don't spend too much on R&D, environmental safeguards, or other niceties. Lay people off at the first sign of economic or market troubles. Wall Street actually likes to see cuts in the payroll; shares often rise after a layoff. Sure, such moves may harm the company (and the taxpayer) in the long run. But most senior executives at publicly traded companies don't have a long run. As of 2020, the average tenure for a C-suite executive at one of America's largest 1,000 companies was less than five years.[4] Many have options or other incentives that pay off in the short or medium term. Long-term investments, such as in sustainable technologies, can take ten years or more to yield profits—a horizon that is far too long to drive today's stock prices.

A second set of tools is obvious only to those versed in public-company earnings management: run the business quarter to quarter. If it looks like you might miss the earnings goal for a particular three-month period, ask your CFO whether the accountants can rejigger the books to increase profits. (There are plenty of legal ways to do this.) If the company runs into short-term trouble—say, an acquisition that didn't work out and so must be written off—cram all the bad news into one quarter, forcing a drop in the share price. Next quarter, when the price recovers, you will be hailed as a great manager.[5]

Stock buybacks. One technique of earnings management has become remarkably popular since it was legalized in 1982: buying back large quantities of your own company's stock on the open market. This is simple, effective, and almost completely at the CEO's discretion. The new demand tends to push the price of shares upward. And because there are now fewer shares on the market, profits per share rise. It's a powerful way of ensuring that you will meet your earnings targets, not to mention your compensation goals.[6]

Of course, buybacks can eat up a company's spare cash. "Buybacks' drain on corporate treasuries has been massive," write economist William Lazonick and his coauthors in *Harvard Business Review*. "The 465 companies in the S&P 500 Index in January 2019 that were publicly listed between 2009 and 2018 spent, over that decade, $4.3 trillion on buybacks."[7] In 2019 the figure was $728.7 billion, or as one reporter pointed out, about the same as 3 percent of US GDP.[8] Over half of the stock buybacks between 2017 and 2020 were financed from the massive tax cuts of 2017—cuts that were meant to stimulate investments but wound up lining the pockets of the already rich.[9] Incidentally, if your company doesn't have the cash for buybacks, you can often borrow the money you need. American Airlines devoted about $12 billion to buy-backs between 2014 and the end of 2019, running up billions of dollars in debt in the process. When the pandemic hit in 2020, it asked the government for billions in bailout money.[10]

For chief executives and their teams, stock-market ownership is a sort of Faustian bargain. They can pay themselves pretty much anything they want to. Friendly boards and their compensation consultants—who naturally want to be hired again—will go along. CEOs can use a variety of tools to manipulate the share price to ensure that their compensation stays high. But they must run their companies in a manner designed to keep Wall Street happy. If they fail at that, they are likely to find themselves out of a job.

THE PERILS OF STOCK-MARKET OWNERSHIP

In 2008 a former McKinsey & Company consultant named J. Michael Pearson became CEO of Valeant, then a small and struggling pharma company. When he started, Valeant's share price was around $11. Between 2010 and 2014 he acquired more than one hundred companies and ran up $30 billion in debt.

He then had to generate cash to pay down the debt. So he raised the prices of his company's pharmaceuticals an average of 50 percent in 2014, and another 65.6 percent the following year. Two drugs for treating a rare disorder known as Wilson's disease rose by 5,800 percent and 3,200 percent respectively, over a period of years. The money rolled in, and Valeant's stock price topped $250 at the end of July 2015.

Unfortunately, all these price hikes generated a lot of bad publicity. Nervous shareholders began to bail out. Pearson was excoriated in Congress for price gouging. Soon Valeant's stock had plunged and Pearson was on the way out—though not without a severance package worth $12 million. (A year later he filed a lawsuit alleging that the company owed him $30 million more.[11])

People have drawn all sorts of lessons from this sorry tale. Michael Pearson was a greedhead. America needs to control drug prices. The system worked—he was exposed and shown the door. The lesson that has escaped notice is about Wall Street. Pearson never lied about his strategy, which was, as the industry calls it, taking price. It was *public information*. He did exactly what he said he would do and what he had an incentive to do: drive the share price up, regardless of the effect on patients or, indeed, on America's healthcare system. Wall Street investors, including some of the Street's biggest names, piled in.

Is It Really Wall Street's Fault?

Defenders of Wall Street—there are many—will take issue with a number of these arguments. Public stock markets, they might say, are one of the world's great inventions. Stock markets enable people who aren't rich to buy shares in their nation's economic growth, and thus to build up nest eggs. Study after study shows that stocks outperform other investments over the long haul.[12] Moreover, the prospect of "going public" makes it easier for founders of innovative-but-risky companies to attract backing from wealthy individuals and venture capital firms. The market thus encourages innovation and entrepreneurship, thereby driving economic growth.

All true—and so far, so good. But other arguments in favor of Wall Street are less cogent:

○ *All those moves—cost cutting, layoffs, and the like—are necessary to keep a company competitive. It isn't Wall Street's fault.* Of course a company has to do whatever's necessary to survive and make a profit. The question is how it balances objectives and where its priorities lie. Are layoffs the last resort—or the first? Does it pursue longer-term goals like building a loyal workforce and investing in sustainable technologies, or does short-term profit trump everything else? A study of more than 600 US companies found that those with a longer-term orientation (about a quarter of the total) outperformed the others over a period of years. "The differences were dramatic," write the authors. "Among the firms we identified as focused on the long term, average revenue and earnings growth were 47% and 36% higher, respectively, by [the end of the study], and market capitalization grew faster as well. The returns to society and the overall economy were equally impressive. By our measures, companies that were managed for the long term added nearly 12,000 more jobs on average than their peers from 2001 to 2015."[13]

○ *Share prices always reflect a company's long-term prospects—so there's really no difference between managing for the short term and managing for the long term.* That might be true if most investors had a long-term outlook. But they don't. They're watching short-term moves, which are affected not only by a company's prospects but by today's economic headlines, by rumors, by the mood of the market, and by a dozen other factors (including the weather).[14] At times, movements in share prices are directly contradictory to the overall economic outlook (as during the pandemic in 2020) and to a company's long-term prospects. Remember the GameStop craze in 2020? The stock of this troubled company suddenly took off because a group of day traders on a particular website decided to push it up—an internet-enabled version of the hoary scam known as pump-and-dump. The stock gyrated crazily, while the company's dubious business outlook never changed. Soon, copycat "meme" investors were pushing up other troubled stocks in what amounted to a sort of Ponzi scheme for stock traders.

○ *High CEO compensation is a small price to pay for the performance of companies such as Apple.* Well, yes. Apple has done exceptionally well in recent years; at this writing it is the second most valuable company in the world, after Saudi Aramco. Apple and many other tech companies also make grants of stock to most or all of their employees, something that few firms outside the tech sector do. But the overall evidence about pay and performance actually points in the *opposite* direction. In a 2016 study, Michael Cooper of the University of Utah and his coauthors found that "industry and size adjusted CEO pay is negatively related to future shareholder wealth changes . . . [and that] the effect is stronger for CEOs who receive higher incentive pay relative to their peers." Other studies, they note, have produced "surprisingly little direct evidence that incentive contracts actually lead to better company returns."[15]

○ *Stock buybacks are merely a way of returning money to shareholders because the companies can't find profitable investments.* Wait a minute—they're "returning" money to shareholders? Most of those shareholders never provided money to the company by buying newly issued shares; they just bought their stock from some other investor. But look at the deeper issue. We live in an era of huge needs and enormous opportunities for innovation—sustainable energy, more effective healthcare, rebuilding infrastructure, and so on. Large public companies, with billions of dollars at their disposal and some of the brightest men and women in their executive suites, can't find anything worthwhile to invest in? What the argument means, of course, is that they can't find anything that will provide the kind of short-term payback that will goose the stock price.

Anyway, shareholders' gain is not necessarily in the interest of a nation's economic health. Those buyback funds could be spent on R&D, on new products, on raising workers' wages or providing better benefits, or on sustainable technologies rather than on a gift to shareholders. Boeing is a sort of poster child for public companies' misplaced priorities. Between 2014 and 2019, reported *Fortune* in 2020, "Boeing spent $43.4 billion on buybacks, compared with $15.7 billion on research and development for commercial airplanes." This is a company that has been plagued by engineering failures and quality issues, reflected in catastrophic crashes. It has even fallen behind its chief competitor, Airbus, in the race to build wholly new ("clean sheet") planes. In 2016, Boeing announced that it would return *all* of its free cash flow to shareholders in the form of buybacks and dividends, rather than boost R&D. "Let's say you only return 50 percent," one disillusioned expert lamented to *Fortune*. "You could have funded an entire airplane program."[16]

And then there are the charges against stock-market ownership that even the defenders of Wall Street don't have much to say about. The two most powerful ones are that it feeds inequality and that it eliminates accountability.

Inequality. Between 1978 and 2019, according to a study by the Washington-based Economic Policy Institute, CEO pay (corrected for inflation) rose 1,167 percent.[17] That was almost half again as much as overall growth in the stock market. It was *eighty-five times* the 13.7 percent growth in the average employee's pay. Of course, it isn't just CEOs. No large company is going to pay its lead dog $10 million or $20 million and the rest of the top team only $100,000 apiece. So the pay of chief financial officers, chief technology officers, and other corporate leaders has ratcheted up accordingly.

Is public company ownership really to blame for this rise? Privately held companies, too, can pay their executives whatever they want, and few outsiders would know the salaries because those companies don't have to report them to the Securities and Exchange Commission. But that observation misses the point. The leaders of private companies are directly responsible to the companies' owners. Family members almost invariably sit on the board; some are executives themselves. Presumably these owners pay their officers whatever they think makes long-term economic sense for the business. In a public company, not many people are thinking long term, least of all those faceless owners. So the company's cashbox is available for the taking.

Accountability. Before we leave the topic of ownership by stock-market traders, ask yourself this question: Who is responsible for the acts of a corporation? In privately held companies, the answer is obvious: the owners. The Sackler family learned this to their detriment when their company, Purdue Pharmaceuticals, was charged with a variety of egregious misdeeds for its role in the opioid crisis. With a publicly traded company, the answer is anything but obvious. Shareholders aren't responsible; under the doctrine of limited liability, they are liable only for the value of their shares. Executives aren't liable, either, unless they commit outright fraud. As long as their actions aren't illegal and are intended to benefit the corporation, they are largely protected by what's known in law as the business judgment rule.

So who is accountable? Well, look for a moment at one famous corporate disaster: the massive 2010 oil spill into the Gulf of Mexico from BP's Deepwater Horizon drilling rig. By its own admission the company was culpable. Settling criminal charges brought by the US Department of Justice, it pled guilty to eleven counts of manslaughter, two misdemeanors, and a felony charge of lying to Congress. These are serious crimes. But you can't put a corporation in jail. And you don't want to put it out of business because many thousands of guiltless employees would lose their jobs. In the BP case, one rig supervisor received ten months' probation for "negligent discharge of oil," and an engineer got six months' probation for damaging a computer.[18] A vice-president was charged with lying to federal agents—he was acquitted—and no other senior executives were charged with anything. Nor did anyone suggest putting the owners—BP's stockholders—in jail, because, after all, they had no responsibility whatever for the conditions that led to the spill.

To be sure, the stockholders paid a financial price. The company wound up paying an estimated $65 billion in penalties and cleanup costs. The share price dropped from about $60 before the spill to a low of $27 two months later, and the company missed paying three successive quarterly dividends. But if you were smart enough to buy BP at that point and hold it for four years, you could have made a 90 percent profit on the share price alone. And since the company resumed paying dividends in 2011, you would have collected an additional five or six dollars per hundred shares every three months.

Remember our statement at the beginning of this chapter: with stock-market companies, the very concept of business ownership essentially disappears. Accountability disappears along with it.

What's the Answer?

We are not proposing to abolish the stock market. It really does offer a low-cost way for people to invest their money. Widely available financial products like index funds allow anyone to invest sensibly, even if they are unsophisticated about finance. Moreover, the prospect of selling stock to the public really does encourage innovation. Nor is ownership by stock-market investors wholly bad. For example, public companies can be more easily made to comply with regulatory requirements than their privately held counterparts; the fact that many people own at least some stock creates a political base for regulation. A few judicious reforms—a tiny tax on each transaction (known as a *Tobin tax*), say, or capital gains taxation that encourages a long-term perspective—might mitigate some of the market's abuses while maintaining its benefits.

But the very thing that makes public companies appealing to many stock buyers and sellers—we probably should quit calling them *investors*, given the arguments we have made—is the fact that the shares are so easily tradeable. Shareholders can sell their stock at any time. And that's what makes them prone to short-term thinking. Owners of private companies, whether they are family members, entrepreneurs, or venture capitalists, have to think longer term because they have no readily available options to sell their stock. Except for the very small number who can do an IPO, liquidity comes only from periodic stock redemptions, earnings distributions, or the eventual sale of the company.

Ultimately, altering public companies' short-term outlook requires more than a few regulations; it requires a different mix of ownership. Suppose, for example, that employees as a group owned a significant fraction of a public company's shares, perhaps through an employee stock ownership plan (ESOP). It's an axiom of public-company governance that even a 10 percent block of company stock enables the owner to exert substantial control over corporate decisions. Putting that much or more in the hands of an employee trust might alter the company's priorities and tilt the balance toward a different time horizon for decisions.

We aren't alone in seeking some such reform. Roger L. Martin, for example, is one of the nation's foremost business theorists. He has been a business-school professor and dean, a consultant and corporate board member, and a prolific author. He has been called the Peter Drucker of his generation, which is sort of like calling a basketball player the new Michael Jordan. In January 2021 Martin published an article in *Harvard Business Review* entitled "It's Time to Replace the Public Corporation." In its place he proposed what he called the *long-term enterprise*. At its heart would be an ESOP, which would partner with a long-term investor such as a pension fund to own the company. Like the investor Warren Buffett, who famously plans to own companies such as GEICO and Burlington Northern Santa Fe "forever," such a company would pursue a long-term horizon and "position chief executives to be incentivized by value enhancement, not stock price movements."

We'll consider the details of such proposals in subsequent chapters. Some arrangement like this for large companies would be good for employees, good for communities, good for society, and good for the companies themselves. It would create real owners, not fictitious ones.

Takeaways

- Shareholders of a publicly traded company nominally own it, but they usually care far more about the share price than the company's operations. Nor are they accountable for what the company does.

- Ownership by Wall Street shareholders gives company executives a strong incentive to focus on short-term financial results—and on manipulating the stock price through devices like buybacks.

PRIVATE EQUITY
Concentrated Ownership

Everything is private equity now.

—*Bloomberg Businessweek*

IF YOU PICK UP A SANDWICH AT ARBY'S, get your printer paper from Staples and your kitty litter from Petco, or trace your heritage on Ancestry.com, the owners of the companies you are patronizing aren't stock-market investors. They are a breed of financial organization known as private equity (PE) firms. Of course, we should add "at this writing" to the examples in this paragraph, and probably to some of the other points we make in this chapter. For if there's one thing to be said about private equity, it doesn't hold still.

The business of PE firms is buying and selling companies. As a group they own retailers and trucking businesses, industrial manufacturers and consumer-goods companies, insurance firms and home-rental companies. Healthcare has been a particularly fertile field for PE buyouts in recent years. "Private equity's purchases have included rural hospitals, physicians' practices, nursing homes and hospice centers, air ambulance companies and health care billing management and debt collection systems," noted an NBC News special report in 2020. Two PE firms "provide staffing for about a third of the country's emergency rooms."[1]

The system of stock-market ownership described in the previous chapter has been around for at least a couple of centuries, and publicly traded companies still dominate the economies of the US and most other developed nations. But that system isn't exactly thriving. The number of public companies in the US has decreased. So has the number of IPOs. Private equity, by contrast, has been expanding. Its net asset value—a measure of how much the companies that PE firms own are worth—has grown more than sevenfold since 2002, twice as much as publicly traded stocks. US companies owned or backed by private equity numbered about 8,000 by 2019, five times the number in the early 2000s—and 2,000 more than all the companies listed on major stock exchanges.[2] In late 2020, PE firms held a total of $4.4 trillion in assets—equivalent to nearly two-thirds of the total assets held by 60 million individuals in their 401(k) retirement plans.[3] The US private equity sector in 2018 employed nearly 9 million workers.[4]

Think about all that: this largely unregulated sector of the economy—and one that receives substantial tax benefits—is now in some ways more important than the stock exchanges we all pay so much attention to. Private equity permeates our economic lives. But is it an improvement on Wall Street's faceless ownership? How does it operate? What are its effects?

How It Works, Part I

From an investor's point of view—and Wall Street is governed by the investor's point of view—buying the shares of stock-market companies has its limitations. There's nothing ordinary shareholders can do about the companies they ostensibly own. They can't change the company's strategy, its cost structures, or its methods of operation. They can't fire the CEO. If they don't like what's going on, all they can do is sell their stock. Activist investors, described in Chapter 2, get around this limitation by buying up such large amounts of stock that they can influence (or replace) the company's management.

But there's another way to solve this problem, provided you can assemble the money. Buy the whole company.

Individual Wall Streeters and investment firms discovered this approach beginning in the 1970s. They began engaging in what were then called leveraged buyouts (LBOs). Put together an investment pool, borrow a lot of the money you need, and you can snap up most or all of a company's stock. You can buy privately held companies in the same way, provided the owners are willing to sell.

Private equity is the institutional offspring of this approach. PE firms create investment funds, typically with a ten-year timeframe. They solicit money from wealthy investors and institutions to bankroll the fund. Meanwhile they scout out potential companies to buy. If a target company is public, they may begin acquiring shares. If it's privately held (as is more common), they approach the owners with what is often a hard-to-resist proposition: cash on the barrel for your entire business.

There are plenty of opportunities for such an approach because—contrary to what you might read in a high school economics textbook—not every company generates all the profit it possibly can. Maybe it is run by an aging patriarch or a sluggish CEO who hasn't invested in the latest technology or who has missed market opportunities. Maybe its payroll has grown bloated over the years and it could run more efficiently with fewer people. Maybe its tax bill is high, and some clever accounting or financial restructuring could reduce the bill substantially. Or maybe it's already quite profitable, and the owner or owners are just ready to sell. The PE firm, staffed with business-savvy MBAs and finance experts, homes in on particular targets, identifying specific opportunities for generating more profit than those companies have produced in the past. Once it has acquired the business, the PE firm typically puts some of its own people on the board, often installs a hand-picked management team, and then begins to implement whatever profit-improvement strategies it has mapped out. Ideally, the new strategies increase the company's value.

And then comes the sale, anywhere from three to seven years later. With its now-more-valuable company in hand, the PE firm considers its options. It may decide to take the company public—selling it, in effect, to Wall Street investors. It may seek out so-called strategic buyers, larger companies in the same (or nearly the same) industry that want to expand their business. It may, and often does, sell to another PE firm, which presumably thinks that it can somehow generate even more value than the first PE firm did. In each transaction, the PE firm typically hopes to double its money. That will provide both the firm and its investors a healthy return, more than they might expect to earn through stock-market investing.

How It Works, Part II

It all seems innocent enough at first glance. After all, publicly traded companies essentially put themselves up for sale every day. If someone decides to accumulate shares in hopes of engineering a buyout, well, that's their right—and it's the risk any public company takes. The owners of privately held companies don't have to sell out unless they want to, but if they do want to, PE firms may offer them a golden opportunity to do so. From an economic perspective, PE firms' ability to generate more profit from the same company would seem to indicate that the company had been operating inefficiently. The subsequent improvements boost efficiency, thus helping the economy grow.

But the devil, as always, is lurking in the details. Those details begin with the PE firms' method of compensation. The usual practice is for a fund to take 2 percent of every dollar that its investors put in, plus 20 percent of any profit they earn from their portfolio companies over an agreed-upon baseline. (If you have ever seen "2 and 20" mentioned in the media, this is what it refers to.) So if a firm raises a $100 million fund, it takes $2 million for itself before it does a thing. The trouble continues with the firms' typical methods of operation. For every straightforward profit-generating improvement implemented by a PE firm—and yes, there are many, including introducing new technologies and more sophisticated management practices—a less admirable practice goes under the rubric of financial engineering. PE firms have become masters of this dubious trade.

One technique is simple: load the company up with debt. When a group of PE firms led by Clayton, Dubilier & Rice bought out Hertz in 2005, they paid Hertz's then-owner, Ford, $14.8 billion. But the firms put up only $2.3 billion. The rest—84 percent of the total—was borrowed money. That deal was unusually big, but the same practice is common in smaller deals as well. Two PE firms acquired Harry & David, the mail-order gift company, for $253 million, including $170 million in debt. Large amounts of debt are characteristic of nearly every PE transaction because it can substantially increase the return on a firm's investment.[5]

The wrinkle here is that the *debt goes on the books of the acquired company*, not on the books of the PE firm. Thus the firm's partners, like the owners of any limited-liability corporation, are not liable for it. The acquired company itself—which is liable—now finds itself saddled with an enormous debt load, meaning that it often must struggle to make the payments. Some pull it off successfully, particularly if they had a big tax bill in the past; since interest payments are tax deductible, their future taxes are likely to be much lower.[6] Others are less successful, since they now have no cushion to fall back on if they run into difficulties. Harry & David went bankrupt seven years after it was acquired. Hertz struggled for years, slashing its payroll again and again, and was finally pushed into bankruptcy by the coronavirus pandemic. Largely because of the debt load, bankruptcies are endemic to the industry. A 2019 study by two business professors at California Polytechnic State University found that companies owned by PE firms went bankrupt at ten times the rate of similar publicly traded companies.[7]

Why would sophisticated owners deliberately put the companies they own into such a risky position? The answer is that they have already rid themselves of much of the risk. And their ultimate job, after all, is to serve their investors, not the companies they own. Financial engineering reflects the magic of ownership: once you own a company, you can do anything you want to so long as you don't break the law. You can, for instance, earmark part of the cash you receive from lenders to pay the owners—yourself and your investors—a dividend. You can even take out additional debt for the same purpose, which is sort of the corporate equivalent of using a credit card to make a cash withdrawal.

Paying yourself back—first. This last is a trick known as a dividend recapitalization, or just dividend recap. If the dividend recap is large enough, you will have *already recouped much of your investment.* You are now playing with the house's money, and anything else you earn is just gravy.

In the Hertz transaction, the PE firms took a $1 billion dividend recap six months after buying the company. Because they put up only $2.3 billion, their exposure was now a little more than half what it had been. With Harry & David, a series of dividend recaps came to more than $100 million, well above the $83 million the PE fund had originally put up. "This guaranteed the investors in Harry & David a 23 percent return no matter what happened to their investment," write Eileen Appelbaum and Rosemary Batt in their book *Private Equity at Work*, widely regarded as the definitive academic study of the industry.[8]

Even in healthcare, not an industry most of us would like to see regarded as a cash cow, such practices are common. "Health-care companies are taking on more debt to pay dividends to their private equity owners, just a year after the start of a pandemic that plunged the industry into crisis," *Bloomberg* reported in early 2021. "Dividend recapitalization is one reason why wealthy investors are drawn to private equity, as they don't have to wait years for a payout."[9]

Debt isn't the only source of cash that can be used for dividends. A second practice is for the PE firm to charge the acquired companies sizable consulting and management fees. (It's the owner of those companies, remember—who's going to stop it?) A third is to restructure the company so as to reduce its tax bill. And a fourth—particularly common when a PE firm buys out a large retailer—is to sell the real estate that the acquired company owns. In 2005, for example, a PE firm called Sun Capital Partners bought Shopko, a Wisconsin-based discount chain with 360 stores and 14,000 employees. The price was about $1.1 billion. Shortly after the buyout it sold Shopko's real estate, forcing the company to pay rent on a property it had once owned. Here's how private equity reporter Dan Primack of the Axios Pro Rata newsletter describes the rest of the deal:

○ Sun also paid itself several dividends, including a $50 million payback in 2015. Plus quarterly consulting fees of $1 million and 1 percent consulting fees on at least six Shopko transactions.

○ That last one is the most egregious, because it applied to the dividends. In other words, Shopko had to pay Sun an extra $500,000 on top of the $50 million dividend—just for the privilege of weakening its balance sheet.

○ And none of this even addresses how Shopko allegedly shortchanged Wisconsin over $8 million in sales tax between 2013 and 2016....

The bottom line: "Sun Capital made irresponsible decisions and made money anyway. That's not uncommon in private equity."[10] Shopko declared bankruptcy in January 2019.

We noted in the previous chapter that chief executives of publicly traded companies pretty much have to manage their business with a hawk's eye on the share price. It's the only indicator of how happy the company's faceless owners are with the CEO's performance. Private equity is completely different in one respect: the owners are very much present all the time, shaping or controlling the decisions of management. In another respect, however, the two ownership structures are very much the same. Companies are run for the benefit of the shareholders, period. The owners' attention is concentrated—focused—on whatever will deliver the greatest financial benefit to their investors, their firm, and themselves. There's nothing devious about this; it's their job.

The Effects of PE Ownership

The fact that so many large and midsized companies are owned by private equity has significant repercussions, not only for how business works but for society as a whole. Consider just a few.

Squeezed companies, compromised owners. A company that is loaded up with debt suddenly faces a narrow range of choices. It has to make the payments or it goes under. If it then has to pay rent for real estate that it once owned—or if its owners decide they need another dividend—the cash squeeze will be even tighter. Such a company can't easily give workers a raise; in fact it may have to lay off part of the workforce. It can't easily invest in future growth or in sustainable technologies and practices. It's at the mercy of both its owners and its creditors. This is not a recipe for a healthy business.

The owners, of course, would very much like their companies to succeed. And to be fair, PE firms have transformed many businesses to make them more productive and successful. But the very structure of ownership means that they must always put the interests of their investors before the interests of their companies if the two conflict. They operate under a timeframe that is somewhat longer than that of a public company—three years (at a minimum) rather than three months—but only somewhat. A few years is rarely enough to put an enterprise on a path toward long-term sustainable growth. And in the meantime, the owners face perverse incentives. As we have seen, they are likely to pursue moves that reduce or eliminate their investors' risks even if those moves put their companies in financial jeopardy. "While the gains accrue to investors in the PE fund, the losses fall mainly on the company's employees, customers, suppliers, creditors, and community," write Appelbaum and Batt in *Private Equity at Work*. "The fund's general partner—the decision maker—has the least to lose in the event that a portfolio company becomes bankrupt."[11]

Job losses. PE firms have a reputation for eliminating jobs through layoffs and other cost-cutting measures. That was an issue in the 2012 US presidential campaign: Republican candidate Mitt Romney, founder and onetime general manager of PE firm Bain Capital, came under fire as a "job destroyer." A good deal of academic research supports this charge, though of course there's a lot of variation from one situation to another. The most comprehensive study was a 2019 analysis by Steven Davis of the University of Chicago and his colleagues, which examined nearly 10,000 private equity buyouts between 1980 and 2013.[12] Half the buyouts were of privately held companies; the rest were spinoffs of public companies. The researchers found that employment was 13 percent higher in the two years after the buyouts in private companies but fell 13 percent in the case of public company buyouts. Overall, jobs fell 1.4 percent, while average compensation per worker fell 1.7 percent (including 6 percent at private companies). A second major study, by Jonathan Cohn and colleagues in 2017, looked at 244 public-company buyouts and 316 private-company buyouts between 1997 and 2007. It found a 13 percent average reduction in within-establishment employment levels relative to peer establishments in the four years following a buyout.[13]

Greater inequality. A key principle of this book is that ownership generates wealth. Ownership in the stock market is at least open to any investor, even though actual ownership is highly concentrated among the wealthy. In private equity, ordinary investors have no chance to invest, except through a pension fund over which they have no control. The beneficiaries of PE ownership are overwhelmingly the institutions, family offices, and rich individuals who are allowed to invest.

Since 2013, it is true, PE firms have tried to expand the range of eligible investors to include both less-wealthy individuals and ordinary workers, in the latter case through their 401(k) and IRA retirement funds. (This is known in the trade as *going retail*.) Since most individuals, even well-off ones, don't want to tie up their money for ten years in an asset that they can't sell, firms have begun to devise methods of packaging their investments in ways that would make them more liquid. But the effort is still in its infancy, and so far the fees are high and the difficulties substantial.

However that works out, the largest beneficiaries of PE investments are always likely to be the same rich institutions and individuals who have benefited in the past. The list of beneficiaries, of course, includes the PE firm itself. The industry's largest firms are now behemoths, and many of their leaders have become billionaires—a testament both to the appeal of this peculiar form of ownership and to its effect on inequality.

Companies as financial assets. We noted earlier that a company, when it is sold, takes on a new and different life. In its early years, a business is likely to be run by its founder. It is likely to be anchored in a community—geographic, professional, or industrial. Its management may regard employees as part of the family, valuing their skills and their loyalty. It may reinvest its profits in building a secure, profitable long-term future. Granted, no one should idealize this kind of ownership—some company founders are as cutthroat and short-term-oriented as anybody. But at least the owners of a new, privately held company are typically on site, involved, and directly responsible for the business's operation.

All that is likely to change when a company is sold. The new owners—Wall Street investors, PE firms, strategic buyers—now view the company purely as a money-making asset. If it doesn't perform to expectations, someone will take action. The business will be restructured. Its workforce may be reduced and other costs cut. Its management may be replaced. It may be sold again, or it may enter bankruptcy. For these companies, the long term no longer exists. Neither does any conception of the business as part of a community, with obligations to other stakeholders in the enterprise. Whole companies will be treated like any other financial asset—bought up, carved up, swallowed up, or sold off.

What the Future Holds

The prospect for private equity's continued rapid growth is uncertain. Its best investment returns "might be in the rearview mirror," said a 2019 report in the business press.[14] Some unions were having second thoughts about investing their members' pension funds in private equity. Congress periodically threatens to regulate the PE industry—in particular, reining in the tax break known as *carried interest*, which allows a PE firm to treat much of its earnings as capital gains rather than as regular income and thus pay lower taxes. Maybe most significant, PE has flourished in an era of low interest rates. Should rates trend higher, the debt that PE firms often load onto a company's books will become more expensive and thus more burdensome.

All that said, no one is expecting the private equity industry to go away, or even to shrink in importance. And though some firms have moved in the direction of social and environmental concerns, their business model ultimately has to trump any other priorities. Luke Johnson, cofounder of a British PE firm called Risk Capital Partners, put the matter succinctly in the *Financial Times*:

> [Private equity] is a pure capitalist pursuit in which investors buy companies and try to sell them for a capital gain. There is an intense focus on returns for shareholders and rather less concern for citizens as a whole. Generally speaking, corporate social responsibility, sustainability, disclosure and environmental issues are not as much a priority as they are to public companies, charities, and government.... Attention is not directed towards the common wealth, but enriching the management, buyout partners and their institutional backers. That is the nature of the game. To argue otherwise is bogus.[15]

The irony here is that—up to a point—private equity plays a useful role by bringing sophisticated business expertise to companies that could use it. As we'll see in Chapter 9, that business model could be adapted to greatly expand a wholly different kind of ownership. In fact—as we'll also see—one prominent PE executive has already taken steps in that direction, with extraordinary results. A substantial opportunity for reforming this quintessentially capitalist enterprise is there for the taking.

Takeaways

- With help from special tax treatment that even Donald Trump decried, private equity investors have turned the buy-and-churn model of corporate ownership into a stockyard full of cash cows.

- Companies owned by private equity too often wind up saddled with debt and forced into layoffs. Their owners typically care little about their long-term health or the communities in which they operate.

PE (NEARLY) DESTROYS A COMPANY

Anchor Hocking was once a premier glassware manufacturer. A major employer, it was an economic mainstay of the small city of Lancaster, Ohio.

Private equity wasn't the only thing that would eventually undermine its position. Foreign competitors began exporting low-priced glassware to the US. Corporate raider Carl Icahn started buying up shares, and Anchor had to pay him a $3 million premium for his stock to make him go away.[16] In 1987, a would-be conglomerate called Newell Co. bought up Anchor and began laying people off. Still, the company remained profitable.

But then PE came along. Cerberus Capital Management, a big New York firm, bought Anchor and two other companies in 2004, building up a large amount of debt that ultimately forced Anchor into bankruptcy. Another PE firm, Monomoy Capital Partners, bought the company out of bankruptcy for $75 million, of which $68.5 million was borrowed money. In 2011 Anchor borrowed another $45 million and paid Monomoy $30.5 million in a dividend recap.

Around the same time, Monomoy bought Oneida, a maker of flatware, and combined the two companies into a new one dubbed EveryWare Global (EWG). Monomoy took out another $10 million in dividends, plus millions in transaction fees. "If you're counting, that's $54 million in known dividends and fees, compared with a combined $12.3 million Monomoy invested . . . to buy the two companies," writes Brian Alexander in his fine book *Glass House*, which chronicles Anchor's—and Lancaster's— sad story.[17] Monomoy took EWG public in 2013, receiving close to $250 million in cash and stock. But EWG was again burdened by debt and entered bankruptcy in 2015.

EWG was then bought by Centre Lane Partners, another PE firm, and rechristened the Oneida Group. In June 2021 Oneida was acquired by the Lenox Corporation, another of Centre Lane's portfolio companies. Meanwhile the Anchor Hocking facilities in Lancaster are decimated, their equipment suffering from years of neglect, the workforce a dim shadow of its former self. The city, as Alexander chronicles in detail, has been plagued by unemployment, drug use, and despair.

PART II

HOW CAN WE CHANGE THINGS?

LET'S IMAGINE THAT WE WANT TO ALTER the structures of ownership—say, by extending it to companies' employees. Is it a reasonable objective? Is it even possible? This part of the book unpacks the questions. It concludes that the answer to both is "yes."

Once the old idea of socialism died out, reformers pretty much gave up on *any* plan for changing the structures of ownership. Instead, some worked to pass regulations, such as the 40-hour week and minimum wage laws. Others—more recently—have tried to change companies' behavior through their investors. If shareholders insist on measures that foster environmental sustainability or other social goals, the theory runs, corporate executives will have to pay attention.

These efforts have been well intentioned, and many have had beneficial results, as we show in Chapter 4. But it has been an uphill battle because the incentives of financial ownership have always pointed in the other direction. Companies are measured above all by their profitability today, this quarter, this year—or in some cases, like biotech, by expectations for large future profits. If they do anything else, such as offering employees better-than-average pay and benefits or investing in green technologies, well, that's nice. But it better not interfere with financial performance.

Chapter 5 looks at the elements that underlie ownership: the assumption of risk, for example, and the value that every stakeholder brings to a company. The key assumption of the past—that ownership should always go to those who provide capital—no longer makes sense in today's economy. Employees in most cases take the greatest risks. They bring the most value. Entrepreneurs who launch new companies should get their reward, of course. But once a company is sold, employee ownership is only logical.

As to its practicality, that gets us into the idea we mentioned in the introduction: the *adjacent possible*. You couldn't invent a microwave oven in 1650, notes the science writer Steven Johnson, no matter how smart you were. You could in the mid-20th century, because the groundwork had been laid. "The adjacent possible is a kind of shadow future," he writes, "hovering on the edges of the present state of things, a map of all the ways in which the present can reinvent itself."[1]

We know that ownership by employees is possible because it already exists. We know that it can be expanded and extended because the mechanisms are either in place or are easy to imagine—and because the idea has widespread bipartisan support. In this case, the process of change is as realistic as the objective.

THE LIMITS OF
(CONVENTIONAL) REFORM

We must not accept the status quo.
It does not work and has to change.

—MARTIN WOLF,
Chief Economics Commentator
Financial Times

SO FAR WE HAVE BEEN PRESENTING an indictment of today's ownership patterns. Where companies of any significant size are concerned, the current systems of ownership mostly benefit the rich and well connected, not the rest of us. They treat companies purely as financial assets, which leads to short-term thinking and (often) bad corporate behavior. But that presents a challenge: If you were charged with changing the way the system works, what would you do?

You might fall back on the traditional path, which is to address business behavior through government regulation. Reformers over the years have nearly always relied on rules and regulations to soften the impact of unbridled capitalism. The list is long:

○ Labor laws, including minimum wages, maximum hours, overtime pay, restrictions on child labor, and antidiscrimination policies

○ Restrictions on other business behavior, including polluting the air and the water, using toxic chemicals, selling dangerous products, and maintaining an unsafe workplace

○ Tax and accounting rules, including (generally toothless) limits on CEO pay

○ Laws and policies favoring labor unions (mostly eased or reversed in the US in the past few decades)

Could you somehow regulate the abuses and absurdities of ownership that we have described? Well, you might impose a tax on short-term stock trading. Or maybe you would change the rules concerning the governance of publicly traded companies. For instance, Senator Elizabeth Warren of Massachusetts and others have proposed that publicly traded companies be required to include employee representatives on their boards of directors. You might also eliminate the tax break on so-called carried interest enjoyed by the private equity industry. Maybe you could even put restrictions on PE firms' ability to buy and sell at will.

But traditional approaches to reform run into two major obstacles. One is that they are fiercely controversial. Liberals and conservatives have fought bitterly over nearly every regulatory measure in the past. In today's divided Congress—and divided country—few new regulations or reforms have a chance at passage. Look at the debate over the federal minimum wage in just the last few years. The level at this writing is $7.25 an hour, the same as it has been since 2009. Corrected for inflation, that's about 20 percent lower than when it was last raised. Yet liberal attempts to increase it have failed. Many Republicans and some Democrats argue that raising the minimum would harm small businesses and lead to cuts in employment and so have held firm in their opposition.

The second obstacle is that such reforms, once implemented, create adversarial situations. The government essentially creates a new policing power. It charges some agency—the Labor Department, the IRS, the EPA, the Securities and Exchange Commission—with enforcing the new law. The agencies increase their bureaucracies accordingly. Meanwhile, the businesses that are being regulated fight back, typically by figuring out how to skirt the law or by challenging it in court. All this eats up time and money, imposing costs on both companies and taxpayers. Over the years, to be sure, most conflicts settle down into some sort of consensus. Few companies these days attempt to pay their employees less than the minimum wage or openly dump toxic waste into a river. But coming to consensus may take a decade or more, and the two sides remain at loggerheads in the meantime.

Like most Americans, we have no interest in returning to a 19th-century version of capitalism in which employees, consumers, and the environment have no protections and companies have few restraints on their actions. But we do believe that pursuing this kind of reform in today's political climate is an uphill battle. And we think there may be more effective ways of changing company behavior than by creating still more adversarial situations, with the government's business police trying to catch the miscreants and haul them into court.

Investor Pressure

So if we see the limits of the regulatory approach, what about a different tack? Leave the ownership structures in place, but try to influence companies' behavior through pressure from shareholders. While this approach is intuitively appealing, it has rarely had the effects that its advocates seek.

This idea goes back at least to 1965, when the Vietnam War was escalating and opposition to the war was growing. Two ministers of the United Methodist Church, Luther Tyson and Jack Corbett, went looking for ways to separate their church from the war effort. Working with a sympathetic financial advisor, they created a new investment fund.[1] The fund would avoid the stocks of companies that profited from the war. The church could put its money into this fund. And who knew? Maybe other churches and antiwar investors would follow suit.

The Pax World Fund, as the two ministers named it, didn't change many hearts and minds on Wall Street or in corporate boardrooms. Still, it was on to something: it was the first socially responsible investment vehicle. Before long, other firms and financial advisors were creating socially responsible investment funds for their clients. And now it wasn't just war-related stocks that were at issue; the new funds would stay away from tobacco companies, gun manufacturers, notorious polluters, and any other company deemed to be operating to the detriment of social goals. Some funds took a more positive approach, seeking out companies with good employee relations, eco-friendly products, and the like. Financial firms began to offer individual investors the chance to pick the particular investment screens that they and their families cared most about.

Partly in response to this phenomenon, some large companies began adopting what were known as corporate social responsibility (CSR) principles. They burnished their reputations among both investors and the public by pursuing—and then touting—good works on the social front. For a couple of decades, CSR seemed to be an integral part of the operation of forward-thinking companies. "NIKE's Sustainability Report Shows Company Reducing Environmental Impact While Continuing to Grow" was one more or less typical press release from several years back. "Coca-Cola Invests in WaterHealth International's Model for Sustainable Safe Water and Partners to Bring Safe Drinking Water to 1 Million School Children" was another. If nothing else, CSR made for good public relations.

And yet, quite suddenly, so it seemed, CSR began going out of fashion. "An archaic and outdated term, CSR today merely resembles a marketing tool, allowing businesses to make symbolic gestures while, in the worst cases, enabling corporate inaction," griped one jaded commentator on an energy-related website in 2020.[2] By then, the new watchword for corporate reformers was ESG.

The ESG movement. *ESG*—the abbreviation stands for environmental, social, and governance concerns—is a more ambitious program of corporate reform. Companies need to set goals in each of these areas, ESG advocates argue. They need to measure their progress toward these goals in publicly available forums. Like the early efforts at socially responsible investing, ESG seemed to tap into widespread discontent with corporate behavior and so became a rapidly growing movement. Consulting firms created a variety of indices by which companies could measure their ESG progress. Financial firms created mutual funds to invest in the stocks of companies that scored high on ESG ratings. Even conventional funds might have an ESG mandate, meaning that fund managers (acting on behalf of the shareholders they represented) would pressure companies to invest in ESG-related improvements.

The specifics of ESG differ depending on who is defining it. But it always reflects a particular idea about how companies should operate. The strictest ESG advocates argue that it's essentially a framework for mitigating the risks posed by climate change and other threats to capitalism. Hence it's just smart investing. Less-strict advocates, motivated as much by social as by financial goals, reflect an older idea known as *stakeholder capitalism*. In this view, companies exist not just to make money but to further the interests of every group they affect—employees, customers, the community, and so on. Old-style CSR advocates believed that companies really ought to do good works, such as protecting the environment and helping the less fortunate. ESG and stakeholder theorists—John Mackey, founder of Whole Foods Market, is one—argue that CSR set the bar too low. Companies' everyday actions *always* affect specific groups, they point out. It isn't enough just to do good works; corporate leaders also need to balance the interests of all the affected groups in making business decisions. If interests seem to conflict, as they often do, leaders should see the situation as an opportunity to create new value by figuring out how to transcend the conflict.

In 2019, the Business Roundtable, an influential organization of big-company chief executives, put its imprimatur on this view, declaring that every company should operate according to the principles of stakeholder capitalism. Investors, presumably, would evaluate companies based on their fidelity to this approach and place their money accordingly.

Evaluating the Investor-Driven Approach

It's an appealing idea in principle: shareholders, the ostensible owners of a corporation, pressure it to behave responsibly, to consider the impact of their actions on all the stakeholders. In response, companies might step up their efforts to operate in sustainable fashion. They might not be so quick to underpay or lay off their employees. And there's no doubt that the ESG movement has in fact led to a number of positive developments, as you can find by inspecting any large company's ESG report. Walmart, for example, reports that it has "engaged thousands of suppliers as well as leading environmental NGOs . . . toward our goal to reduce or avoid emissions in our supply chain by 1 gigaton by 2030." Big banks, led by JP Morgan, were investing more by 2021 in green bonds and loans than in fossil fuels.[3] All this has been accomplished with few new rules or and regulations.

But how much is changing? In our view, the investor-driven approach to business reform suffers from four drawbacks:

○ *Confusion.* What counts as ESG? Acts designed to protect the environment are pretty easy to see and to applaud. But what about the "governance" and "social" aspects? A study financed by the Ford Foundation argues that the signatories of the Business Roundtable statement "have done no better than other companies in protecting jobs, labor rights, and workplace safety during the pandemic, while failing to distinguish themselves in pursuit of racial and gender equality," according to a summary in the *New York Times*.[4] Then there's the fact that BAT—formerly British American Tobacco and current parent of cigarette maker R. J. Reynolds—was named the third-highest ESG performer in a 2021 global ranking. Said the press release: "BAT has been on a transformation journey to A Better Tomorrow, putting sustainability front and center and winning over 200 awards in 2020, and is the only company in its industry in the prestigious Dow Jones Sustainability World Index."[5] The manufacturer of a product that kills millions of people every year wins an ESG award? We're speechless.

○ *Weakness.* The effectiveness of ESG ratings depends on two things: investor opinion, which is notoriously fickle, and corporations' willingness to take the ratings seriously. Harvard Business School professor Lynn S. Paine points out that the Business Roundtable statement contains "no mention of changes in corporate governance or management practice to implement the new stance"—and so, she adds, it is hard to see how the statement "can have much bite."[6] Others have noted that no publicly traded company can afford to make socially minded investments on a scale that might harm the stock price. Many shareholders would flee, and activist investors would likely pounce.

○ *Limited impact.* A number of people have pointed out that the "S" in ESG gets short shrift, in part because it's hard to define. Job security? The CEO of Salesforce, Marc Benioff, is a well-known and vocal advocate of stakeholder capitalism. That didn't stop Salesforce from laying off about a thousand employees five months into the pandemic. (So much for those stakeholders.) And what about wealth security? CEO pay? Stock buybacks? The short-term focus of so many public companies? ESG has little to say about issues like these. Nor does it offer any way of influencing the thousands of large privately held companies, which will pursue ESG only to the extent their owners wish to do so.

○ *Restrictions.* Pension funds, one of the largest holders of corporate stock and one of the few institutional holders with the clout and resources to hold corporate feet to the fire, are limited in what they can advocate by US Department of Labor (DOL) rules. As the DOL said in 2021, these rules "generally require plan fiduciaries to select investments and investment courses of action based solely on consideration of 'pecuniary factors.'"[7] Plan fiduciaries—those in charge of operating the plans in the best economic interest of plan participants—can make an argument that not following some aspect of ESG constitutes an economic risk, but investments cannot be selected because of ESG policies per se. Other large institutional investors, including mutual funds and university endowments, may come under similar, if less binding, constraints from their owners, who want to see the value of the investment put first.

Pressure from investors has no doubt made a difference in some areas of corporate behavior. But no one should hold their breath in anticipation of more far-reaching changes.

Redistribution

Finally, let us say a word about *redistribution*, which has been the most common approach to boosting economic security among lower-income people. Cash-based redistribution takes many forms in successful capitalist economies: child tax credits, welfare programs, social security, the direct payments made during the pandemic. Some reformers go so far as to advocate a guaranteed annual income. Redistribution can also come in the form of service provision, such as medical care for the elderly or for low-income families. Here, too, liberals and conservatives fight fiercely about the size of these payments and who should be eligible to receive them. But nearly everyone agrees—whether out of altruism or out of concern that support for capitalism would vanish without them— that some sort of redistribution is necessary and inevitable.

In developed nations, redistributive programs have been an essential part of life since their inception in the 19th century and especially since their expansion during and after the Great Depression. But while they have been of great benefit to many people, they have left us with the crippling wealth insecurity and the pervasive sense of economic unfairness described earlier in this book. In principle they could be made substantial enough to address these problems, but the cost to taxpayers would be enormous and the political will to get there unimaginable. By itself, redistribution will never get us to a more sustainable and more equitable capitalist system.

The Heart of the Matter

So now let's edge up to the real subject of this book: a different kind of ownership.

Changing who owns a company, after all, is potentially the most effective and far-reaching way of changing its behavior. Owners set the terms and incentives for the decisions of boards and CEOs. If owners are involved with the business, they are accountable for its actions. Moreover, ownership is a form of wealth. Spread ownership more broadly and you automatically decrease economic insecurity. You give more people a stake in the system, because they share in its rewards.

Despite these obvious benefits, ownership has mostly been missing from reformers' agendas on both sides of the aisle. Incredibly, few political leaders and policy folks around the world give much thought at all to who owns their nation's businesses. Nor do they ponder how the structures of ownership might be altered to bring about a fairer economy. Maybe they're worried about being called socialists, even though socialism in the old sense—government ownership of every large enterprise—has been thoroughly discredited. Or maybe they just don't know how to go about reshaping the structures that determine who owns and controls a business. The economy of today, after all, is very different from the economy that gave birth to conventional ownership, and it requires some new thinking. In the following chapter we'll examine what's needed.

Takeaways

○ Conventional approaches to corporate reform, from regulations to ESG-related investor pressure, have awakened people to the need for change. They have also encouraged companies to consider interests other than those of their shareholders.

○ But ultimately, it is ownership that sets the terms and incentives under which companies must operate. Unless reformers address the issue of ownership, their impact will always be limited.

BENEFIT AND B CORPORATIONS: ESG ON STEROIDS

In recent years a majority of US states have passed laws enabling companies to become *benefit* corporations. Directors of a benefit corporation must consider the business's impact on all stakeholders and must file an annual report assessing their ESG performance. Meanwhile—and separately—a nonprofit organization called B Lab offers certification to companies that want to be known as B corporations. Applicants to B Lab must complete an exacting questionnaire relating to their environmental, labor, and community practices. They won't pass the test unless they score sufficiently high, and they must recertify every three years.

The legal status of benefit corporation is relatively new, and the laws' effects on corporate behavior have yet to be assessed. As for B Lab certification, skeptics point out that companies don't get docked for negative actions; that there is no liability if they don't go along with their professed beliefs; and that there are plenty of companies—the handicraft marketer Etsy is one—that have quietly dropped their certification because of potential objections from investors. Despite these quibbles, there's little doubt that both legal benefit status and B Lab itself have pushed the ESG movement a big step forward. B Lab, for instance, now has about 3,500 certified members worldwide.

What about ownership? Benefit corporations and certified B corps are public, private, and employee owned—there's no requirement for any specific ownership structure. But employee ownership is a logical complement to both. A study by the Democracy Collaborative found that 20 employee-owned B corporations outperformed 20 similar but not employee-owned companies by 21 percent on B Lab's assessment tool. "The employee-owned firms had average worker impact scores nearly twice those of non-employee-owned firms, and average environmental impact scores on par with their peers," said the researchers.[8]

OWNERSHIP IN TODAY'S ECONOMY

*Not by logic but by history, owners of capital have
become the owners of the enterprise.*

—CHARLES E. LINDBLOM,
Politics and Markets

THE PAST HAS A WAY OF LAYING DOWN TRACKS that we
trudge dutifully along, unaware that they represent historical choices—
choices that may or may not make sense in the contemporary world. So
it is with ownership. Our assumptions about how companies should be
owned have become cast in stone through familiarity and repetition. Yet
on inspection the assumptions turn out to be full of cracks and flaws,
perhaps even ready to crumble. Let's look at where they came from—and
how poorly they fit the economy of the 21st century.

The Evolution of Capitalism

The fundamental assumption about ownership in capitalist societies
has always been this: a company naturally belongs to the people who
provide the capital.

As we noted earlier, the belief obviously doesn't have to hold true. An entrepreneur or a team of partners could start a business and get a loan for the money they need. The lenders would doubtless insist on a generous return, but they would have no ownership claims. Still, ownership by those who provide the capital is by far the most common form of enterprise. Why so?

To answer that, let's go back to the late 18th century, the era when businesses were just beginning to grow larger than a single workshop. Europe in that period wasn't far removed from feudalism, and the feudal model of enterprise—primarily agriculture—would have seemed as logical to the people of the time as capitalism does to us. The lord owned the land. So he owned the product of all the people who worked on the land. That's just the way it was. Why should things be different in any other type of business?

Moreover, financial capital was scarce in those days. The people who controlled it—wealthy landowning families, a handful of rich bankers— were in a strong bargaining position vis-à-vis anyone who wanted their money. They would have known not just of the feudal model but also the model of international trade, which had begun well before the Industrial Revolution. Investors would fund a ship's captain to embark on trading expeditions to the far reaches of the globe. If a voyage was successful, those investors would now own the ship's cargo—spices, tea, silk, whatever it might be. The captain, of course, got a cut (and on 19th-century US whaling ships, so did the crew). But the investors dictated the terms and collected most of the profits. Why would anything be different in the operation of a factory?

As capitalism evolved, the investor-based model of ownership spread. It was facilitated by 19th-century laws allowing the establishment of corporations and granting them the status of legal persons. The laws provided limited liability for corporate shareholders. If the company went bankrupt, was sued and lost, or had other liabilities it could not cover, creditors could not get their money from individual shareholders. That limited liability made it both practical and appealing for investors to put their money into corporations as compared to other business forms such as partnerships.

So an entrepreneur's backers regularly insisted on an equity stake in the form of shares as compensation for the risk they were taking. (*Equity* in this context just means ownership.) They could then trade those shares at will. The very idea of *stakeholder* capitalism would have seemed absurd. Customers had no organized power. Governments stayed mostly on the sidelines, acting primarily as contract enforcers and tax collectors. Employees in the big factories of the 19th and early 20th century were for the most part a faceless lot in the eyes of the owners. Many workers were just off the farm, many illiterate. Some were children. In the United States, many were recent immigrants with limited English. One mission of enterprise managers and engineers in those days was to make jobs as simple as possible (*deskilling*, economists call it) so that a new hire could get up to speed quickly. Labor turnover was high, and no company wanted to spend any more time and money training the newbies than it absolutely had to.

The 21st century. Today's economy could hardly be more different. For one thing, the world is awash in capital. Wealthy investors and fund managers scour the globe for profitable uses for their money. They compete to fund promising new ventures. A thriving midsize company that wants to expand will find potential investors and lenders lined up at the door. The balance of power has shifted—not completely by any means, but not negligibly either—from the owners of capital to the people who can actually run a successful enterprise.

Then, too, we already live in a sort of half-baked stakeholder economy, just because stakeholders other than investors are far more important to the system than they once were. National governments fund research and development. They closely regulate some economic sectors, such as pharmaceuticals and food production. Through contracts, they spend immense amounts on defense, healthcare, and other goods and services. State and local governments in the US have contracts of their own to hand out; they also devote large sums in the form of tax forgiveness and public investments to entice companies to move to, remain in, or expand in their jurisdictions. (These handouts were estimated to total anywhere between $65 billion and $90 billion a year in 2011 and

2012; they are likely more than that now.[1]) Even customers have more influence than they used to, thanks to organizations such as Consumers Union (publisher of *Consumer Reports*) and to the countless customer-oriented sites available on the web.

The situation with labor—the term itself has come to sound archaic—is more complex. When economists first identified what they called a dual labor market several decades ago, the concept referred to the disparity between unionized workers at large companies, who generally had good pay and benefits, and nonunion workers at smaller companies, who usually earned considerably less. Today the dual labor market is different, and it has spawned even starker disparities. On one side are the millions of people who staff the offices of corporations, banks, hospitals, and so on. The group includes programmers, market-ers, sales reps, technicians, medical personnel, engineers, managers, and many other occupations. Many of these "knowledge workers" are well paid. Many, in fact, create most of the value in their companies. Businesses that trade primarily on intellectual property and expertise rather than on factories or distribution networks depend completely on their knowledge workers.

But there are still plenty of more traditional companies around. They make, transport, and distribute goods. They provide people with everyday services such as restaurant meals and hotel rooms. So on the other side of the labor divide are hospitality workers, truck drivers, warehouse employees, retail clerks, lower-level medical personnel, and the like. The disparity between the two groups showed up starkly during the coronavirus pandemic. Many of the knowledge workers (very much excepting medical professionals) were able to work from home and so weathered the pandemic with relative ease. Many of the things-and-people workers, by contrast, lost their jobs for the duration. Others had to go to work or risk being fired. While there, they were in constant danger of infection. Unions once helped to improve the pay and working conditions of employees in this category. Today, they are unable to help much. Only about 6 percent of private sector workers even belong to a union, and companies resist new unionization efforts aggressively.

Of course, no simple categorization like this is complete. Factory workers, for example, can fall into either group. Many modern plants still require a great deal of semiskilled hand labor. But they also require people who can operate, monitor, and repair sophisticated machinery, automated assembly lines, and other high-tech equipment. On top of that complexity, there's a sizable and growing category of labor that scarcely existed in the past: the people who staff the so-called gig economy. They work for Uber, Grubhub, TaskRabbit, and numerous other companies that provide software platforms for the people who actually do the work. Those workers aren't quite employees; they aren't quite independent contractors either. The legal definition of this category has been the subject of legislation, lawsuits, and even one statewide referendum, in California. So far, gig workers are generally not covered by regulations governing minimum wages, overtime, and the like.

The Implications for Ownership

One way to look at ownership is to determine who creates the most value in an enterprise. The early capitalists clearly brought the most value to the businesses they created. They had the initial idea, often developing new technologies. They assembled whatever money was needed; many risked much of their own. They hired and trained a labor force at a time when most people were accustomed only to farm work. Little wonder that the laws and practices of the day were happy to assign them ownership of the businesses they built.

You can see the same principle at work in some ownership structures today. Contemporary start-ups, like those of early capitalism, are usually owned (entirely or mostly) by their founders. Businesses in professional services like law or accounting are typically organized as partnerships, because it's the professionals who generate the greatest value. Agricultural co-ops like Land O'Lakes or Ocean Spray are owned by their members, who are farmers—and it's the farmers who create most of the value.

71

But established companies too often betray this principle. The stockholders who are the ostensible owners of public companies bring no value at all. The family members who own established family-owned companies bring value only if they work for the business, and even then they may bring no more than any experienced outsider. Private equity firms sometimes bring value in the form of better management or insights into profitable new investments. But often the only "value" they provide lies in the financial engineering techniques that reduce their investors' risks and promise an early payoff.

The idea that ownership should reflect value is one strong argument for ownership of established businesses by their employees. Companies once depended on the backing of financial capitalists. They once depended on big factories, expensive machinery, and distribution networks. Today capital is easy to come by, and all the other elements of business can be easily purchased or farmed out to third parties when necessary. The one component that distinguishes a successful company from an unsuccessful one is the quality and commitment of its employees—and by employees we mean everyone in the organization, not just senior executives and highly paid specialists. In a great company, ideas crop up at every level and address all sorts of matters, from new products to better ways of serving customers. Successfully implementing those ideas is what sets the company apart from its competitors.

So that's where most of the value in a business now comes from: the dedication and imagination of the human beings who are a part of it. According to one study, less than 20 percent of the value of the S&P 500 companies comes from tangible assets; the rest comes from intellectual capital such as patents, reputation, and software.[2] CEOs have always loved to say that their company's most important asset is its people. Today that's more than a platitude—it's reality. Common sense suggests that all those people should own the product of their labors; without them there is no company.

Ownership and risk. A second approach to ownership turns on risk. It's widely assumed that owners deserve the rewards they get because they take all the risks. Because capitalist owners risk their money, they should get all the profits.

This belief reflects a fact known to any student of business: entrepreneurs who launch companies from scratch really do take enormous risks. They may work brutally long hours. They typically put much of their own money into the venture, sometimes taking out large personal loans or second mortgages. They put their own credibility and trustworthiness on the line with investors, lenders, suppliers, customers, and employees. If the venture fails, they will have betrayed the faith of all these people. Silicon Valley, it is true, thrives on maxims like "fail fast" and "never trust an entrepreneur who hasn't had a failure." But the world isn't Silicon Valley, and most companies involve something more than designing the latest smartphone app. The failure of a serious start-up can be devastating to all concerned.

Since entrepreneurs really do take big risks, they are entitled to big rewards if the venture succeeds. That's what capitalism is about. But that's also where the risk-reward assumption ends. Anyone who then buys the company pretty much knows what they are getting. The risks aren't nearly as big. And those other "owners"—public-company shareholders—take no risk at all other than losing some money if the stock price tanks.

Start-up entrepreneurs aside, the biggest risks in today's economy are shouldered not by investors or other stakeholders but by a company's employees. Investors can sell their shares. Customers can buy from somebody else. But whenever people take a full-time job with a company, they are preparing to devote 40 or more hours a week to the enterprise. They may spend years learning the skills required by a particular company and getting to know all the different people involved. They may be promoted to supervisors or assistant managers or even senior positions. They may buy homes near their jobs, enroll their kids in the local schools, and build a social fabric in their communities, all of which would be difficult to replace if they had to move to find new jobs. In a sense, employees are investing the most precious things anyone has—their time, their lives, their families' futures—in their choice of jobs. Yet *they can be let go at any time,* usually with little warning or compensation. They have no control over these decisions, and they have no say over the business strategies that led to the layoffs or the firings.

And it isn't just employees of troubled companies who are in jeopardy. Those 1,000 people laid off in 2020 by Salesforce, mentioned in the previous chapter? The company had just experienced a profitable quarter, bringing in more than $5 billion in quarterly revenue for the first time. Its stock rose 26 percent. The layoff was just a reallocation, explained a company spokesperson: "We're reallocating resources to position the company for continued growth. This includes continuing to hire and redirecting some employees to fuel our strategic areas and eliminating some positions that no longer map to our business priorities."[3]

Ownership sets the priorities. A third and final way of looking at ownership points in the same direction. What does the United States want from its economy today? It's a rhetorical question, of course, because citizens and their organizations want many different things. Still, you can adduce some "wants" by looking at what happened and what was most valued at any given time.

In the 19th century, for instance, the nation seemed to want growth at all costs, much like what China and other developing nations seem to want today. For much of the 20th century the US seemed to want steady jobs, with good pay and good benefits. Today our priorities have changed. We want innovation and entrepreneurship, for sure. We want economic rewards that are commensurate with work and skill. But we also want businesses that behave in socially responsible ways and owners who are accountable for their actions. Most of all we want the economy to provide citizens with opportunity and with a measure of economic security, benefits that are too often missing from millions of people's lives. These are objectives that in most cases can't be realized through wages and salaries alone. Ownership has to be one element of a financially secure and economically responsible life. Any country, not just ours, might well want the benefits of ownership to be distributed as widely as possible.

How to Get from Here to There

Reformers who sketch out a vision of a better future often assume that their job is done. We call it the "If I ran the world . . ." syndrome. The assumption is that everyone will see the logic of your argument and will somehow—in the words of Captain Jean-Luc Picard of the starship *Enterprise*—make it so. We don't want to fall into that trap—and anyway, the idea of spreading ownership among employees raises all kinds of practical issues as to how it could be implemented. So the remainder of this book will show in detail how our nation can escape those rutted tracks of history and get from where we are now to a fairer, more equitable capitalist economy, one in which owning stock where you work is as common as owning a house.

Fortunately, we already have a big head start.

Takeaways

○ Companies came to be owned by capitalists—those who provided the funds—at a particular point in history. We have trudged along in these same ruts for too long.

○ When you look at who should own companies, measured by who takes the biggest risks and who adds the most value, the arrows all point in one direction: the employees.

THE FATE OF "ENLIGHTENED CAPITALISTS"

It's a recurring dream of reformers: a visionary entrepreneur or CEO creates a company that serves its employees as well as its shareholders and that operates in an innovative, socially responsible fashion. We have seen plenty of such attempts in recent years, including TOMS (giving away a pair of shoes to needy children for every pair sold) and Dr. Bronner's (environment-friendly products, great employee benefits including profit sharing, a $7,500 child-care allowance, and free vegan lunches).

But the historical track record isn't so great, as management professor James O'Toole points out in his pathbreaking book *The Enlightened Capitalists*.[4] From Robert Owen's New Lanark on through James Cash Penney, Milton Hershey, Robert Wood Johnson (of J&J) and a dozen others, nearly all of O'Toole's innovators created successful businesses that operated on more inclusive and more responsible principles—until they didn't. The moral of the story is that visionary businesspeople can run things differently. But if they get distracted, grow bored, or die, the companies will revert back to the customary methods of capitalism. The record is equally mixed today. Family-owned Dr. Bronner's, like many others, is thriving. TOMS—also like many others—got itself into trouble and was taken over by creditors in 2019.

What's the answer? Change the ownership structure, says O'Toole. "After studying the careers of enlightened capitalists for the better part of my career, I have concluded that ownership is far and away the most significant predictor of virtuous business practices, and especially the key to their sustainability."[5]

PART III

REINVENTING CAPITALISM FOR THE 21ST CENTURY

THIS PART OF THE BOOK—THE PAYOFF, we hope, for which earlier chapters have prepared the ground—introduces you to a different (and better!) form of ownership: ownership by a company's employees.

In some cases employees own whole companies, as we'll see. That form of ownership awaits *extension* into more and more enterprises. In other cases—particularly in publicly traded corporations—they might own only a piece. That form can be *expanded* so that employees as a group become significant shareholders.

We wish you could accompany us on the many visits we have paid to employee-owned companies over the years—TDIndustries, say, a big mechanical-construction firm in Dallas, or maybe the Newport Restaurant Group (NRG), headquartered in Rhode Island. At first glance the facilities look like any other business. But look a little closer. You might find the walls papered with employee photos, as at TD. You might see an employee-ownership flag flying alongside the Stars and Stripes, as at NRG's flagship inn.

And when you talk to people, you hear things that you seldom hear at conventional companies. "I love this job!" "I've been here 20 years and hope to be here another 20." "We pull together—after all, we own the place." Employees might show you the walls where the latest financial results are posted. They might let you sit in on an idea session, where people put their heads together to figure better ways of doing things. Chapter 6 describes some of these companies and spells out their benefits.

Like any social invention, employee ownership has a history, recounted in Chapter 7. It caught on slowly at first, then quickly. It had some growing pains, and it spawned some myths and misconceptions. But today it is ready for expansion. Chapters 8 through 11 show how easy it would be to make this form of ownership much more common in America—and elsewhere. Chapter 12 recounts other countries' experiences and experiments with the idea, most of these efforts still in their infancy.

Hope—optimism about the future—can be hard to come by these days. And employee ownership is hardly a panacea for all the ills that face humankind. But it is one big step—one huge step—in the direction of a fairer, more productive economy, one that works for the many and not just for the few. This part shows how it works, and how it could easily be expanded.

A DIFFERENT KIND OF COMPANY

*Because we each receive an ownership interest
in the company, we realize that we are investing
in ourselves. We all work for one another.*

—TRINA PARKS
Craft Training and Development Director,
McCarthy Building Companies

BACK IN 1983, NO ONE WOULD have expected much from a small company with the outsized name of Springfield ReManufacturing Center Corporation. It had a little more than 100 employees and sales of about $16 million. It was in the gritty business of remanufacturing heavy-duty diesel engines. It was facing a mountain of debt, the result of a recent buyout.

Today, that company is known as SRC Holdings Corp. (usually just SRC), and it's a phenomenally successful operation. It employs nearly 2,000 people. It generates more than $650 million a year in revenue. It operates 10 different subsidiaries, not just in remanufacturing but also in such areas as warehousing, logistics, and technology. Its value has grown over the years from 10¢ a share to a split-adjusted value of $767. Its "Great Game of Business" system of open-book management has attracted the attention of executives and business-school professors from all over the world.

What's sometimes overlooked in the writeups is that SRC is wholly owned by its employees. The company's iconic CEO, Jack Stack, set up an employee stock ownership plan soon after he and several other managers bought the business from International Harvester. The plan was originally a minority owner but has owned 100 percent of the shares since 2011. So SRC's employee-owners have enjoyed the benefits of owning a growing, profitable business. Many have retired, in some cases cashing out more than a million dollars' worth of stock. Others remain as employee owners, building up comfortable nest eggs. "We have distributed close to $160 million to people who cashed out their stock," Stack told us. "That money goes right back into the community."

The Remarkable World of Employee Ownership

SRC is a particularly prosperous example of a phenomenon that all too few Americans know about: the flourishing world of employee-owned businesses. You could think of all these enterprises as a kind of economy in waiting—a business sector based on a wholly different kind of ownership, and one that holds immense promise for a more equitable future.

A quick survey of this world would reveal more than 13,000 enterprises with some degree of employee ownership, including perhaps 2,000 that, like SRC, are entirely owned by the people on the payroll. The overall numbers are relatively small compared to the whole US economy. Still, employee-ownership companies are in every state of the union and in nearly every industry. If you shop at Publix, WinCo Foods, or any of a dozen other grocery chains, you're buying from an employee-owned supermarket. If you drink Harpoon or many other craft beers, you're patronizing an employee-owned brewery. If you bake with King Arthur flour, with grains from Central Milling, or with Bob's Red Mill products, you're using ingredients produced in employee-owned facilities. If you stop for gas and coffee at places like Wawa (middle Atlantic states), Stewart's Shops (New York, Vermont), or Huck's Food & Fuel (midwestern states), you're a customer of (largely) employee-owned convenience stores.

And it isn't just consumer-oriented companies that are employee owned. The 18,000 employees of Amsted Industries, a global manufacturer of heavy industrial components such as railroad-car undercarriages, own their company. So do the 11,000-plus employees of W. L. Gore & Associates, whose innovators have given us not just Gore-Tex fabric but new products in electronics, cable, medical, and several other fields. Eight of the 20 largest engineering firms, including Burns & McDonnell, Parsons, and Black & Veatch, are largely owned by their employees; so are dozens of construction companies, such as St. Louis–based McCarthy Building Companies and San Francisco's Swinerton. Ohio-based Davey Tree Expert Company and several other tree-service firms are employee owned. Recology, in the San Francisco Bay Area, is a leader in waste management. The Coordinating Council for Independent Living in Morgantown, West Virginia, is one of the largest providers of home healthcare services and management in its region. Axia Home Loans, in Seattle, is a full-service mortgage banking firm. All are wholly owned by their employees. The three largest contractors to the United States Agency for International Development (USAID)—Chemonics, Abt Associates, and DAI—are all 100 percent employee owned; so are many other government contractors.

The Implications of Employee Ownership

The companies we have mentioned so far are owned—in some cases partially, more often wholly—through an *employee stock ownership plan (ESOP)*, an innovative organizational structure that, so far, is unique to the United States. It's the most common and in many ways the most effective form of broad-based employee ownership. At this writing there are about 6,500 of these plans covering over 14 million employees (Figure 3).[1] There are plenty of other forms of employee ownership as well: profit-sharing trusts that invest in company stock, plans that grant stock directly to employees, and worker cooperatives, to name three common examples. We'll say more about these in a moment, and we'll examine them all in subsequent chapters. But before we get into the details, take a moment to consider what the existence of so many ESOP companies means for the future of capitalism.

FIGURE 3: ESOPs by the Numbers

PLAN TYPES	PLANS	PARTICIPANTS	PLAN ASSETS
Privately held companies	5,864	2,014,771	$186,218,000
Small plans (under 100 participants)	3,421	147,971	$16,358,000
Large plans (100+ participants)	2,442	1,866,800	$169,860,000
Publicly traded companies	638	12,035,803	$1,273,710,000
Total	6,501	14,050,574	$1,459,928,000

Source: National Center for Employee Ownership, 2021

Things don't have to be as they are. The conventional structures of ownership—individual, family, stock-market—are so familiar as to seem inevitable. Even private equity is a perfectly logical outcome of the system of tradeable shares. As long as shares of stock and whole companies can be bought and sold like so many properties on a Monopoly board, we will be left with the absurd systems of ownership chronicled in the first part of this book.

But no ownership structure is natural or inevitable. All are creations of human beings and the laws they enact. In the case of ESOPs, the US government established certain procedures and incentives for the owners of private companies to sell their businesses to the employees through this structure. Several thousand owners have taken advantage of the policy and in the process have created an immense variety of employee-owned businesses. Nearly all of these companies have thrived under their new structure. They are a market-tested alternative to the other forms of capitalist ownership. They work.

Employee-owned companies broaden the benefits of ownership. Remember what we said about ownership at the very beginning of this book. It transforms people's lives. It provides a level of security that most wage workers never attain. It makes some people rich. WinCo Foods, the Idaho-based supermarket company, boasted on its website in 2021 that the company's employee-ownership plan included "more than 500 millionaires." The website of Jasper Holdings, an engine remanufacturer in Indiana, informed us that more than 700 of its 2,600 employee owners held over $100,000 worth of stock in their accounts, while another 500 or so held more than $50,000. Numbers like these aren't uncommon among ESOPs. According to an analysis of company filings with the Department of Labor, the average account balance of ESOP participants in 2019 was $132,362.[2]

We have spoken with individual workers at hundreds of employee-owned companies over the years, and most are naturally reticent to reveal the details of their family finances. But the few who do share those details seem both proud and incredulous at the fact that they have earned far more than they ever thought possible. José Juan Alvarado, a veteran blue-collar employee at a Texas specialty manufacturer called Polyguard, acknowledged "several hundred thousand dollars" in his ownership account. Leo Szlembarski, a lathe operator at Illinois-based Scot Forge, once told us that it wasn't uncommon for blue-collar workers at Scot to retire with $700,000 or $800,000. He himself, he confessed, had "a little more."

Later in the book we'll look at comparisons between ESOPs and other kinds of retirement plans, such as 401(k)s. For now, note that the benefits of ownership accrue quickly, even for young workers. A survey that looked at workers' economic circumstances over time compared 28-to-34-year-olds who had employee ownership to their peers who did not. The study found that the former group enjoyed 92 percent higher median household wealth, 33 percent higher income from wages, and 53 percent longer median job tenure.[3]

The benefits are more than financial. Ownership, of course, provides more than financial rewards. People who own companies feel like they're working for themselves rather than for some distant owner.

Here's how Nancy Prewitt, a technical support specialist at Polyguard, puts it:

> *Working for an employee-owned company makes you take more pride in your work. You look out for the overall benefit of the company because you know that if you do your part, it will ultimately help that project and bring in the sales dollars that increase the overall worth of the company.*

And this is what Mike Perri, an operations manager at Davey Tree, says:

> *Employee ownership is a great way to look after my future and to feel the rewards of my hard work. All the hours you put in are returned back, and that's rewarding. You certainly focus your attention on each individual task more. You pour more of yourself into what you are doing.*

Rosanne Wheeler-Flint, a customer care specialist at employee-owned Web Industries, in Massachusetts, says,

> *Each person has a stake in the company—you can see it, you can feel it. Not only am I happier at work, but I now have a financial plan for my future in my ESOP that I didn't have before and never expected to have.*

In a world where so many people feel insecure and alienated from their job, it's hard to put a price tag on sentiments like that.

Employee ownership builds stronger companies. It boosts a nation's productivity and international competitiveness.

Researchers have studied employee-owned companies for many years, and their findings are remarkably consistent. These firms really do perform better. One study reports that employee-owned companies grow about 2.5 percentage points per year faster in sales, employment, and productivity after they set up their ownership plan than would have been expected if they had not done so.[4] Other studies have found productivity increases of between 4 and 5 percent, on average, in the year a plan is adopted.

Companies with employee ownership also have higher survival rates. A study tracking the entire population of such companies over ten years found that privately held employee-owned companies were only half as likely as firms without employee ownership to go bankrupt or close. They were three-fifths as likely to disappear for any reason.[5] For comparison, remember the Cal Poly study reported in Chapter 3? Private equity companies went bankrupt at 10 times the rate of similar publicly traded companies.

How to account for these gaps in performance? For one thing, employee-owned companies are nearly always off to a good start. Struggling businesses are rarely able to convert to employee ownership and probably couldn't get financing for the transaction if they tried. Then, too, some employee-owned companies also get continuing tax benefits, established by Congress to encourage this form of ownership. But the strength of employee-owned companies seems to be largely attributable to how they run their operations. It's well established in the business world that participatory management—including helping employees to understand the company's economics and involving them in workplace decisions—leads to better results. But it's hard for conventionally owned corporations to get the level of engagement from employees that this approach requires; workers understandably ask, *What's in it for me?* If employees own a chunk of stock, that question answers itself. So a participative orientation is far more common in these companies than in conventionally owned firms, with corresponding differences in outcomes.

Employee-owned companies reorder their priorities. You can see some of the differences in how they treat employees—fewer layoffs, for example. Since 2002, the quadrennial General Social Survey has tracked layoffs among respondents who say they participate in some kind of employee ownership plan in their company. The survey consistently finds that employee-owners are much less likely to report being laid off in the previous year. In 2014, for instance, the layoff figure was 9.5 percent for all working adults compared to 1.3 percent for employee-owners.[6] In other words, typical wage earners at that point were seven times as likely as employee-owners to lose their job, along with healthcare coverage and whatever other benefits it might have carried. A similar pattern showed up during the pandemic. In June 2021, a study looking specifically at ESOP companies found that they laid people off at one-quarter the rate of similar non-ESOP firms.[7]

Compensation and benefits at employee-owned companies tend to be better as well. That study of 28-to-34-year-olds mentioned earlier found that those who own shares through ESOPs earn one-third more in median wages compared to employees who are not in ESOPs.[8] Broader studies show employees making 5 to 12 percent more overall than workers in matching but conventionally owned companies.[9] As for retirement security, ESOP participants have more than twice as much just in their ESOP accounts as employees in non-ESOP companies have in their 401(k) plans (Figure 4). And ESOP companies are as likely to have *secondary* retirement plans, such as a 401(k), as comparable companies are to have any plan at all. Once they set up an ESOP, moreover, these companies typically make few changes in what they contribute to the secondary plans.[10]

FIGURE 4: ESOPs and 401(k) plans

EMPLOYEES WITH ESOPS HAVE TWICE AS MUCH IN THEIR ACCOUNTS AS EMPLOYEES IN COMPARABLE COMPANIES HAVE IN THEIR 401(K) PLANS...	
Average ESOP account balance	$132,362
Average 401(k) account balance in companies with only a 401(k) plan	$63,925
...AND EMPLOYERS CONTRIBUTE 2.6 TIMES AS MUCH PER YEAR.	
Average employer contributions to ESOP per participant	$6,567
Average employer contribution to 401(k) per participant in companies with only a 401(k) plan	$2,507

Source: National Center for Employee Ownership, "Measuring the Impact of Ownership Structure on Resiliency in Crisis," January 2022, *https://esca.us/wp-content/uploads/2022/01/ESCA-Report-FINAL.pdf.*

But the real contrast lies in a company's perspective. The owners of public and private equity companies, as we have seen, have a purely financial interest in the business, and a short-term one at that. They expect executives to produce profits quarter to quarter or year to year with little regard for how those profits are produced. If the executives' actions weaken the company over the long haul but produce better results right now, so much the worse for the long haul. Private equity sometimes drives companies right into the ground, as with Anchor Hocking and many others.

A company that is owned by its employees, by contrast, naturally takes a longer view. The differences between this kind of outlook and the stock-market or private equity outlook are stark:

It's the difference between investing in long-term capital improvements, including environmentally sustainable practices, versus expecting a one-year or two-year payback.

It's the difference between balancing the long-term interests of financial backers, employees, customers, and the community versus serving shareholders' short-term interests.

It's the difference between maintaining a healthy balance sheet versus loading the company up with debt to pay for dividends and buyback shares.[11]

It's the difference between building a loyal, committed workforce through training, skill development, and participation in management versus treating employees as no more than interchangeable hired hands.

It's the difference between a company whose employee-owners cash in their stock when they leave—and then use it to buy a house or a car, send kids to college, or help out a loved one and still have money left for retirement—versus a company whose employees leave with little or nothing.

It's the difference between working for a company that is likely to treat you like an owner, to seek out and listen to what you think, and to share information about how the company—your company—is doing versus working for a company that does none of those things.

Employee-owners naturally want profitability and growth. They are less likely than financial owners to want profitability and growth right now at the expense of the enterprise's long-term health.

WHAT'S IT LIKE TO MANAGE AN EMPLOYEE-OWNED COMPANY?

Listen to what some CEOs and front-line leaders say.

- McCarthy Building Companies is the 13th largest construction company in the US, with more than 6,000 salaried and craft employees. Headquartered in St. Louis, it has operations across America. McCarthy has been wholly owned by its employees since 2002. "It's a place where everybody believes, acts like, and operates as if they're a principal," says former McCarthy Chairman and CEO Mike Bolen. "They own the place, and as owners they must be able to trust one another and be trustworthy. An ownership culture drives people to care about not only what they're doing today, but also about what that means two, three, four, five, ten years from now."

- Hypertherm is a New Hampshire–based manufacturer of industrial cutting systems and software—equipment that is used in shipbuilding, construction, and many other industries around the world. It employs nearly 1,900 people and sells its wares in more than 60 countries. It has been 100 percent employee owned since 2013, and has grown steadily. Larry Kennett, a front-line manufacturing leader, has been with the company all that time. "As for being an owner, we're all heavily invested," he says. "So we're always trying to choose the right thing to do, the right decisions. You can pretty much count on everybody to have that mindset.... If you invest in something, then you want to see it succeed."

○ Torch Technologies, based in Huntsville, Alabama, is a contractor to the US Department of Defense and other agencies. With 1,250 employees and more than half a billion dollars in revenue, it is one of the largest federal contractors in the country. "We believe that level of success is achieved by giving every employee owner a stake in the outcome," declares the company's website. Employee ownership, says cofounder Bill Roark, "creates a level of teamwork that I would never have imagined possible."

○ Manos Home Care started in 1986 to provide minor home services such as cleaning. Over the years it developed capabilities in senior care and then in services for individuals with developmental disabilities. Today it employs 1,700 workers including 1,100 employee-owners; more than 85 percent of the company is owned by the direct care providers. Manos, which services California's East Bay region, provides services to about 1,600 clients in their homes each year. "Manos employees continue to enjoy the benefits of our employee ownership, both financially and as the basis for our corporate culture," says executive director Kevin Rath.

Other Forms of Employee Ownership

A formal employee stock ownership plan is in many ways the most widely applicable embodiment of the concept, which is why we led off with companies like SRC and the others. But the business world is a complex place, and there are plenty of other ways to get equity into the hands of a company's employees. For example:

○ **Private companies** can and often do give employees restricted stock—that is, shares that are subject to some vesting requirement, such as working at the company for a certain number of years. They can give employees stock options, meaning the right to buy shares for some number of years at the price when the option was granted. Or they can give employees synthetic equity, the right to either the value of a certain number of shares or the increase in share value. Chobani, the fast-growing yogurt producer, had about 2,000 employees in 2016. CEO Hamdi Ulukaya awarded shares to all of them; the stock amounted to about 10 percent of the company, with individual awards based on tenure. In 2021, when Chobani filed for an initial public offering, *Forbes* reported that the average payout for those employees would be roughly $150,000. The earliest employees' stakes, the magazine added, "could possibly reach over $1 million."[12]

○ **Some startups**—particularly those seeking backing from venture capital firms and aiming at an IPO or other sale of the company—award restricted stock or stock options to most or all of their employees. After all, they're asking those employees to work long hours, often for less than they could make elsewhere, in hopes of sharing in the company's success. And if the company does succeed, the payouts can be enormous. When Facebook (now Meta) went public in 2012, it created hundreds—possibly thousands, no one's quite sure—of millionaires on the spot. Of course, most startups never seek or get VC funding, and most never achieve anything like that level of business success. So instant riches of this sort are rare. Anyway, the bulk of the equity, even in these startups, often goes to senior executives and highly skilled employees like scientists and programmers, not to rank-and-file workers.

○ **Some publicly traded companies** have programs designed to make their employees into owners. They may award stock options or restricted stock directly. (Starbucks's Bean Stock program is an example.) They may offer company stock as a match—usually 50 percent or less—for whatever employees put into their tax-sheltered retirement accounts, such as 401(k)s. (This was much more common in the 1990s than it is today.) They may also create so-called employee stock purchase plans, which enable workers to buy stock at a discount, profit-sharing plans that invest in company stock, or an ESOP.[13] We'll discuss all these in Chapter 8.

○ **Worker co-ops** get a lot of attention in the media and often are the first thing people think of when you mention employee ownership. Cooperatives are a form of shared business ownership based on membership; members have governance rights as well as rights to a financial return. They have been encouraged by initiatives in New York, Philadelphia, and several other cities as a means of retaining small businesses and providing jobs for excluded workers. Right now, the US Federation of Worker Cooperatives conservatively estimates that there are roughly 500 co-ops in the country, employing a total of about 8,000 people. Even if both numbers are somewhat larger than these estimates—they probably are—co-ops still constitute a small part of the employee ownership landscape. There's more on co-ops in Chapter 10.

In later chapters we'll show which structures are most appropriate in specific business situations. But it's a good thing that so many different methods are available. The ownership landscape will continue to be a crazy quilt for the foreseeable future. If we want to spread the benefits of ownership to more people, we'll need a variety of tools at our disposal.

A Bipartisan Alternative

When Americans are asked by pollsters whether they would support employee ownership, the results are remarkable. In 2015, for example, a poll of 853 registered voters showed that 68 percent supported "the concept of companies being owned by their employees so that all workers at a company share in its success." Only 13 percent opposed the idea, while 19 percent were unsure. A majority of respondents from both major parties supported employee ownership. The poll also found that 58 percent of Americans would support legislation that makes it easier for employees to own a part of the business where they work, and 50 percent of Americans think the government should do more to encourage the growth of employee-owned companies.[14]

A broader poll, included in the 2018 General Social Survey, identified Americans' attitudes toward *shared capitalism*, defined as employee ownership, profit sharing, or both. About 60 percent said they would probably or definitely take a job with these benefits, compared to about 10 percent who said they would probably or definitely take a job without them. Asked whether they would favor working at a job where the company was government owned, investor owned, or employee owned, more than 70 percent chose employee owned. In all cases, attitudes toward employee ownership differed little by political identification. In the job question, for example, self-identified liberals showed a 64.8 percent preference, while self-described conservatives came in at 58.9 percent.[15]

Even the world of professional politicians shows bipartisan support for employee ownership. Liberal senators such as Ben Cardin of Maryland and Kirsten Gillibrand of New York have been enthusiastic supporters. So have conservative Republicans such as Rob Portman of Ohio and Charles Grassley of Iowa, not to mention Ronald Reagan himself. The 2012 Republican Party platform, titled "We Believe in America," explicitly endorsed the idea:

> Republicans believe that the employer-employee relationship of the future will be built upon employee empowerment and workplace flexibility, which is why Republicans support employee ownership. We believe employee stock ownership plans create capitalists and expand the ownership of private property and are therefore the essence of a high-performing free enterprise economy, which creates opportunity for those who work and honors those values that have made our nation so strong.[16]

But all this raises thorny questions. If both parties agree on employee ownership, and if public opinion supports it, why is it such a back-burner issue in every political campaign and agenda? Why aren't more pundits and journalists writing about it? Somehow, political and thought leaders are content to pat the idea on the head, as they would an adorable pet, and stop there. Then, too, why are there not more employee-owned companies? Given the widespread discontent with the US economy, why has this commonsensical idea not yet caught on among many more people? It's easy enough to imagine a more equitable kind of capitalism based on employee ownership, and it's easy enough to point out the harms and abuses of the current system. But it seems hard to move from one system to the other.

So what are the obstacles? And where are the most fruitful opportunities for spreading the idea? The chapters that follow will try to answer these questions—and point the way toward a more thoroughgoing transformation.

Takeaways

○ Ownership by employees—usually through an ESOP, but also through several other mechanisms—is already widespread in the United States.

○ Employee ownership changes how companies operate. It changes how people feel about their work, and it enables them to build significant wealth over time.

WHY SELL TO AN ESOP?

Litehouse Inc. is a 100 percent ESOP-owned manufacturer of salad dressing and other food products. With facilities in four US cities and remote workers across the US and Canada, the company has grown steadily since the ESOP was launched in 2006 and now employs about 1,300 workers. Why the ESOP? CEO Kelly Prior told us that the previous owners got many other inquiries from potential buyers. But, he added, "Our founders never had an interest in selling to a strategic buyer or PE firm because they were concerned that in either case Litehouse would eventually be relocated out of the small communities in which it operated. They witnessed many companies over years lose their values and culture because of a sale to another party." Instead of having to relocate or give up their jobs, Litehouse's employees are now owners. By 2020, everyone who was there at the start of the ESOP in 2006 had surpassed $100,000 in account value.

WHY ISN'T THERE MORE EMPLOYEE OWNERSHIP?

*Labor is the source of subsistence, capital is the
source of affluence. My idea is to make everyone a
capitalist, and therefore, financially secure.*

—LOUIS O. KELSO
Inventor of ESOPs

PEOPLE MAY SUPPORT THE IDEA of employee ownership in the
abstract, but most know little about it in practice. Say the word *ESOP*
to someone who has never heard it before—a group that unfortunately
includes a majority of Americans—and you will likely be greeted with a
blank stare. Spell out the acronym, *employee stock ownership plan*, and
the response may be no different. Say what?

Things are only a little better in the world of business and finance. A
lot of people in these parts have at least heard of ESOPs. But though they
can't plead complete ignorance, their reaction is likely to be an eyebrow
raised in skepticism. "Some sort of retirement plan, right? Seems pretty
risky to me." We can't count the number of times we have heard variations on this theme.

Seldom has a pathbreaking social invention been so greatly misunderstood and so dramatically underestimated. Of course, we can't be sure. Maybe when the founders used words like *republic* and *democracy* they were met with a similar combination of ignorance and skepticism.

The facts are simple enough. An ESOP is simply a legal vehicle—a kind of trust—that enables people to own stock in the company they work for and to get that stock *at no cost to themselves*. It works like this:

○ The company first sets up the trust, which isn't so different from the kind of trust it might create for the funds in an ordinary retirement plan, such as a 401(k). But with an ESOP, employees won't make any contribution; the trust will be funded entirely by the company.

○ The trust's purpose is to buy shares in the business from whoever owns it. So the company either puts cash into the trust or borrows the money it needs to buy the shares.

○ The trust then credits the shares to individual employees' accounts according to a formula. (If it has bought the shares with borrowed money, it credits them to individuals as the loan is paid off.) Government rules ensure that the formula is fair.

○ At a minimum, every full-time employee who has been on the job for a year gets an account, and shares can be added to that account each year. Once the account is fully vested—that can take up to six years—the shares belong to those individuals.

○ The company is legally obliged to buy back those shares for cash at their current value (sometimes paid out over a few years) when employees leave or retire.

Think about all that for a moment. Once the transaction is complete, a new legal owner, the trust, now holds part or all of the shares. Since the trust represents the interests of employees, it naturally has a long-term interest in the health of the company. Over time, workers can build up significant amounts of wealth as their shares grow in value and more shares are added to their accounts. That's what we saw at SRC and the other companies described in the previous chapter.

So is the ESOP a retirement plan? Well, sort of. It's certainly a way for people who don't earn high salaries to build up a sizable nest egg that they can draw on later in life. But it's different from conventional retirement plans, which require employees to contribute part of their paycheck. An ESOP costs employees nothing—zero—yet provides them with a chance to accumulate substantial sums. Anyway, it's far more than a retirement plan. ESOPs have the potential for reshaping the ownership landscape, as they have already begun to do. They change a company's priorities. They spread the wealth. They are one key to a fairer, stronger form of capitalism.

To be sure, there's risk involved, because not every company succeeds. And no one would want their long-term savings to be in only one company's stock, which is why most ESOP companies offer a conventionally diversified 401(k) as well. But remember: with an ESOP, it isn't the employees' contributions that are at risk, because there aren't any contributions.

As for how ESOPs came to accomplish their financial magic—and why, in light of the benefits they deliver, they aren't as common as pigeons in the park—well, that's the story of this chapter. It begins in the middle of the 20th century, with an iconoclastic character named Louis O. Kelso.

Kelso's Invention

Kelso was a dapper man: his conventional attire was a well-tailored suit graced with a polka-dotted bow tie. Born in 1913, he trained as a lawyer, served in the navy during World War II, and spent most of his adult life working in law and investment banking. But he had come of age during the Great Depression, and he developed a lifelong ambition to understand and reform the capitalist economy. How could a nation have so much productive capacity lying idle? Why weren't there jobs available when so many people wanted work? His questions and concerns continued into the 1950s, even though the postwar world brought a return to prosperity. Would automation, then looming on the horizon, throw people out of work? If it did, what would they live on?

Already, he argued, capital was playing an increasingly important role in production. As the trend continued, the rich would prosper, because they owned most of the capital. But wages might stagnate, and technological change would jeopardize many workers' jobs. The resulting disparity between the rich and everybody else was a sure-fire recipe for discontent; it might even touch off some sort of socialist revolution. This, in his view, was the capitalist system's fundamental weakness.

So Kelso, a devout capitalist himself, set out to redress the balance. He wrote a book called *The Capitalist Manifesto*, published in 1958, coauthored with the well-known philosopher Mortimer Adler. It hit the bestseller list, and he followed it up over the years with several others. The prose in his works can be dry and the arguments abstract. But the fundamental idea underlying all of them was simplicity itself. *No one should have to live on labor income alone.* If more people enjoyed what the rich already enjoyed, namely ownership of capital and the income that flowed from that ownership, they would get along just fine. If you have enough stock, after all, you don't worry so much about losing your job. And if everyone had an income regardless of whether or not they had a job, they could continue to buy things. The economy would be that much less likely to collapse the way it did in the Depression.[1]

So how to get capital into the hands of people who couldn't afford to buy it? Kelso offered a wealth of proposals, some of which involved large government programs. But his simplest and most practical idea was what came to be known as the employee stock ownership plan, or ESOP.

Look, said Kelso (in effect). People who depend on an ordinary worker's wages will never be able to buy much stock. If a company gives them a few shares of stock, they'll just sell it, because they need the money. Only the best-paid wage earners could ever hope to accumulate enough capital to replace or even meaningfully supplement their labor income just by stashing a little away each year.

So let's try another idea. Suppose employees were to buy a portion— or indeed all—of the company they worked for. They couldn't afford it on their own nickel, of course. But suppose they paid for their ownership out of the company's future profits. You'd have to set up a legal entity of some sort to borrow the money that was needed and to ensure that employees were credited with ownership as the loan was repaid. But that seemed eminently practical, and in fact Kelso's investment banking firm organized a number of such buyouts starting in the mid-1950s.

Still, Kelso wasn't satisfied. He wanted to reform the whole system, not just a few companies. He gave speeches and interviews, even appearing once on *60 Minutes*. He bent the ear of every politician who would listen to him. Finally, one night in 1973, he had dinner with the powerful senator Russell Long, a Democrat from Louisiana and son of the legendary populist Huey Long. Dinner lasted three or four hours. Kelso outlined his ideas. Long listened and then began to talk. He told anecdotes about Huey. He expounded notions of his own. His father had been a "Robin Hood" populist, he said. He himself wasn't a Robin Hood populist, but he liked the idea of more people becoming capitalists. A couple of hours into the conversation, Long's tone changed. "Louis, you've made your sale," he said. "Now, what can I do to help you?"

Long (and others) make it happen. From that moment forward, Kelso's ideas were a live issue in Washington; they would be written into a series of legislative initiatives over a period of years. Long began by trying to get employee ownership into the Regional Railroad Reorganization Act. But other senators were leery because the rail unions weren't on board, and Congress ended up deciding only to sponsor a study of the idea. Long then inserted provisions regarding ESOPs into the Employee Retirement Income Security Act (ERISA), the landmark legislation that has governed company-sponsored retirement accounts ever since its passage in 1974.

This was a turning point. Until then, Kelso and his associates had been setting up legal entities known as stock bonus plans, which borrowed money to buy stock from retiring owners. They argued that the law permitted this. But lawyers often disagreed, so Kelso found it difficult to sell his ideas to many companies. ERISA—which happened to be the bill that was moving through Congress and that Long felt he could use to make such transactions legal—finally put the government's imprimatur on Kelso's ideas. ERISA was the "tax train leaving the station at the time," as one expert puts it, and Long's expertise and inclination naturally pointed him in the direction of supporting ESOPs by writing them into tax law. That's why ESOPs are a "retirement program."

Over the next dozen years, Long was instrumental in passing numerous pieces of ESOP-related legislation. Some of that legislation has come and gone, amended beyond recognition or simply allowed to expire, but the net effect was a series of ever-increasing tax benefits for ESOPs. The key, ironically, was a provision that Kelso had never imagined. In 1979, one of this book's authors, Corey Rosen, was working for the Small Business Committee of the US Senate. A man named Ed Sanders came into the office. Sanders owned a 20-employee plywood distributor in Alexandria, Virginia, called Allied Plywood. He wanted to sell the business to those employees through an ESOP, but he wasn't happy with one part of the deal. If another corporation bought his company and paid him in stock, he noted—John Deere and others had made offers—he could defer capital gains tax on the proceeds. But if he sold to the ESOP, he'd have to pay the taxes right away. That didn't seem fair. He himself would sell to the ESOP anyway, he said, but he thought that other company owners should get a better deal if they did the same.

So Rosen drafted a bill allowing for deferral of capital gains taxes for owners of private companies who sold at least a certain percentage of their stock to an ESOP. At first, Long and his staff didn't think the provision was important—they wanted to focus on ESOPs in publicly traded companies. But another committee member, Donald Stewart, a liberal senator from Alabama serving out the remains of a fill-in two-year term (he was not reelected), did introduce the bill and got Long and others to go along with it. And though it didn't pass right away, the provision survived; in 1984, almost as an afterthought, it was tossed into a late-night conference-committee agreement on a tax bill that contained a number of ESOP amendments. In fact, Long made the requirements even more lenient than Rosen had suggested. That provision—deferring taxes on the sale of private-company stock to an ESOP—is known as the

1042 rollover, after the relevant section of the tax code. It has been a key incentive for the creation of thousands of such plans.

The Advantages for Workers

So right there is the magic of the ESOP: over time, employees come to own the business without spending a dime of their own money.

Compare this to the dominant form of retirement plan in the US, the 401(k). Although both plans make everyone eligible after working (at most) 1,000 hours in a year, and both can vest benefits over up to six years, they differ greatly. In an ESOP, the company funds the plan; in 401(k) plans employees typically put up about two-thirds of total 401(k) funds. In an ESOP, allocations of contributions are based on relative pay or a more level formula. In a 401(k) plan, allocations are usually based on how much an employee puts in each year. So 401(k) plans tend to skew sharply toward better-paid employees; many lower-paid workers don't participate at all. In an ESOP, everyone gets an allocation just because they work there.

The result? As we showed in the previous chapter, employees in ESOP companies accumulate well over twice the retirement wealth that employees with other employer-sponsored retirement plans accumulate in similar non-ESOP companies. That is impressive enough, but keep in mind that half the private sector workforce does not participate in *any* retirement plan. ESOP employees also are laid off much less frequently, and they get paid somewhat more. And about 80 percent of their employers offer a secondary retirement plan in addition to the ESOP. The employers can do this because ESOP companies perform better. Everyone wins.

Alternatively, compare ESOPs to other ways employees can get stock. As we noted earlier, many companies grant equity rights to employees. Unlike with an ESOP, however, they can give whatever they want to whomever they want on whatever terms they like. Though there are exceptions, ordinary employees rarely get much from these programs. As we'll see in Chapter 8, employees in many public (but not private) companies can buy stock at a discount. Trouble is, most don't have the money to do so. Only ESOPs cover people so broadly.

Note how different the ESOP is from most programs aimed at reforming capitalism. It requires no big government program. It involves no new taxes. It doesn't redistribute wealth—it *predistributes* it.[2] The owners get a fair price for their business, along with the various tax benefits spelled out by law. All it requires on a government's part is a set of rules and incentives that enable and encourage this form of ownership. The US government has already created some of those rules and incentives, which is why employee ownership has spread as far as it has.

And yet, the spread has slowed. Right now, companies with significant employee ownership account for only a small fraction of the US economy. The number of ESOPs has plateaued in the last several years, though the number of individual participants in the plans has continued to grow. If Louis Kelso and Russell Long were alive today, they would be surprised and dismayed to see that their great idea has not yet reshaped more of the business landscape.

Why Not More?

We'll look here at the reasons for the ESOP's limited impact to date. And then—because every limitation presents an opportunity—we'll look in subsequent chapters at the vast possibilities for expanding the idea.

Right now, nearly every new ESOP depends on an individual business owner's decision. Virtually all of the ESOPs created so far are in privately held companies. (The small number of ESOPs in publicly traded companies present another set of challenges and opportunities, which we'll examine in the following chapter.) ESOPs come into existence because individual business owners decide to sell their companies to their employees using this device. Later in the book we'll discuss policies and programs needed to make this option better understood and more appealing; first let's look at why an owner might (or might not) go down this road.

There are plenty of reasons for selling to an ESOP. The employees who helped build the business get a reward, ownership. The seller gets cash representing the business's fair value, as determined by a third-party appraiser. Selling to the employees ensures that the company will continue as an independent business—no risk that it will be immediately swallowed up by some giant corporation, with people on the payroll given the ax. A sale to an ESOP is thus a way of maintaining the owner's legacy. (Maybe the family name will still be on the door.) The tax incentives don't hurt, either. Even if another buyer would, for its own reasons, pay a higher price, the difference in taxation may help equalize the financial calculation.

But there are also plenty of reasons why an owner might choose a different route. Some companies are just too small—the regulations and expenses associated with ESOPs would be too burdensome. Some aren't profitable enough to buy the shares, either directly or by paying off a loan. Some owners don't know about ESOPs or are misinformed about how they work. Others just don't like the idea. Many worry that sale to an ESOP is cumbersome and expensive—though in fact every sale of a sizable business is a cumbersome and expensive transaction, and sales to other buyers usually end up costing more and involving more contingencies on the sale than selling to an ESOP. Finally, owners who want to sell all of the shares will find that banks won't finance 100 percent of such a transaction. So they will have to finance part of the deal themselves, typically by taking back a note—that is, the company promises to pay the rest of the purchase price (with interest) over time.

Also, of course, a buyer may come along that views the business as far more valuable than an ESOP appraiser would or could allow.[3] The resulting offer may outweigh whatever tax benefits an ESOP can provide.

ESOPs are irrelevant to a lot of business owners. The "owners" of public companies aren't likely to care about whether their company sets up an ESOP. They don't care about much of anything other than the stock price. The owners of thousands of other companies don't fit the ESOP model, either. Some are large corporations that operate their subsidiaries as independent businesses. Warren Buffett's company,

Berkshire Hathaway, is the best-known example of this phenomenon, but nearly every large company owns many subsidiaries and is likely to buy or sell some every year. Other owners are private equity firms. Private equity's business model is based on buying and selling companies, but few of them even consider selling to an ESOP. (We'll examine the specific challenges and opportunities of private equity in Chapter 9.)

Many professional advisors ignore or disdain ESOPs. Owners of closely held companies often look to accountants, attorneys, or business brokers for help in figuring out how to sell their company. But many of these specialists don't understand ESOPs. They may provide misleading information about them to their clients, or they may simply tell them that an ESOP wouldn't be a good fit. (We human beings tend to think that something we don't understand is probably not a good idea.) Accountants may fear losing business if the company is sold to an ESOP. And business brokers, for their part, have a clear disincentive to encourage ESOPs: they get paid a commission by the seller, anywhere from 3 to 10 percent of the selling price. Sale to an ESOP wouldn't generate a fee because the broker didn't find this buyer—it was right there all the time. Most ESOP professionals tell us that advisor ignorance or misrepresentation is the biggest single barrier to the spread of ESOPs.

Every year, in short, companies worth untold billions of dollars are bought and sold. And ESOPs never even appear on the sellers' radar.

ESOPs got off to a rocky start (especially in the media). The history of ESOPs goes back to the 1970s, but it took a few years for them to attract much attention in the press. When that attention came, unfortunately, it created a misperception that in some quarters has persisted to this day.

In late 1983, a lead story in the *Wall Street Journal*, archly titled "The Grapes of Rath," described the bankruptcy of Rath Packing Company in Waterloo, Iowa.[4] Rath had been an 8,000-employee meatpacking outfit, known for its bacon. But persistent underinvestment by its prior owners left the company in a money-losing downward spiral. The United Food and Commercial Workers Union local agreed to wage concessions and a reduction in the workforce; the employees got 100 percent ownership in return. Things looked promising at first, but the arrangement didn't work out and Rath was forced into bankruptcy.[5]

Around the same time, National Steel Corporation, reeling from losses endemic to the US industry at the time, sold its integrated steel mill in Weirton, West Virginia, to an ESOP. The mill's roughly 8,000 employees agreed to a 20 percent wage cut and a six-year wage freeze while keeping their jobs and their pensions. In the next few years, Weirton became profitable. Morale was high, and the company was a pioneer in employee involvement programs from the shop floor to the boardroom. Many employees were able to retire in the ensuing years with full pensions. The company also embarked on a substantial modernization program. Even so, Weirton was not immune to the steel industry's growing difficulties. It was able to restructure and return to profitability, doing a public offering for 51 percent of its shares in 1994 and ultimately selling itself to the Dutch company Koninklijke Hoogovens NV three years later. It finally went bankrupt in 2003. But at least the business hung on longer than most of its competitors, saved thousands of jobs for several years, enabled thousands of employees to retire with pensions, and gave the small town of Weirton time to adapt.[6]

Weirton and Rath both generated substantial media coverage. They were typically portrayed as examples of a larger trend: employees trying to rescue troubled companies through buyouts. Several other steel companies, including Northwestern Steel and Wire, Republic Steel, and Erie Forge & Steel, became partly or wholly owned by ESOPs, invariably funded by wage concessions. Several airlines also had these plans: Western Airlines, Braniff, PanAm, Eastern Airlines, TWA, Northwest, Continental, and PSA (names many readers may no longer remember). A few trucking companies did as well. Generally, employees got between 15 percent and 40 percent of the stock and a voice on the board. A few of the companies, notably Eastern Airlines, went out of business; most of the others recovered enough to be sold.

And, of course, in 1995 employees bought United Airlines—a widely publicized but misbegotten ESOP that failed for countless reasons, including the facts that one of the airline's three major unions never agreed to it and a new CEO was skeptical of the whole idea.[7]

As a group, these buyouts had mixed success. Some lasted for just a few years, some for several years. Some, like Weirton, did well enough to retain most of the jobs, at least for a time. Many have been sold off; a few are still doing well today. But the ESOPs at all these companies weren't anything like what we recognize as ESOPs today. Many of the companies had a record of poor labor relations and troubled finances. Giving employees stock was little more than a way of getting workers to agree to wage or work-rule concessions—never a good idea. The plans were far from what Kelso had in mind, and far from what the employee ownership community has learned over the years about what makes an ESOP work. Employee ownership was never enough to rescue companies in dying industries or those that had suffered systematic neglect.

Whatever the results, the perception in the media at the time was this: *employee ownership is mostly a way to rescue failing companies.* Even back then, that wasn't the case. These plans were outliers. One of us (Corey Rosen) talked to reporters at the *Wall Street Journal* and the *Today* show for stories on Rath and emphasized that the troubled-company buyouts accounted for less than 1 percent of all ESOPs at the time. Nonetheless, both stories said just the opposite. When Rosen complained, the reporters said—shockingly!—sure, they knew that. But the troubled-company theme made the story more interesting.

While all this was going on, another small-but-well-publicized group of ESOPs were created out of divestitures or sales of large companies. Some, like Burlington Industries and Cone Mills, had been publicly traded. A few, such as Avis and Simmons Bedding Company, were owned by private equity firms like Wesray Capital Corp. (William E. Simon, former US Secretary of the Treasury, was the "Wes" in Wesray.) Avis was employee owned from 1987 to 1996, when it was sold to another company. Still others, including hospital chains Epic Healthcare and Health-Trust, were divisions of larger companies before becoming ESOPs.

Here, too, the record was mixed. Some of these companies improved their performance dramatically. During Avis's employee ownership years, profits increased substantially; employee involvement programs came up with ideas such as no-smoking cars and traffic-law tips for renters; customer complaints dropped 35 percent.[8] HealthTrust, a chain of rural hospitals that corporate parent HCA did not want, did so well that it bought ESOP-owned Epic, which had also done well, at twice what Epic's most recent value had been; it then sold itself to Columbia/HCA, a company formed from an earlier merger of Columbia Healthcare and HealthTrust's former parent. Other companies, like Simmons, Burlington Industries, Charter Medical, and Cone Mills, did much less well. Some of the deals ended up in court, particularly over the role the private equity firms played in engineering them. (With only a few small exceptions, this was the last time private equity would use ESOPs.) Ironically, one of the private equity firms that did a handful of ESOP deals like these was none other than Kelso & Company. Louis Kelso was no longer involved, and the company used ESOPs only in return for wage concessions. It ultimately dropped out of the ESOP business altogether.

This early ESOP history was in many ways a time of growing pains. The concept was still new and, partly as a result, sometimes produced mixed or damaging results. By the end of the 1980s, using ESOPs to save companies or to bolster highly engineered financial deals was no longer so common—the structure just doesn't work well for either purpose. In fact, employees have not used an ESOP to buy a troubled firm for at least 20 years. Today's trucking industry, for example, includes several successful ESOP companies ranging from fewer than 100 employees to thousands. None came from buyouts of troubled companies. Nevertheless, the ESOP's mixed early experience still colors its perception today, particularly among the political and business leaders who remember those times.

Finally, governments have little direct political incentive to broaden employee ownership. In theory, the US government (or any other government) could craft rules, incentives, and institutions that address all the limitations catalogued here. People have already proposed a number of these, and we'll discuss them later in the book. But Congress and other legislatures respond to political pressures, and employee ownership has rarely been high on any politician's list of priorities. Many reforms come about because some interest groups—labor unions, environmentalists, business organizations—push hard for them. Professors and policy analysts debate the proposals; the media publicize them. Employee ownership was different. It came about because Louis Kelso whispered in Russell Long's ear, and because Long was an unusually powerful and well-respected senator. It has always lacked a grassroots political base, and it has always lacked currency among policy mavens.

This may be changing. The last few years have witnessed a proliferation of groups advocating employee ownership—trade associations, nonprofits, state-level information-and-advocacy centers, and others. (We list some of these groups in the book's conclusion.) Widespread concerns over how to address economic insecurity and the widely perceived unfairness of the economy are encouraging new ideas. What was once a small band of dedicated activists has now mushroomed into a significantly larger and more influential group. Moreover, the challenges to the US economy—stagnant wages and insecurity for much of the population even while people at the top grow ever richer—are increasingly hard for politicians to ignore. At some point employee ownership may be an idea whose time finally arrives.

• • • •

So now let's look at the opportunities. Employee ownership has grown past its adolescence. We know how it works, and we know how to avoid the pitfalls that cropped up in its early years. The United States currently has 6,500-plus companies with ESOPs covering 14 million employees. But there are more than half a million companies with 20 or more employees in this country. There are about 125 million workers in the private sector. So the ratios of coverage are still relatively small. What if we could expand them by a factor of three or five or even ten? We would be on the way to a better, fairer economic system. And the opportunities to do just that are legion.

Takeaways

○ The ESOP was a great idea—it's the only way a lot of wage earners will ever get an ownership stake. It spreads the wealth of free enterprise without compromising the system itself.

○ Though Congress has been generous in encouraging ESOPs, their growth has been hampered by misconceptions, lack of familiarity, and their checkered early history. But the need—and the opportunities—have never been greater.

WAS KELSO RIGHT?

In their 1958 book *The Capitalist Manifesto*, Louis Kelso and Mortimer Adler argued that, as investment in capital increased, returns to wages would decrease. That was a violation both of accepted economic theory and economic history. In a 1975 *60 Minutes* story on Kelso, the famed economist Paul Samuelson declared that Kelso was an "amateur crank" and ESOPs were just a form of "economic alchemy."

ESOPs were hardly a form of alchemy, and Kelso wasn't a crank. But unlike many economists of the time he was deeply concerned about the differential impact of technological change. People who worked for a living were often vulnerable to automation—they could lose their jobs and their livelihoods. Those who owned capital often benefited from change. After all, capital was mobile. Owners could always move their money to the most promising investments.

Economic developments of the past several decades have borne out Kelso's concerns. Beginning in the late 1970s, US companies began investing heavily in production overseas. That investment benefited workers in those countries but harmed many wage earners in the US as factories shut their doors.

Unions lost membership and power and were no longer able to push workers' wages up. Many former factory workers—or their children—moved into lower-productivity service jobs.

The result? Wages and productivity, which had risen more or less in lockstep since the end of World War II, began to diverge (Figure 5). The owners of capital prospered as stock markets rose. Those who worked for a living—particularly if they had only a high-school education—got the short end of the stick. Kelso's answer, of course, was to find a way for ordinary people to become owners.

FIGURE 5: Productivity Growth Has Outpaced Worker Pay Since 1980

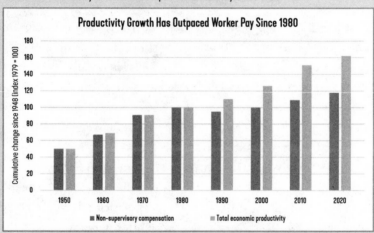

Source: Authors. Data from Economic Policy Institute, "The Productivity–Pay Gap," August 2021, https://www.epi.org/productivity-pay-gap/. The data are adjusted for inflation.

OPPORTUNITY #1
Employee Ownership on Wall Street

I hope the day may come when these
great business organizations will truly belong to
the men who are giving their lives and their efforts
to them, I care not in what capacity.

—OWEN D. YOUNG
Chairman and CEO, General Electric Company (1927)

THE IDEA THAT EMPLOYEES SHOULD OWN STOCK in large publicly traded companies goes back nearly 150 years. Leland Stanford, railroad magnate and founder of Stanford University, favored it. So did John D. Rockefeller Jr. The list of companies that began giving or selling stock (at a discount) to their employees included Procter & Gamble, DuPont, Kodak, GE, and many other blue-chip enterprises of the time. Some corporate leaders no doubt hoped that sharing ownership with workers would forestall union organizing drives. Others seem to have believed it was the right thing to do, maybe even the wave of the future. When he was a US senator, Stanford introduced a bill to encourage employee ownership. "What I believe," he explained in an 1887 interview, "is, the time has come when the laboring men can perform for themselves the office of becoming their own employers." GE's Owen Young would echo him 40 years later.[1] (For a fascinating look at the early history of sharing ownership in the US, see the book *The Citizen's Share*, by Joseph R. Blasi, Richard B. Freeman, and Douglas L. Kruse.[2])

Today, the status of employee ownership in stock-market companies is a sort of glass-half-full, glass-half-empty picture. Employees own more of the businesses they work for than any casual observer of the Wall Street world might imagine. Yet that ownership has encountered a variety of obstacles and limitations, which you can see in every one of the methods companies have used to distribute stock to workers. So there's a kind of double opportunity here. One is to improve and encourage existing methods of employee ownership in public companies. The other is to craft a wholly new structure for the ownership of large corporations, and ultimately to scale back the follies of stock-market ownership. We'll take these points up one at a time.

Getting Stock into Employees' Hands

Employee ownership in all its forms is a lot more common than most people think. A 2018 General Social Survey report found that nearly one-third of US workers in companies that have stock enjoy some level of ownership. The figure includes 14 million who participate in ESOPs and 25 million who have purchased or received shares through some other means. The survey found that the average value of the stock held by workers was about $75,000 and the median value $15,000. Among ESOP participants the average worker held $134,000.[3]

The surveys don't break out this ownership by public-company versus private-company employees. But there are reasons to believe that employee ownership in public companies is much more common than in their privately held counterparts. Owners of private companies must make a decision to sell or give stock to their employees. If they do so through an ESOP—the most common form—they must comply with a variety of regulations, and they must sell at least 30 percent of the shares to realize all the tax benefits provided by law. As we noted, there were about 6,000 private-company ESOPs in the US as of 2021. But this number is a small fraction of the total number of midsize companies, and most of those companies probably share little or no ownership.

Public companies are in a different situation. They can offer stock in multiple ways without running into costly securities-law rules. And it just isn't that big a deal for them to provide stock to the workforce. These companies have thousands of shareholders already, and (if management is worried about it) employees will rarely if ever accumulate enough shares to have a meaningful role in corporate governance.

Companies have plenty of methods to provide their employees with stock. For example:

The ever-popular 401(k). The plans known as 401(k)s are the most common form of retirement plan in the US. Employees set aside part of their pay, deferring taxes until they take the money out of the account. Companies may choose to match those set-asides up to a certain amount, often 50 percent. They can use their own stock for the match; if they are publicly traded, they can also offer their stock as an investment option for the employees' money. A study in the mid-1990s found that, wherever company stock was offered as a match and an investment option, about one-third of employees' account balances was invested in these securities.

This particular glass, however, soon began emptying out. By the end of 2018, just 5 percent of 401(k) assets were invested in company stock.[4] Fewer than one-third of all 401(k) participants worked in companies that offered their own stock, and only 40 percent of these employees held any company stock at all. We can only make back-of-the-envelope extrapolations from these data, but the calculations suggest that, of the 60 million or so US employees participating in 401(k) plans, about 5 or 6 million own about $350 million worth of their employer's stock. In other words, not much.

Why so sharp a decline? Well, maybe you remember Enron. Enron's contributions to its 401(k) plan were entirely in its own shares; employees were also encouraged to purchase more shares, which many did. In addition, Enron had an ESOP that covered part of its workforce and that was entirely invested in Enron stock. By 2001 the two plans owned over 25 million shares. And then came Enron's collapse, a result of widespread fraud at the company's highest levels. When Enron went bankrupt, the shares were worthless; many employees lost most of the money they had planned to retire on.[5]

In response to Enron and other debacles, Congress passed the Pension Protection Act of 2001. That law included several measures that effectively discouraged company stock in 401(k)s. Then, after the financial crisis of 2009 and the failure of many leading financial firms, employees who had lost money in company stock mounted lawsuits. Though nearly all of these suits failed, they were enough of a nuisance that companies continued to back away from using their own stock in retirement plans. Employees continued to move away from it as well.

Public-company ESOPs. About 90 percent of ESOPs in the US are in privately held companies. Most own at least 30 percent of the company's shares, and many as much as 100 percent. ESOPs in public companies have a lot of participants but don't own much company stock. In 2019, the NCEO found that there were 638 ESOPs in public companies with a little more than 12 million participants.[6] These plans held $1.27 trillion in assets, but just $133 million of that was in employer stock.[7]

Here, too, the glass has emptied out over time. In the late 1970s and early 1980s there were about twice as many public-company ESOPs as today. Laws at the time gave public companies a tax credit for contributions to ESOPs, basically allowing the companies to put a percent or two of workers' pay into an ESOP and have the government reimburse them. That was a hard deal to turn down—it was almost like free money. The policymakers' idea was that public companies would like the idea of employee ownership so well that they would add more to the employees' accounts. Unfortunately, the very first research report issued by the newly created NCEO showed that nothing of the sort was happening. That finding helped spur Congress to drop these incentives and use the money to fund incentives for privately held companies to set up much more substantial ESOPs.

Still, ESOPs have hung on in a significant number of public companies. Most are combination plans, an ESOP linked with a 401(k). In 2019, the median account balance in combination plans was $82,000, compared to only $25,775 for public-company employees with 401(k)s but no ESOP.[8] Still, only a small fraction of those balances was held in company stock; the rest was diversified.

So what's going on? For the most part, public-company ESOPs are used to fund the match in employees' 401(k) accounts. This arrangement offers a couple of advantages to a company. Most dividends, for instance, aren't deductible from a company's taxable earnings—but dividends paid to shares held in an ESOP are deductible. Also, the ESOP can borrow money to buy shares. Doing so was common a few decades ago, partly because a 1986 law allowed banks to exclude from their taxable income half the interest they received on loans to ESOPs. Banks loved this provision and took out full-page ads in the *Wall Street Journal* trumpeting their ESOP loan capacity. Companies liked it, too, because banks would negotiate lower rates—no small matter in that high-interest-rate era. But this party came to an end in 1989: Congress modified the law, and the accounting profession soon changed its rules about how companies accounted for the stock they put into an ESOP. As a result, a few hundred companies just dropped their ESOP and funded the 401(k) directly with company stock.

Employee stock purchase plans (ESPPs). Participants in an ESPP set aside part of their pay over a period of time and then use the money to buy company stock, usually at a discount. NCEO data suggest that about 40 percent of public companies offer the plans, with perhaps eleven million participants in all. In a typical ESPP, employees enroll in the plan and designate how much is to be deducted from their paychecks. At the end of a specified offering period (almost always 6 or 12 months), the accumulated funds are used to buy shares, often at a discount of as much as 15 percent. Many plans have a look-back feature: the price the employee pays is based on either the price at the beginning of the offering period or the price at the period's end, whichever is lower. Employees pay no tax until they sell the stock.

ESPPs seem like no-brainers at first glance: participants are virtually guaranteed a good return because of the discounted price. But surveys suggest that only about a third of people who are offered such plans participate in them. Many employees can't afford the deductions. Most companies don't spend a lot of effort promoting the plans. And if a 401(k) is available, that's likely to be an even better deal because of the potential match and the tax benefits. Maybe that's why the amounts involved in ESPPs are generally small. A study by Ilona Babenko and Rik Sen found that, in companies with ESPPs between 1998 and 2007, the average annual contribution of participating employees was only $1,630 per year.[9]

Equity grants. Back in the 1990s, the word was out: if you worked for one of the young tech companies, you'd receive stock options or shares as part of your pay. Options or other forms of equity became an essential currency to attract employees at every level in an industry where workers could easily move from one company to another. But though tech was a leader in distributing stock, it wasn't alone. Starbucks created the program known as Bean Stock, which has continued to this day; Bean Stock distributions can amount to tens of thousands of dollars over time for employees who stay with the company. Pfizer, DuPont, Merck, and other old-line companies also granted shares, though often in small amounts and often at management's discretion. The NCEO estimated that about 1 million public-company employees got equity awards in 1991; by 2001 the number had grown to about 9 million.

But then—the half-empty glass again—the trend reversed itself. Joseph Blasi, one of the leading scholars of employee ownership, found that in 2002, "58 percent of the employees of the U.S. computer services industry were employee owners of their company, while 57 percent held company stock options. By 2010, only 20 percent of employees were employee owners in the computer services industry and only 17 percent held employee stock options."[10] Some major tech companies still do provide broad-based equity, including Alphabet (Google's parent company), Microsoft, and Meta, but the practice is no longer so pervasive. And Starbucks is now a distinct outlier among non-tech companies in offering broad-based equity to its employees. At this writing the NCEO estimates that just a few million employees now receive stock grants.

Here, too, accounting rules changed in a way that discouraged companies from handing out options. The major stock exchanges changed their rules as well, making it harder for companies to gain shareholder approval for equity-sharing plans. There was also a subtler but no less important shift in the view of who in a company really matters. Back in the 1990s, if you went to meetings on equity compensation in public companies (as one of us always did), the mantra from compensation professionals was "Share ownership widely." Employee ownership was good for corporate America. But once the new rules made shares more difficult to hand out, the professionals' tune changed. Now the common view was "Don't waste equity on people who don't have a direct role in how the company performs. Focus on your 'talent.'" The argument was that only key employees really deserved equity and that employees didn't much understand or value it anyway. It was a convenient notion, given that these consultants were hired by the very executives whose stock awards they were justifying.

Does It Matter?

So there's the half-a-glass picture. On the half-full side, we have lots of big-company employees with an ownership stake in their business—many more than you might have imagined. We also have several convenient vehicles for getting more stock into workers' hands (Figure 6). Employee ownership of a sort is thus well established in corporate America. On the half-empty side, however, the employees' stakes are relatively small, and the number of workers holding stock has declined significantly over the last couple of decades. During that time, wages have continued to stagnate and inequality has worsened. Bolder, more far-reaching programs of employee stock ownership could have put more money in workers' pockets, boosted Americans' economic security, and helped to mitigate inequality. But Congress hasn't enacted major new legislation to encourage broader employee ownership since the late 1990s.

FIGURE 6: Employee Ownership on Wall Street

PLAN TYPE	HOW EMPLOYEES GET STOCK	HOW MANY PARTICIPANTS (NCEO ESTIMATES)
Employee stock purchase plan	Purchase of shares at a discount	9 million
401(k) plans	Employee deferrals into company stock and/or company contributions	3 to 4 million
Stock options or other grants to most or all employees	Company grants rights based on a formula it creates	2 to 3 million

Source: Authors, based on National Center for Employee Ownership data

The half-empty glass has another cost as well. Companies that share ownership, profits, or both with their employees tend to perform better than others. They are more competitive in the global marketplace. You can see this anecdotally in any number of cases: the rapid growth of the tech giants, built on equity sharing; the remarkable accomplishments of Starbucks, whose stock rose 160-fold between 1992 and 2016, a period when the market was only quadrupling; the pack-leading performance of Southwest Airlines, known for its generous profit sharing and widespread share ownership among its employees.

You can also see it in the research. Indeed, there is a rich body of academic literature on the impact of employee ownership in public companies. The studies show a small but consistently positive impact on company performance and on employee job stability.[11]

○ One significant piece of research asked the question, "How Did Employee Ownership Firms Weather the Last Two Recessions?"[12] Authors Fidan Ana Kurtulus and Douglas Kruse looked at all publicly traded companies in the US between 1999 and 2011. They divided the sample into those with ESOPs, profit sharing, and 401(k) plans with employer stock compared to companies without these benefits. They then looked at the average yearly change in employment for each group. When the unemployment rate ticked up by one percentage point, they found, companies without any employee ownership reduced employment (on average) by 3 percent; firms with any employee ownership reduced it by 2.8 percent; and ESOP firms lowered it by only 1.7 percent. (Only the ESOP results are statistically significant.) The higher the amount of employee ownership in the plans, the stronger the impact. Companies were also about 20 percent less likely to go out of business during the study period if they had an ESOP.

○ The most comprehensive analysis of ESOPs and company profit was done in 2008 by E. Han Kim and Paige Ouimet.[13] They found that ESOPs led to an 8.12 percent increase in company valuation relative to the industry median.

○ The major study on the effect of broad-based option plans on company performance was by Yael V. Hochberg of the Kellogg School of Management at Northwestern University and Laura Lindsey at the W. P. Carey School of Business at Arizona State University. These researchers found that companies granting options to a broad base of employees showed a significant improvement in industry-adjusted return on assets, whereas companies that granted options more narrowly showed a decline in performance.[14]

The many other studies on this issue largely confirm these results. Companies that share ownership widely with employees do better; those that offer ownership to only the few at the top do worse. Right there would be enough of an incentive for a responsible CEO to implement or expand employee-ownership plans. Of course, we have to ask: If it is economically rational for companies to do that, why do most content themselves with plans that favor only senior executives or individuals with special skills? Because what is rational for the company is not necessarily rational for top leadership. Say you are the CEO and you have 100,000 shares available for equity grants. You could give out 90 percent to the rank and file, and perhaps your stock grows 9 percent a year over time. You and other top executives get 10 percent of that. Alternatively, you could keep 90 percent for yourselves and watch the stock price grow just 8 percent per year. You come out way ahead by taking this path, even though your shareholders pay a price. So it's better for you and your senior colleagues to maintain the fiction that it's just the "key" people who deserve equity.

What to Do, Part I

The US Congress could easily nudge large corporations into broadening and deepening their employee-ownership policies: more stock for more people. Doing so would have a salutary effect on Americans' economic health and on companies' performance.

A skeptic might argue that Congress shouldn't meddle with corporate compensation policies. But it already does. In 1993, it passed a law limiting the deductibility of pay for a public company's top five executives to $1 million a year. That had little enough effect all by itself; deductibility, it turns out, just isn't that big a deal for giant corporations.[15] But the law also had an escape clause: "performance based" pay did not count against the cap. If a company larded up its executive pay with equity awards or bonuses—even if they were easy to earn—it could deduct the full cost of these execs' compensation.

That clause was repealed in 2017. But anyway, why not take a different tack and link the deductibility of executive equity pay to broad-based equity plans? The company could get a deduction only if it provided an ESOP or equity grants to (at a minimum) all full-time employees with a total value at least equal to what the executives get.

That isn't the only simple reform that would make a difference. Other provisions in the tax code could easily encourage employee ownership among public companies with little negative effect on the budget. Congress and state legislatures could also provide a contracting preference for companies that provide broad-based equity awards. Companies could be required to report on their ownership structure so that investors and consumers could find out how much of each corporation is owned by employees. (Those with ESOPs already have to do this.)

Investment advisory firms could get in the act as well. Right now, these firms focus on limiting equity awards. As the data shows, that is just wrongheaded. The firms' focus should be on how broadly equity is distributed. Companies with broad-based equity plans aren't just good for employees and society, they are good for investors. Of course, investors themselves don't have to wait for the advisory firms' advice. They should be urging companies to adopt broad-based ownership plans and then voting with their proxies and their dollars to make it happen. Pension funds in particular could see ownership as an opportunity to align their financial and social interests. For that to happen, the Department of Labor would need to rule that this investment choice is consistent with current pension laws that limit or prohibit the funds from taking social goals into account.

What to Do, Part II

In the long run, the idea of stock-market ownership—like the idea of any kind of financial or absentee ownership—may run its course. As the economist David Ellerman has pointed out, it makes no sense to have ownership separate and disconnected from the business for which the owners are nominally responsible.[16] And it makes both moral and economic sense for the people who actually operate the business, the executives and specialists and front-line employees, to reap the rewards of their efforts.

But the long run is by definition some time away, and the immediate question is how to move publicly traded companies in this direction. We have two simple ideas.

ESOP as dominant shareholder. Many companies, though publicly traded, have a single dominant shareholder. The dominant shareholder is usually the founder—think Mark Zuckerberg of Meta—or a group of the founder's heirs (such as Sam Walton's descendants). Sometimes these shareholders' control is protected by a two-class stock structure.

They own the shares that have most of the votes. Other shareholders are essentially along for the ride, hoping to benefit from dividends, an increase in the share price, or both.

What if, over time, the ESOP became the dominant shareholder? A sizable ESOP—by definition an owner with a long-term perspective—would act as a source of patient capital, discouraging activist takeovers and encouraging management to develop longer-term strategies for profitable growth. As to other effects, who knows? Executives who feel themselves partially accountable to employee owners might not jump quite so quickly to layoffs and outsourcing when the bottom line needs a boost. They might be more receptive to "good jobs" strategies like those described by MIT's Zeynep Ton and Harvard Business School's Dennis Campbell and his coauthors.[17] They might seek to create employee-centered cultures like those at Southwest Airlines and furniture maker Herman Miller. The research has already revealed that public companies with ESOPs hire more slowly and fire more slowly, creating a more stable—and presumably more loyal—workforce.

Maybe an ESOP would even have a dampening effect on executive pay. Once upon a time, unionized companies felt constrained as to how much they could pay their CEOs and other top executives, knowing that some of those same execs would have to sit across the table from labor in collective bargaining negotiations. The presence of a good-sized ESOP might act as a similar restraint.

Taking public companies private through an ESOP. Every so often, a group of investors takes a company private—that is, they buy up the shares and remove the company from the public markets. Sometimes the goal is to maintain private ownership over time. More often, the goal is to restructure the company out of the glare of Wall Street so that it can eventually be resold to public investors at a profit.

But suppose an ESOP were able to take a company private and keep it that way.

This is the idea proposed by Roger L. Martin in an influential *Harvard Business Review* article published in early 2021. (We mentioned this article—"It's Time to Replace the Public Corporation"—in Chapter

1.) Publicly traded corporations, Martin says, no longer serve the interests they ought to serve. Their focus on short-term earnings gains betrays the interests of long-term investors such as pension funds. Their concentration on financial results to the exclusion of employees' interests betrays the very people who create the most value. What to put in its place? "I believe," Martin writes, "that the most likely successor is what I call the *long-term enterprise (LTE)*, a private company in which ownership is limited to the stakeholders with the greatest interest in long-term value: retirement investors and employees." Here's Martin:

> It would work like this: An employee stock ownership plan (ESOP), whether existing or specifically created for this transaction, would partner with one or several pension funds to acquire the company and take it private. Governance would focus on real long-term performance rather than on short-term stock price fluctuations—because there would be no stock price. Other classes of long-term investors might also find the model attractive. The likes of BlackRock, Fidelity, and State Street, for example, could create vehicles whereby their IRA investors could invest alongside ESOPs.

ESOPs are a natural vehicle for privatization, Martin points out, because they are already well established and well regulated:

> Little or no new regulation would be required to roll out ESOPs on a large scale. A robust infrastructure is already in place to protect the interests of individual employees enrolled in them. (An ESOP is not equivalent to an employee retirement plan, which should not be wholly or even largely invested in company stock. It is, rather, a way to reward and motivate employees for value creation.) All shares vest after six years, and ESOPs are required to have a third party establish the fair value of the shares once a year so that when employees leave, their shares will be bought by the plan at a fair price, enabling them to benefit from capital appreciation much as employees of public companies do. Retiring employees benefit in the same way and enjoy favorable tax provisions for rolling the proceeds into their retirement accounts.

Martin's proposal continues to allow for outside investors. But the ESOP would be a major inside shareholder, just as we proposed, and would thereby have a significant role in governing the corporation.

• • • •

Publicly traded companies aren't going to disappear any time soon. But they can be reformed by greatly increasing the role of employees in ownership. It's a relatively simple way of spreading the wealth, boosting corporate performance, and reshaping companies so that they concentrate on long-term value creation rather than short-term stock movements. Congress, take note.

Takeaways

○ Broad-based employee ownership is common in stock-market companies, especially through various share purchase mechanisms, but it's limited. It makes a difference for the employees who own stock, but it isn't an economic game changer.

○ ESOPs offer a convenient vehicle for reshaping the fundamental ownership structure of stock-market companies—that *would* change the game.

OPPORTUNITY #2
Private Equity and Impact Investing

This is the right thing to do.
It also happens to be good business.

—PETE STAVROS
Co-head, Private Equity for the Americas
KKR & Company

PRIVATE EQUITY AND EMPLOYEE OWNERSHIP are some-
times viewed as competitors—business owners looking to sell their
companies may contemplate selling to an ESOP or to a PE firm. But
this competition isn't necessarily a zero-sum game. Sometimes, as with
Louis Kelso, all it takes is one individual to show that things don't have
to be the way they are.

Pete Stavros, who turned 47 in 2021, might seem an unlikely pioneer.
A graduate of Duke University and Harvard Business School, he rose
through the ranks of the investment world to become (at this writing) a
co-head of private equity for KKR. KKR is among the largest investment
firms in the world and was once known for its take-no-prisoners style
of operation. One of its earlier megadeals—the hostile takeover of the

tobacco and food company R. J. Reynolds—was chronicled in the 1989 bestseller *Barbarians at the Gate*.[1] Even if you never read the book (or saw the subsequent movie), the title conveys how KKR's approach was perceived at the time.

Stavros had a different idea. As the son of a Chicago-area construction worker and a secretary, he became intrigued with employee ownership when he was a young adult. His dad, who operated a road grader for 40 years and earned an hourly wage of $15 to $20 an hour, was disillusioned with two aspects of his job. First, he couldn't build wealth on his labor alone. Second, he saw a huge misalignment of incentives with his employer. Employers wanted jobs done well, at the lowest possible cost, and completed on time. Employees wanted more hours, because that was how they got paid. If a job fell behind, or if it had to be reworked, well, so what? The workers would get more hours, maybe even overtime at time-and-a-half. Because of this conflict, companies had to monitor employees closely. All those layers of supervision sapped morale and productivity and added to the company's costs. Pete's dad always wanted some form of profit sharing to align the incentives of his union with those of the construction company, but he was never successful.

After college, Stavros worked in investment banking at Salomon Brothers and then made his way into the private equity world. The first investment he worked on was a company called Gleason Corporation, which had a history with ESOPs. He was fascinated by the idea, he says—he liked the concept of all the employees participating in ownership and the government providing tax incentives to foster a movement. Later, while a student at Harvard Business School, he called one of us (Corey Rosen) for help with a paper he was writing on the history of ESOPs. The whole idea just seemed so logical, and not only because it would put more money in the pockets of people who needed it. In the current system, conflict in the workplace was unavoidable. But employee ownership put everyone on the same side, and it made possible a more participative style of management, with fewer supervisors. In a 2021 interview Stavros said to us, "If companies share equity and provide information to employees at all levels about the metrics of the operations they are working on, employees have a reason to care." It was just a better way of doing business.

By 2011 Stavros was well established at KKR and ready to start experimenting with employee ownership. By 2021 he had led nearly a dozen buyouts, each of which involved sharing equity with all of the acquired company's employees. In 2013, for instance, KKR acquired Gardner Denver, a Milwaukee-based manufacturer of pumps and flow-control equipment. Gardner Denver had been a public company, and at the time of its acquisition only 86 of its 6,000 employees owned stock. But KKR set aside some shares for all the workers. Four years later, when the firm took the company public, all 6,000 employees were awarded this stock, which was worth a total of $100 million at the time. In 2020, Gardner Denver merged with old-line manufacturer Ingersoll Rand, taking the latter's name; all 16,000 employees received another $150 million worth of shares. With the stock market rising—and with the company's stock outpacing the market—the two batches of stock together were worth about $500 million.[2]

Stock was just the most visible symbol of the PE firm's new employee-centered approach. At C.H.I. Overhead Doors, in Illinois, the management team installed by KKR first changed the company's staffing model, reducing the seasonal layoffs that had been the bane of the workforce for years. Then it air-conditioned the factory, which had been hitting 120 degrees in the summer. Then it made other investments—in safety training, in new breakrooms, in an on-site health clinic and a cafeteria with healthy food options. C.H.I. also began sharing financial information with employees and providing training to help people understand the numbers. It gave employees a certain number of stock options, and it allowed those earning above a certain income threshold to buy additional shares in the company. Finally, it provided employees with financial literacy training to help them make optimal use of the proceeds from stock ownership. On May 16, 2022, KKR announced the sale of C.H.I. to Nucor. The stock employees had received was worth $360 million in total, with individuals receiving anywhere from $20,000 (for the most recent hires) to $800,000.

Like Kelso, Stavros is an evangelist. In early 2022 he launched a nonprofit called Ownership Works with $40 million in initial funding, including $10 million from himself and his wife, to stimulate interest in employee ownership. He said that other private equity companies were beginning to take notice, in part because KKR's model had been remarkably successful in improving margins and share values but also because more people seemed to believe that sharing ownership was the right thing to do. "Business can be a major driver of greater social and racial equity," he told us. "I have found that leaders of companies we work with find that an appealing idea—they want to do more than just make money. They want to make a difference." By March of 2022, Ownership Works had 37 PE firms involved in the project; each had committed to three or more deals in the coming year that would provide employees with equity worth at least 6 months—and in some cases 12 months—of pay. Operating companies were taking notice as well. Harley-Davidson engaged KKR to consult on how it can use the equity sharing model; it set up a plan in 2021.

Equity Sharing—Or ESOP?

The KKR approach is limited compared to an ESOP. (Stavros calls it an "in-between" model.) As with an ESOP, the employees do get equity at no (or very little) cost, and the entire workforce is included. But employees typically end up with only 10 percent or so of the company's stock, sharing ownership with the private equity firm, public investors, or both. Like the private equity model in general, the KKR program is oriented toward a big payout when the company is sold or taken public and employees can sell their stock.

ESOPs, by contrast, nearly always involve something between 30 percent and 100 percent of the equity. Though ESOP companies can be—and sometimes are—sold, resulting in a one-time payout to the employees, most continue to operate as independent private businesses. That allows employees to build wealth over many years until they retire.

Despite these limitations, no one should dismiss Stavros's innovations. Thousands of good-sized businesses are bought and sold every year. These transactions are nearly always times of stress for the companies involved and for their employees. Sellers may be looking to cash out, which means that longtime owners or managers may be leaving. Workers fear for their jobs and for the future of the business. Local officials worry that plants and other facilities will be closed or moved. No one knows what the new owners will do. An ESOP sale instantly mitigates those fears: now the workers own part or all of the business; most of the company's leaders typically stay on; and everyone can expect a relatively stable future. But Stavros's equity grants and the employee-centered culture have a similar effect, at least for a while. They put money—sometimes substantial amounts—in employees' pockets. They say, *We're the new owners, and we care about you. For the next few years, we are all in this together. And when we sell the company, you will share in the profits.* It's a powerful message. And as Stavros has shown, it is highly likely to boost the company's performance, particularly when coupled with participative management.

Still, the KKR method raises a question. Why shouldn't Stavros—and by extension, every other corporate seller of a business, including other PE firms and companies that are divesting themselves of a division or a subsidiary—consider setting up an ESOP? Then they could eventually sell their businesses to those companies' employees, not just spreading the wealth but raising the odds that the company they nurtured would survive and prosper for many years into the future. They would essentially close the circle: buying a company, sharing the equity, developing a culture of employee involvement and long-term thinking, and then enabling the employees to take full ownership through a buyout.

Why corporations and PE firms don't sell to ESOPs. The answer to this question reveals one significant set of limitations to the current ESOP structure—and one sizable opportunity for expanding the number of employee-owned companies.

Imagine yourself in the position of a corporate seller of a business. You're on the divestiture team of a large company, responsible for selling off unwanted divisions. Or you work for a PE firm and you're looking for buyers for a company your firm has invested in. Remember in either case that you are a financial owner: regardless of your own values, you are accountable to your bosses and your company's investors for your decisions.

Now, if you sell the business to another corporation or another PE firm, you pretty much know what to expect. The buyer will provide you with cash. It may see unrealized value in the company you're selling, particularly if the deal complements its other businesses, and so offer you top dollar. You know that the buyers' representatives are like you—sophisticated businesspeople with access to capital and managerial skills. Your superiors will likely applaud such a sale.

But suppose you wanted to sell to an ESOP?

There are obviously some advantages. You don't need to shop around for a buyer. Employees would probably welcome the move and would quit looking for other jobs. If you represent a private equity fund structured as a partnership, as most are, your investors can get a capital gains tax deferral on the sale if they reinvest the money in other stocks and bonds. But there are barriers as well. As a government-regulated entity, the ESOP is only allowed to offer a price (determined by an appraiser) that represents the current market value of the company to a financial buyer—a buyer who would operate the business as a standalone entity. However, other potential buyers, known as strategic buyers, may see additional value in the company. Maybe they can reduce costs by combining it with another of their businesses. Maybe the acquired company opens up a new market for them, or gives them greater market power. Such potential synergies can add considerable value to a business, and so the strategic buyer may be willing to offer a higher price.

Then there's the issue of finance. An ESOP buyout would need to be financed mostly or entirely with debt; employees themselves would rarely be able to buy the shares outright, and they might not want to take the risk in any event. But banks won't finance 100 percent of such a deal—half or less is more likely. So the sellers would have to lend the company money, and would undoubtedly require a high rate of interest. Is this something you want to ask your firm to do? And if you saddle the company that you're selling with all that debt, will it still be profitable?

Bottom line: your superiors will be highly skeptical of an attempt to sell to an ESOP. Even Stavros, who counts himself a fan of ESOPs, prefers his in-between model for most corporate sales. ESOPs take a lot of time and money to set up, he argues. They may not be price competitive. His partners and others in the PE world don't like all the rules and regulations involved in an ESOP, such as requirements for eligibility, share allocation, regular contributions to the plan, and Department of Labor oversight of the whole thing.

Overcoming the obstacles. In principle, none of these obstacles has to be a deal breaker. An imaginative PE firm or corporate acquirer could find several ways to build long-term employee ownership into one of its portfolio companies through an ESOP. For example:

- It could buy a controlling interest in a company but share part of the ownership through an ESOP. That's a lot like KKR's approach. But with an ESOP to hold the equity on the employees' behalf, the acquired company's present and future employees would have a long-term interest in the business. The ESOP can also provide tax advantages both to the company and to the employees, depending on how the plan is structured. When the time comes for the PE firm or corporation to sell its interest, the ESOP would be well established. It could buy the rest of the shares, or it could remain as a minority shareholder if the company goes public or is acquired by another buyer.

- A PE firm could also be a minority investor in an ESOP. The mechanics of this can get complicated, so we'll summarize them very briefly here. Say the ESOP buys 100 percent of the common stock. It is now a non-taxable entity (that's the law, not some clever legal gimmick). The PE investor buys what's called a *warrant*, meaning the right to buy shares in the ESOP-owned company for some years into the future at the price established by the warrant. If the share value goes up, as it usually does in an ESOP, the investor can cash the warrants in at the new, higher price. Models of such a transaction suggest that PE investors could get a very good return.

○ The PE firm could participate in a joint venture with an existing ESOP company. The ESOP company would set up a subsidiary firm and (usually) own a majority of the stock. The PE firm would buy the remaining shares. Employees in the subsidiary would be in the ESOP. The PE firm's interest would be bought out several years later. A handful of cases follow this model, but it is not well known in the PE community.

○ Finally, the PE firm could provide the debt financing for an ESOP buyout. PE investors are typically looking to double their money in about five years, so they would have to charge an interest rate of almost 15 percent. That's far more expensive than bank loans, but banks won't finance a 100 percent sale. So if sellers want to get all their money out right away, the PE firm's expensive loan could supplement whatever they can borrow from the bank. Of course, maybe a savvy PE firm would notice that the risk of ESOP loans is lower than nearly any other unsecured corporate debt. NCEO data show that the default rate on ESOP acquisition debt is vanishingly small (two per thousand per year).[3] That seemingly unsecured debt is actually quite secure, and a more moderate interest rate could actually be a good investment.

So methods are available. But the question of motive remains. Why would PE partners or corporate divestiture teams concern themselves with any of this?

Some, like Stavros, might be motivated by the wish to make a difference. This isn't quite as far-fetched as it sounds: ESG is a watchword for many investors, and the firm could tout its accomplishments on this front. (Social goals are already the basis for what's called *impact investing*, which we'll turn to in a moment.) The dealmakers might also notice what Stavros has already seen: employee ownership and a culture of involvement make for better financial results.

But here's the opportunity lurking in all these difficulties: the motivation would be far stronger

- if there were financial incentives to do this kind of deal,

- if ESOPs were less cumbersome to establish and maintain,

- and if government-guaranteed loans were available to finance the transaction.

As we noted, thousands of companies are bought and sold each year. If a significant fraction of them could be converted to employee ownership, the economy would be that much fairer, and millions of employees would gain greater economic security. We'll explore the incentives and institutions that could lead to more such conversions in Chapter 11.

Impact Investing

Until we have such incentives and institutions, most PE firms are likely to continue on their present course, acquiring companies from private sellers and then seeking out conventional buyers. However, there are some signs of change. By late 2021, reported *Bloomberg BusinessWeek*, "a record 132 'impact' funds" sponsored by PE firms were in operation. Most focused on categories such as alternative energy, healthcare, affordable housing, and the like.[4] But some were looking at ESG criteria, often at the request of clients such as pension funds. Other investors—wealthy individuals and families, foundations, specialized mutual funds, even insurance companies—were also setting out to invest their money where it could do some good as well as earn a reasonable return. All these impact investors were beginning to have an effect on the corporate landscape.

An example that's relevant to this book is Taylor Guitars. On January 11, 2021, this company's 1,200 employees learned through a video conference that their company had just been sold—to them, at no cost, through an unusual kind of ESOP.

Founded in 1974 by Bob Taylor and Kurt Lustig, Taylor Guitars had become one of the premier guitar makers in the world. It was known both for its fine instruments and for its emphasis on environmentally sustainable sourcing. It was profitable and growing, with $122 million in sales. So it was an attractive target for competitors or private equity firms looking for acquisitions. Taylor and Lustig, however, didn't like the idea of selling to a buyer who might not share their values and who probably wouldn't reward the employees who helped build the company. An ESOP offered them a way to sell their shares, gradually ease out of the business, reward the workers, and preserve their legacy. "Who will be the best people to guide [Taylor] forward into the future?" Lustig asked in a video shown to the employees. "Who will keep our company true to our values and maintain the culture we love? While Bob and I still have many good years left to dedicate to the company, we wanted to make sure we put the company in the best possible position for future success, to give it the best chance to be around for the next 100 or maybe even 200 years."[5]

Unlike some company owners, Taylor and Lustig wanted to sell all of their shares at once. But it isn't easy to sell 100 percent of a company as big as Taylor to an ESOP. No bank would finance such a deal because the company couldn't provide enough collateral to back the loan. In principle, the founders could have used some combination of a bank loan, mezzanine financing (usually loans from private investment sources at three to four times the interest rate of the bank loan), and seller notes (agreements by the sellers to be paid with interest over time) to do the transaction. But Taylor and Lustig worried about loading up the company with too much costly debt.

So their investment bank turned for help to a Canadian organization called Social Capital Partners (SCP), a nonprofit impact-investing advisor with a strong interest in employee ownership. SCP's Jon Shell reached out to the Healthcare of Ontario Pension Plan to talk about getting involved. Pension plan officials were receptive, and the resulting deal benefited both parties. The pension plan got a relatively safe long-term investment: it offered a 10-year term, with no principal payments during the life of the loan, at a rate of interest that met the needs of its members. The company got favorable terms and a level of flexibility that were not available from other lenders. If it needed cash to grow, for example, it was allowed to skip an interest payment. When the deal was complete, Taylor announced that not only would US employees be included in the new ESOP but Mexican employees would be as well. That made Taylor one of the first US companies to extend its ESOP across international borders.[6]

The Taylor deal is the largest example of investors supporting employee ownership. But others, too, have expressed interest. By 2021, at least 14 impact investment funds were involved in some way. Some of these funds focused on converting smaller companies—particularly those with lower-wage workforces—to worker cooperatives. Others were looking more toward ESOPs.[7]

Impact methods. Jon Shell, the SCP representative, has become knowledgeable about impact investing, and he points out both its limitations and the opportunities it presents. One limitation is simply that impact investors right now have far less money at their disposal than private equity funds and other mainstream investors. So impact investing is likely to be a marginal player in the world of employee ownership conversions. Moreover, many funds concentrate on small-scale co-ops or other businesses in low-income or otherwise disadvantaged communities. That fits with their social mission, but it necessarily limits their impact on the overall economy. (We'll discuss co-ops in greater detail in Chapter 10.)

Shell and others argue that the best role impact investors can play is this: making it easier for large capital providers like the Ontario-based pension fund to provide more and better debt for ESOPs. He suggests three methods:

○ Impact investors can provide *first-loss capital*, meaning that, in the unlikely case of a default, their loans would be paid off last.

This greatly lowers the risk for other lenders. Loan guarantees can achieve the same goal.

○ Impact investors can fund the cost of leading and structuring deals on behalf of other long-term investors, allowing those investors to participate in the deal without managing it themselves.

○ Foundations and universities invest billions of dollars and could commit some of those investments to ESOP lending. Since these organizations do not pay income tax, they should receive appropriate returns through long-term, market-rate ESOP lending.

So far, the Kendeda Fund foundation has taken the lead in this kind of ownership-related investing: it announced in 2019 that it would commit $24 million to promote conversions of companies to employee ownership. It provided these funds to four organizations that focus primarily on worker cooperatives, especially for low-income workers in industries such as home healthcare, laundries, retail, or childcare. Cleveland's Evergreen Cooperatives, for example, has launched three businesses employing over 250 people. In late 2018, it initiated the Fund for Employee Ownership as a new method of expansion; the fund has used capital from Kendeda and others to acquire and convert four businesses to employee ownership.

Impact investors have a lot of choices about using their money, of course. So why employee ownership?

For one thing, investing in employee ownership is not a zero-sum choice. Funds like the Ontario plan can earn a good rate of return in a relatively safe investment and then use that money to fund other endeavors. These investments can spread ownership widely without the need for grants or subsidies. Then, too, ESOPs provide every employee with shares, almost always at no cost to them. The research shows that this is one of the best, and often the only, way that lower-income people can accumulate a capital nest egg. Finally, ESOP companies are good for their communities. They stay local; they lay people off at lower rates;

and they often provide large payouts to employees who can use them to buy houses, cars, and education.

Greater involvement by PE firms, money from large investors such as pension funds, and more interest from other impact investors can all move the needle. They won't get us to where we want to be by themselves, but they are surely part of the solution.

Takeaways

○ Led by KKR, some private equity investors have concluded that sharing ownership broadly is the right thing to do and that it boosts the performance of the companies they own. This development could lead to major change, but it isn't as far-reaching as ESOPs are.

○ Impact investing has largely ignored issues of ownership. It's past time for these investors to make it a priority.

SPREADING THE WEALTH

When KKR bought a company called Capital Safety in 2012, there were 35 owners among the company's 1,250 employees. Those owners received a total of $157 million, with the two principal owners getting $60 million for themselves alone. "It's a microcosm of the industrial world," says KKR's Pete Stavros—"the vast majority of employees barely getting by on an hourly wage and a small segment with ownership, that's the group getting ahead."

Three and a half years later, KKR sold Capital Safety to 3M Co. Thanks to the firm's equity sharing program, all the employees had ownership stakes, including 200-plus who received more than $100,000 and 44 who got over $1 million.

OPPORTUNITY #3
Trusts, Co-ops, and the Gig Economy

Many working people want to own the place that they spend most of their working lives. I started thinking about worker ownership as a different strategy for worker empowerment.

—ERIK FORMAN
Cofounder, The Drivers Cooperative

EMPLOYEE OWNERSHIP, as we have tried to show, is not an all-or-nothing proposition. Advocates like us don't expect to see some utopian day in which every last company is wholly owned by the people on its payroll. Just as there's a crazy quilt of ownership today, there is likely to be a crazy quilt in the future. We hope only that more—many millions more—of today's wage earners will one day be able to enjoy the benefits of ownership. As we have said, it would make for a stronger, fairer capitalist system.

Right now, ESOPs are the broadest and most-traveled avenue toward this more equitable future. They are numerous, well established, and market tested. The law supports them. So does a network of advocates, attorneys, accountants, and other experts. But ESOPs do not fit every business, nor are they the only path to employee ownership. KKR's equity grants—Pete Stavros's in-between model—are another. So are the structures we describe in this chapter: trusts, worker co-ops, and the platform co-ops that could eventually transform the so-called gig sector of the US economy.

Employee Ownership Trusts

The John Lewis Partnership may be one of the best-known employee-owned companies in the world. Its eponymous department stores and Waitrose groceries dot the United Kingdom. It employs some 95,000 people. But it isn't an ESOP—the UK doesn't have American-style ESOPs. Rather, it's owned by an independent trust charged with operating the business for the benefit of John Lewis employees. Those employees, unlike participants in an ESOP, don't own shares as individuals, and so they can't accumulate equity in the business over time. But they do receive an annual share of the profits, and they vote for a network of councils that ultimately run the organization. Hundreds of other companies in the UK have a similar structure, encouraged in recent years by tax incentives somewhat similar to those that apply to ESOPs in the US. (See Chapter 12 for more detail.)

The idea of trust ownership isn't new even in the United States. One of the first such trusts was set up in 1922 at American Cast Iron Pipe Company, now known simply as American, in Birmingham, Alabama.[1] John Eagan, the company's owner, was a deeply religious man who created an employee-friendly enterprise. He paid better-than-market wages, instituted new safety measures, and provided a variety of social services for his workers. He also established a trust that would own the company after his death; the trustees were charged with running the business for the benefit of the company's employees as well as its customers. That trust is still in place today, and its effects can be seen in the way American operates. Employees get an annual share of the profits. They elect a 14-person "board of operatives" to act as an intermediary between themselves and senior management; four members of this group sit on the board of directors. The company has frequently won awards as a best place to work.[2]

For decades, Eagan's company was an outlier. But the trust idea has slowly been spreading in recent years, even though trusts in the US enjoy no special tax advantages. At this writing there are a dozen or so examples of the model.

One example is WATG, a company whose acronymic name reflects the names of its founders. It's an architecture and design firm that started in Honolulu. Today it's a global operation, with 500 professionals, offices in 9 locations around the world, and projects completed in 170 countries.

Some years ago, a would-be acquirer offered to buy out WATG's internal shareholders, who were all members of the company's senior leadership. The price was attractive: more than three times the company's book value. WATG's leaders looked hard at the offer but ultimately rejected it. "None of us wanted WATG to be dissolved," said Mike Seyle, who was company president at the time. "And we had all seen what happens to a firm's culture and identity when businesses are acquired." Seyle and the others considered sale to an ESOP, but decided against it because of the ESOP's costs and legal requirements. Even an ESOP, they noted, can sometimes be forced to sell to an outside buyer if the offer is high enough.[3]

So WATG established a trust. It did so in the UK, where it had an office. The company invited Graeme Nuttall—author of the government report that has been the blueprint for employee ownership policy in the UK—to speak at a meeting of the company's board of directors. Nuttall presented the case for ownership through a perpetual trust modeled after John Lewis; when the proposal was accepted, he helped WATG set up the trust. The company took out a bank loan and gifted the money to the trust. The trust then bought roughly 60 percent of the shares from the existing owners at a price reflecting an adjusted book value. But the goal was always to have the trust own all of the shares. Now, when WATG's board decides to facilitate the purchase of more shares, the company will set a sale price and allow existing shareholders to decide how many shares they want to sell. The trust's founding document notes that its purpose is to hold shares of WATG "as a permanent part of [WATG's] ownership and governance arrangements." In short, the company is not for sale.

Smaller companies are using trust structures as well. In early 2016, Metis Construction founder Matthias Scheiblehner sold all of the company's shares to a trust, the first owner to do so using US law. The sale price was calculated to reflect the time and money Scheiblehner had invested in establishing the company. Metis is based in Seattle, and the trust is a so-called noncharitable purpose trust, a legal form that exists in many but not all states. Of the company's 34 employees at the time, 18 immediately became beneficiaries of the trust; the other 16 employees were on track to become so if they remained at the company for five years. Scheiblehner saw the structure as the right thing to do because, as he put it, "any other organization misses the point of who is doing the work and who is making the profit."

Trusts versus ESOPs. At WATG, employees of the company are beneficiaries of the trust, regardless of where in the world they are based. If the trust ever liquidates its assets or dissolves, those employees will receive their share of the company's value at the time. But since the trust is supposed to endure forever, employees benefit from business success mostly by receiving a share of annual profits. The board of directors determines what the bonus percentage will be each year, and every employee from the receptionists to the CEO receives the same percentage of base pay.

A fan of ESOPs might ask whether the WATG arrangement is really ownership, since employees don't accumulate wealth from an increase in share value. WATG leaders argue that employees get most of the benefits of ownership. They vote for the company's board of directors and vote on major changes to the business. They participate in formulating business strategy through local representatives who regularly communicate with management. They receive regular reports on the company's plans and financial performance, and they receive a share of the profits. The part of ownership they forgo is cashing in shares at an appreciated value when they leave. Proponents of trusts argue this is a worthwhile tradeoff because the company can't be sold—and because an employee's share of the company's value is paid out in annual distributions rather than in future growth of the share price.

Chris Michael of EOT Advisors is the leading expert on employee trusts in the US, and one of the idea's chief advocates. Trusts, he points out, take much less time to implement than ESOPs. They require no ongoing valuations, and they are not subject to the rules and requirements of ERISA. The benefits are immediate and easy to communicate to employees, and the flexible rules allow founders to incorporate social or environmental goals as they see fit. "Most private company owners place a high value on privacy and flexibility," Michael argues. Trusts "are not restricted to a retirement plan. And the transaction is private, as opposed to the quasi-public nature of an ESOP transaction where multiple parties are weighing duties and responsibilities—and examining corporate financial documents—under the light of federal law."

In the US, trusts get no special tax benefits, and there are no specific rules as to how they must operate, who has to be in the plan, how much stock the seller must provide to the trust, how employees are allocated financial rights, or how the plans are governed. (If they were to get tax benefits, those benefits would undoubtedly come with rules much like the rules governing ESOPs.) As Michael suggests, the absence of rules is part of their appeal to some company owners. Still, the absence of tax advantages may limit their growth to owners who are philosophically aligned with the concept. Also, whether trusts represent "real" ownership depends on how you define the term. A company owned by a trust exists for the benefit of employees. It rewards them with both profits and job security. Employees do not build up equity rights, however, so those who seek long-term wealth must depend on benefits such as a 401(k) match, if the company decides to implement such a plan, and their own savings.

Worker Co-ops

Employee-owned cooperatives—worker co-ops—have long been a dream of those who would reform capitalism.[4] Imagine a company wholly owned and controlled by the people who work there. Imagine workplace democracy, with employees voting for their leaders and having a say in how the company is run. The dream dates back to the early days of the industrial revolution, and since then worker co-ops have taken root in a number of places. Several European countries, notably Italy and Spain, have modest-sized but thriving cooperative sectors. Spain's giant Mondragon Corporation, with more than 80,000 employees around the globe, is the world's biggest and best-known worker co-op. (There's more on Mondragon and other European co-ops in Chapter 12.)

Cooperatives can be difficult to categorize. They have a different logic than conventional businesses, a logic that informs both the opportunities and the challenges involved in using them to build worker wealth. Cooperative expert Margaret Lund writes, "Cooperatives differ fundamentally from other business entities in that they do not promise unlimited—or even particularly high—rates of return in exchange for the risk of ownership. Instead, cooperatives offer their members the advantages of a democratically governed enterprise directed toward meeting the needs of participants."[5] Co-ops often form and grow where some sort of market failure leaves critical needs unmet. For instance, farmer cooperatives, rural electric cooperatives, and credit unions played an important role in developing rural economies in the United States.

Worker co-ops in the United States—there are several hundred—present a puzzling picture. They draw a great deal of media attention. They enjoy a lot of philanthropic and political support. New York City, for instance, has pledged $15 million to help community-based organizations develop cooperatives. Berkeley (California), Durham (North Carolina), Madison (Wisconsin), Boston, Miami, Minneapolis, and Philadelphia also have city programs designed to encourage co-ops; so do the states of Colorado and California. Foundations have contributed tens of millions of dollars to the effort. Active and effective nonprofit organizations, including the Democracy at Work Institute, Project Equity, and the Democracy Collaborative, have used grant funds both to develop tools and training that strengthen co-ops and to encourage more support from cities and states.[6]

Yet worker co-ops account for only a small fraction of the employee ownership landscape. Unlike ESOPs, co-ops do not have to file with any central government agency and may employ a variety of legal forms. So it is difficult to determine just how many there are. As noted earlier, the US Federation of Worker Cooperatives conservatively estimates that there are roughly 500 worker cooperatives employing a total of about 8,000 people. For comparison, the US has several thousand ESOP companies employing millions of people. At least a dozen majority-owned ESOP companies *each* have more than 8,000 employees.

What are we to make of these disparities? On the one hand, the appeal of the cooperative model to many people is undeniable: an egalitarian, democratic company, one-member, one-vote, with everyone sharing in the wealth they create. It's an ideal that has long captured reformers' imagination. But supporters are taking on a difficult task, simply because co-ops can be hard to start, hard to run, and hard to scale. We'll look here at how co-ops work, what difficulties they face, and how some have succeeded in spite of the obstacles.

How co-ops work. Worker cooperatives are not specifically defined in most state laws, so there are variations in how these companies are organized. The common feature is that all are owned and controlled by their worker members, each of whom has one vote at the governance level. Workers typically become members by making a member equity contribution, either out of pocket (when they join the company) or out of future earnings. The equity contribution varies widely from one co-op to another but may be as much as several thousand dollars and is returned to the member on departure. While members, workers get a profit share based on their "use" of the cooperative, typically measured by hours worked.

Unlike workers in an ESOP, co-op employees don't have a claim on the equity value of the company—that is, they do not hold shares that go up and down in value. They instead have individual internal capital accounts, with profits distributed and losses deducted yearly. Cooperatives are designed to be perpetual member-serving institutions; they are not created to be sold. But if they are sold, the equity value could be divided accordingly, among those who are members at the time. (Some co-ops specify that the equity value be divided among everyone who was ever a member.) Unlike ESOPs, cooperatives do not have to include all employees as members.[7] Each member votes for the board of directors; employees usually participate in other areas of governance as well. Worker co-ops don't have all of the tax benefits of ESOPs, but if owners of closely held companies sell to co-ops, they can defer taxes on the gains just as with ESOPs.

Why they are scarce—and usually small. Most co-ops employ fewer than 20 people, and most are in the retail sector (bakeries, restaurants, food stores) or the care sector (childcare, home care). Only a few are in businesses that require significant capital investments. The small size and limited scope of co-ops reflects a number of difficulties that any co-op must confront:

- **Purpose.** A cooperative's primary purpose is to meet its members' needs. It's a form driven by principles and committed to democratic control by members, not necessarily (or exclusively) to maximizing profit. This purpose isn't always a great fit with the modern business environment. It leads to tensions— between members' individual interests and the interest of the business; between cooperative principles and market demands; and between democratic member control and the imperatives of management.

- **Start-up.** Starting any business is hard. Starting a co-op is even harder. The new members may disagree on strategic directions and business priorities. Banks will be reluctant to lend money to the fledgling business. Equity capital will be hard to come by as well, since an investor gets no control. So co-ops may be undercapitalized from the outset. Social impact capital and foundation investment can be used to finance a co-op's startup or growth, but that support is unlikely to reach the scale of capital available to conventional small businesses or ESOPs. Then, too, many co-ops choose to impose strict limits on the pay ratio of management to nonmanagement employees. Such rules may make it harder to attract qualified managers, especially because equity incentives are not available.

Because of these obstacles to start-ups, many co-op efforts in recent years have focused on converting existing businesses to the cooperative form. But similar difficulties apply. It is often hard to find lenders to finance the transactions. And the fledgling co-ops will still have to attract skilled managers and funds for expansion.

○ **Growth.** All these difficulties only intensify as an organization grows. Money to finance expansion may not be easily available. Experienced managers may be reluctant to deal with the democratic constraints imposed by a co-op. If the organization gets significantly bigger, it may have to streamline its management and governance processes for the sake of efficiency—moves that are likely to provoke controversy. If it fails to do so, the staff meetings and other procedures required to make decisions democratically can become cumbersome.

Faced with such obstacles, co-ops often choose to remain small. Worker co-ops that have grown to considerable size generally streamline processes for member participation in governance, prioritize skilled and experienced management in their industry, leverage their cooperative advantage to build their market (for example, with customers who share the co-op's values), and create an ecosystem of affiliates to strengthen the enterprise.

○ **Political issues.** One internal challenge that faces many co-ops is what to do about nonmembers. Almost all worker cooperatives have a trial period for new workers before they become members. But beyond this, should the organization allow nonmembers to work there indefinitely? And if it does, doesn't that contradict the fundamental belief in one-member, one-vote? How should non-members be compensated—just with wages, or should they get a share of the profits as well? Issues like these have plagued even successful co-ops, since the founding members may be reluctant to share the wealth they have created with those who are newer or who seem less committed. Anyway, not all workers are interested in the demands of becoming a member.

Co-op Success Stories

For all that, some worker co-ops have flourished, usually in industries, times, and places where they serve an unmet need. The form often makes sense for very small businesses, companies that are too small to take on the legal and administrative costs of an ESOP. They are also appropriate for sectors such as childcare that are made up mostly of small independent providers. The providers can gain operational efficiencies by forming a cooperative that shares marketing, administrative, and financial tasks.

CHCA. In the US, the leading example of a worker cooperative is Cooperative Home Care Associates (CHCA), in New York City. At this writing CHCA has some 1,700 employees (down from 2,000 due to the pandemic), about half of whom are owners. Founders Rick Surpin and Peggy Powell started the business back in 1985 out of a concern that the jobs created in the growing home-care industry were poor—low pay, little stability, few benefits or opportunities for advancement. They believed that a for-profit cooperative structure would allow for better-quality jobs while providing high-quality care. They also wanted the co-op to be a model employer, offering not just better wages and services but employee participation and control of the board—and, when possible, a share of the profits.

So Surpin and Powell plunged in, beginning with a workforce of 12 home-care aides and a contract for services from a Bronx-based hospital. The first two years were a struggle, but soon their business started to grow and become modestly profitable. By the third year of operation, they had started a home-care aide training program, which proved to be a key element in the company's development: the program provided an edge over competitors who did not provide training and who faced rapid staff turnover. It also provided an entry point into the cooperative's participative culture, a culture that was reinforced as participants advanced from trainee to home-care aide and, for many, to worker-owner.

Over time, CHCA has continued to grow. Its employees became unionized through Local 1199 of the Service Employees International Union. It built an organizational ecosystem around its "Quality Care through Quality Jobs" approach, including an affiliated nonprofit agency for industry-specific training, workforce development, and policy advocacy. The pandemic naturally created obstacles, but it also presented a substantial opportunity that CHCA was well positioned to seize.

Namasté Solar. CHCA and some other co-ops received significant funding from foundations and other philanthropists, which makes them hard to replicate. Namasté Solar, based in Boulder, Colorado, is in some ways more typical of the cooperative movement: it started—and has succeeded—with no outside involvement. Cofounder Blake Jones believed deeply in the cooperative model, and when he and his partners started Namasté in 2004, he hoped he could help shape what was then a new industry. "We started with our own version of employee ownership, a very unique form, where we invented our own wheel," he told an interviewer in 2013. "It was based on one-member, one-vote. Then two years ago, on January 1, 2011, we officially converted into an employee-owned cooperative, also called worker cooperatives."[8]

Namasté Solar members base their operations on a series of principles:

- They hold quarterly, full-day Big Picture Meetings, known as BPMs, to make decisions, review financial statements, discuss high-level matters, and facilitate team building.

- They build transparency through open-book management and access to all company information (except for information protected by government privacy regulations).

○ They maintain a six-to-one maximum ratio of highest-to-lowest total pay per employee.

○ They practice what they call Frank, Open, and Honest (FOH) communication.

Co-owners receive positive or negative patronage dividends each year depending on profitability. As a Colorado public benefit cooperative and Certified B Corporation, however, Namasté Solar explicitly measures its accomplishments not just by profit but by its effects on higher quality of life for employees, a superior experience for customers, and positive impacts on other stakeholders, including its community and the environment. In 2021, with support from CEO Jason Sharpe, members added "come as you are" and "equity" to their core values in an effort to build justice, equity, diversity, and inclusion, and to cultivate an environment in which people felt comfortable bringing their "authentic selves" to work.

Employees who petition to join the co-op begin a year-long candidacy. Candidates participate in BPMs and leadership meetings; they also enroll in a curriculum known within the organization as the Namasté Solar MBA. This education includes financial literacy, solar technology, and unconscious-bias training. Candidates who wish to become co-owners are voted in by the existing owners; they then buy one share of voting common stock, which enables them to participate in annual profit sharing and in democratic decision-making on the basis of one-member, one-vote.

As of 2021, Namasté Solar had over 200 employees, roughly half of whom were owners. The company has consistently been named a best place to work and is the largest solar contractor in the Denver area. Importantly, Namasté was the first in a family of cooperative enterprises that now includes the Amicus Solar Cooperative (a purchasing cooperative for solar equipment) and Amicus O&M Cooperative (a maintenance cooperative for Amicus members). The Kachuwa Impact Fund, Blake Jones's most recent project, is also structured as a cooperative; it's designed to support co-ops and other social ventures with mission-aligned, long-term, non-controlling capital. This method of network building is common among cooperatives.

SIMILARITIES AND DIFFERENCES

Trusts, co-ops, and ESOPs are similar in some ways, different in others. Figure 7 shows some of the critical variables.

FIGURE 7: Employee Ownership Trusts (EOTs) and Worker Co-ops versus ESOPs

	EOTS	CO-OPS	ESOPS
Tax benefits to seller	No	Yes	Yes
Tax benefits to company	Contributions are deductible.	Contributions are deductible.	Contributions are deductible; plan can borrow money in pre-tax dollars; 100% ESOPs pay no tax.
Employees can vote shares.	In some plans	Yes	Generally only on limited issues
Share allocation	Company sets rules.	One person, one share	Based on relative pay or more level formula

Source: Authors

Co-ops in the Gig Economy

The rise of the so-called gig economy—platform companies such as Uber or TaskRabbit that employ individuals on a contract basis to deliver services—is surely one of the major developments of today's labor market. Granted, no one is quite sure how big this sector is: estimates range from about 7 percent of the workforce to as much as 36 percent.[9] And nobody really knows how gig work pays compared to conventional employment. Some studies say it pays more, some say less; others conclude that comparisons are fruitless because gig workers may have different preferences about hours, flexibility, and other goals. The only thing researchers agree on is that gig workers usually lack the benefits, such as health insurance, enjoyed by many regular employees. Gig employers have fought tooth and nail to avoid having their workers classified as employees, largely because paying benefits and other labor-related expenses would significantly raise their costs.

Given this book's focus on ownership, we have a different perspective. Many gig companies have enjoyed huge run-ups in value, evidenced by high stock prices. Uber, for instance, was worth more than $80 billion in late 2021. But the people who deliver the services that ultimately create that value have not shared in the wealth. Rather than arguing over whether those individuals should be classified as employees or contractors, everyone might be better off figuring out how they can share in the companies' ownership. As it happens, a different kind of cooperative model might be exactly what's required.

Although worker co-ops are few in number and typically quite small, organizations known as secondary co-ops play a significant role in the US economy. Sunkist, Land O'Lakes, Ocean Spray, and other agricultural processors are owned by the producers who supply them. Ace Hardware is a national co-op owned by local hardware stores. In secondary co-ops like these, the members are businesses rather than individuals. Since members usually have equal votes, the companies are democratic in structure, though in practice they are run much like other large businesses.

Platform co-ops. Secondary or platform co-ops might be just what the gig economy needs, and some organizations are already testing these waters. One of the most successful is the Canadian stock-media agency Stocksy United, a royalty-free photo, video, and illustration cooperative committed, as the company says, to "empowering the creative class's pursuit of meaningful work."

Stocksy's founders had earlier started a company called iStock, which they sold to Getty Images in 2004. Later, they found themselves unhappy with the way the industry was changing: it seemed to be undercutting both artistic integrity and artists' pay. So they created Stocksy, aiming to disrupt the stock industry with a different business model and policies that would restore the trust and creative freedoms of its members. Users of Stocksy can purchase rights to digital, royalty-free content for prices from $15 to $400, depending on size and format. Artists earn between 50 percent and 75 percent of the license fees. If the cooperative earns a surplus, members receive a profit share based on how much their images and videos have contributed to the surplus. By 2021 Stocksy had more than a thousand members and was paying out several million dollars a year in royalties and profits to those members. The company has a traditional elected board; members each have one vote.

Another promising new platform co-op is The Drivers Cooperative in New York City, launched in 2020. The co-op developed its own software to provide an alternative to Uber and Lyft. It takes a 15 percent cut of ride fares, compared to 20 to 25 percent for the two giants (these percentages can be higher for shorter rides). Erik Forman, who helped start the cooperative, told us in late 2021 that it had 4,000 drivers, a few hundred of whom were providing regular rides, and it had recently won a contract with the city to do 1,200 trips a day for paratransit, a deal expected to make the co-op profitable. Co-op leaders plan to make its software available for driver cooperatives in other cities under a common brand. Other small-scale experiments, like New York's Brightly cooperatives (housecleaning) and Chicago's CoRise Cooperative platform (childcare providers), combine a digital platform with a franchise business structure. Using these platforms, independent workers in the service economy join cooperatives that provide back-office support and a customer-facing brand.

Trebor Scholz of the New School in New York estimates that there are about 400 platform cooperatives around the world. Most are very small, but an active group of proponents is promoting the idea. The New York City–based Platform Cooperativism Consortium, for instance, provides advice and technical support to co-op launchers. To be sure, platform co-ops face significant hurdles. Someone with the right skills and ambition needs to start them. They must attract the software developers and marketers who can build and launch the platform. Money is likely to be a problem as well: venture capital firms won't be interested because co-ops have no stock that can later be sold to the public or another buyer. Some have relied on foundation funding, others (like Stocksy) on social entrepreneurs who are willing to forgo some of the potential rewards of their creation. But both sources are small. Alternatively, governments at the local or national level could provide the funds, as the federal government once did for rural electric cooperatives.

Melissa Hoover, executive director of the Democracy at Work Institute, told us that "platform coops meet an immediate need for the workers who actually provide the service, but longer term they also reorient the conversation . . . in a more sensible direction: actual humans doing work that meets needs for other actual humans. Without quality drivers or quality home-care workers or quality photographers or whatever else the platform provides, there are no customers."

• • • •

All of these opportunities—trusts, worker co-ops, and platform co-ops— are currently no more than a drop in the US economy's bucket, and they pale in importance in comparison with ESOPs. But employee ownership comes in many forms, and you can't always tell which ones will catch on with business owners, legislators, and the public at large. We ourselves consider all these experiments worthwhile, and we think they are all worthy of the kinds of support that we'll outline in the following chapter.

Takeaways

- ○ ESOPs aren't the only model for broad-based employee ownership. Worker co-ops are a practical alternative for many small companies. Platform co-ops are a promising idea that could transform the gig economy. Trusts are right for some companies.

- ○ These other models are just a start. By focusing on broadening ownership, would-be reformers will undoubtedly create more models that work for more situations.

AN EMPLOYEE-OWNERSHIP NETWORK

Western North Carolina has long been one of America's premier textile and furniture manufacturing regions, but it took a serious hit when many of the area's companies moved production to other countries. Now an organization called The Industrial Commons is working to rebuild the state's heritage industries by taking an ecosystem approach, with employee ownership as one of its pillars.

The Industrial Commons is a nonprofit that partners with a broad array of organizations, including community colleges and economic development agencies as well as local businesses. Its workforce development programs train workers in everything from production to open-book management practices. In 10 years it has helped to spawn several enterprises along the supply chain and dozens of jobs. The group's startup period was modestly funded by private philanthropy and public money. But it aims—and is on track—to be a self-sufficient organization that employs public resources such as economic development funds but is not reliant on them.

The Commons also launched the Carolina Textile District (CTD), a member-governed and member-driven network of values-aligned textile manufacturers in North and South Carolina that (as its website says) "connects makers, designers, and entrepreneurs to a reliable domestic supply chain in order to make quality products here at home." CTD includes well-established businesses such as Valdese Weavers, owned by its employees through an ESOP; worker co-ops such as the fast-growing Opportunity Threads; and conventionally owned small businesses such as TS Designs. "We're trying to usher in a renaissance of our state's traditional industries, building on new labor models and partnering with other values-based businesses," says Molly Hemstreet, co-executive director of The Industrial Commons.

OPPORTUNITY #4
Policies and Programs for Spreading Employee Ownership

Bring on those tired, labor-plagued, competition-weary companies and ESOP will breathe new life into them. . . . It will revitalize what is wrong with capitalism. It will increase productivity. It will improve labor relations. It will promote economic justice.

—RUSSELL B. LONG
United States Senator, 1948–1987

THREE THINGS ARE WORTH REMEMBERING before we plunge into this chapter.

Number one: although some successful businesses will be passed on to family members for a generation or more, every other company that doesn't close its doors will be sold. When a company is sold, the ownership changes—and so there's an opportunity to change the structure of ownership. Almost all the ESOPs in the United States came into existence when a company owner decided to sell the business to its employees.

Number two: no ownership structure is somehow natural or inevitable. Every structure is created and maintained by law. Laws make it possible for entrepreneurs to form corporations, thus limiting their liability and accountability. Laws make public stock-market ownership practical and (relatively) safe for investors. Laws facilitate the buying and selling of companies. (For example, private equity investors can characterize what is really ordinary income as "carried interest" and pay a lot less tax than even Donald Trump once thought they should.) So when we suggest tinkering with laws and tax codes to encourage more employee ownership, we're not proposing anything radical, just a reorientation of the legal framework to make a fairer economy.

Number three: employee ownership isn't a partisan idea. As we were writing this chapter, the US Senate's Armed Services Committee inserted a provision into the National Defense Authorization Act that extended small-business contracting preferences to companies wholly owned by an ESOP. The striking part about the provision wasn't its scope—it was pretty modest—but its political parentage. It was initially sponsored by Elizabeth Warren, the liberal Massachusetts Democrat, then introduced to the committee by Jeanne Shaheen, a Democrat from New Hampshire. But it was also sponsored by Republican Tommy Tuberville, the former football coach from Alabama who is as far ideologically from Warren as any senator could be.

This bipartisan support has served employee ownership well over the years, with 18 different laws from 1974 through 2019 providing tax and other benefits for ESOPs.[1] The ideas we outline in this chapter aren't particularly ideological, either. They would make a big difference to employee ownership, which has so far been limited in its impact. But they would not require major changes to US (or most other countries') tax laws and business regulations. Nor would they impose significant new costs on taxpayers. Given employee ownership's popularity and its strong bipartisan backing, the proposals are very much within the realm of political reality.

With these precepts in mind, let's look at what governments—particularly the US federal government—can do to turn many more wage earners into owners.

Leveling the Playing Field for Company Sales

One set of proposals focuses on the key to a lot of employee-ownership conversions: facilitating sales to an ESOP or similar structure.

When a company is sold, the acquirer usually borrows money to finance the deal. But it's just like when you take out a mortgage to buy a house: the bank won't lend you the full amount. So a buyer has to come up with some other source of funds for the remaining part of the purchase price. That's no problem for a PE firm or a large corporation, both of which have plenty of cash and other assets they can draw on. They also are likely to have ongoing relationships with banks and other lenders, so arranging for loans isn't hard either.

ESOPs are at a distinct disadvantage in this situation. In most ESOP transactions, a bank will lend only 30 to 50 percent of the purchase price. The typical company can't put up enough collateral to justify a larger loan. So the rest has to come from somewhere else. The seller might agree to be paid over several years—to take back a note, in financial parlance. (For technical legal reasons, the seller may also have to jump through some expensive hoops to get the full benefit of the tax deferral available to owners who sell to ESOPs.) To get the money up front, the company might take on what's known as mezzanine debt, meaning loans from specialized lenders who (in case of trouble) are repaid only after the bank has been repaid. These loans naturally carry a significantly higher interest rate. So if you're a company owner and you sell to an ESOP, you might have to wait to get your money, or you might have to let the company take on high-cost debt. None of these conditions hold if you sell to a larger corporation or PE firm.

Loans and guarantees. But here's the thing: government programs are already in place that provide capital to smaller businesses. These could easily be adapted to facilitate ESOP transactions and thereby level the playing field.[2] Small Business Investment Companies (SBICs), for instance, are private companies set up to invest in small enterprises. The government's Small Business Administration (SBA) lends these SBICs two dollars for every dollar the SBIC raises, and the SBIC then invests the money in qualifying small companies. A simple tweak to the program could define transitions to majority ESOPs, worker cooperatives, or employee ownership trusts as entities that are eligible to receive the funds. The recently enacted State Small Business Credit Initiative (SSBCI), similarly, provides funds that states can use to support small companies. In November 2021 the Department of the Treasury issued guidelines allowing these funds to be used "for the purchase of an interest in an employee stock ownership plan . . . , worker cooperative, or related vehicle," provided that employees wind up holding a majority interest in the business.[3]

These programs are for smaller companies, meaning (in most cases) businesses with fewer than 500 employees. But a lot of company sales involve significantly larger enterprises, well outside the scope of "small business." So three experts in the field have developed a different approach, this one focusing on so-called middle market companies.[4] Middle market companies typically have $50 million to $1 billion in annual revenue and may have as many as several thousand workers. They account for a sizable fraction of the value of companies that are sold every year.

The government, these authors point out, has a long history of guaranteeing loans that serve certain social objectives. A prime example is the series of initiatives that provided guarantees for home mortgages. Why not put the same idea to work in favor of employee ownership? An Employee Equity Investment Act, or EEIA, would create a new program, housed either in the Treasury or in the Department of Commerce rather than in the SBA. The program would license privately owned and operated investment companies, much like SBICs, that would offer a combination of private capital and federal loan guarantees for ESOP conversions. Maybe, for instance, a seller could finance 40 percent of the transaction through a low-priced bank loan. EEIA funds could then be used to guarantee a portion of a mezzanine lender's debt, thus lowering the interest rate to a point where the deal made financial sense.

Such a program would be especially important for divestitures of operating businesses by large companies. In the US, more than 2,000 divestitures are reported in a typical year, with a total value ranging from $172 billion to more than $400 billion. Other corporations buy about three-quarters of these companies; most of the rest are snapped up by PE firms.[5] Companies that are doing divestitures will rarely be willing to sell to an ESOP, which must borrow money to pay for part of the deal and pay the rest over time. Other buyers, after all, will pay a good price with cash on the barrel. The EEIA would level this part of the playing field, enabling an ESOP to be a bidder. Some public-company sellers might favor the ESOP because they want an ongoing supply relationship with the business they are divesting or because they believe that sale to an ESOP sends a better message to their remaining employees.

Because of the very low default rate on employee ownership transitions, these changes in loan programs would cost little. Indeed, state governments could enact their own programs along the same lines without raising anybody's taxes. Combined with existing federal tax incentives, loan programs like these could generate a large number of new ESOPs each year.

Tweaking the Tax Code a Little More

Congress has been generous in the past to ESOPs and worker cooperatives. But a handful of additional changes could broaden the effect at little cost. Some of these changes might even generate revenue.

One measure is simplicity itself. Right now, owners of C corporations can defer taxation on the gains they realize from selling to an ESOP. Owners of S corporations cannot.[6] The difference between the two forms turns largely on tax law. C corporations pay a corporate income tax. S corporations pay none, but stockholders are taxed personally on their share of the company's profits. Many owners of S corporations, for various reasons, do not want to convert to C status. So when they look to sell, an ESOP is less attractive. Allowing these owners to defer the tax would spark more ESOPs—we would guess another 50 to 100 transactions per year.

A second tweak could correct the imbalance between corporate buyers and ESOPs. Corporate buyers will often pay what's called a synergistic price for an acquisition. The price reflects additional benefits the buyer hopes to realize from the purchase, such as lowered costs from combining the two companies. An ESOP transaction creates a standalone business that can't capture these hoped-for synergies. And even if an ESOP is competitive with other buyers on price, sale to an ESOP can take longer than a sale to other buyers because of the ESOP's additional regulations and requirements. To make sales to an ESOP more attractive, Congress could declare that some percentage of the seller's capital gains from sale to an ESOP are fully exempt from taxes (rather than just tax deferred).[7] The UK already exempts taxes on sales to employee ownership trusts.

Congress might even restore a provision in ESOP tax law that existed between 1987 and 1992. That provision allowed lenders to exclude 50 percent of the interest they received on ESOP loans from their taxable income. It actually sparked tens of billions of dollars in loans to ESOPs, but it was repealed as Congress tried to deal with the recession of the early 1990s. Restoring it could be particularly important for mezzanine debt, which carries higher interest rates.[8]

Beyond ESOPs, Congress could look to current tax rules for deducting executive pay. Right now, pay over $1 million per year is not deductible. An easy but potentially powerful reform would enact a simple tradeoff: if a company awards stock compensation to any of its top executives, bringing the total to more than $1 million, the funds are deductible only if at least that much is allocated to all full-time employees with (say) a year or more of service. The awards could be channeled through an ESOP or distributed directly based on the same allocation rules that apply to ESOPs. At worst, companies would pay more in taxes. At best, hundreds of millions of dollars in equity would go to employees. The arrangement would have no negative effects on a company's performance; it might even improve results if the companies took their new employee ownership program seriously.

Finally, many public companies currently offer stock to employees at significantly discounted rates. (We discussed these employee stock purchase plans in Chapter 8.) Employees specify a payroll deduction over a period of three months to two years; at the end of that time they can use the money to buy shares at a discount. The discount is normally 10 to 15 percent, but sometimes it's considerably more. Because of the programs' structure, employees have an opportunity to build significant equity stakes in addition to their pension or 401(k) benefits. Yet only about a third of eligible employees participate. Some may find it hard to afford the deduction. Many may not understand the program. If companies seeded the first two years of participation with a $1,000 grant to buy shares, employees would likely see the "guaranteed win" nature of the offering and participate at much higher rates. To encourage this, the government could provide a tax deduction for these grants, and perhaps offer a tax incentive for price discounts over a certain level. Also, these plans would be more effective if they all included a look-back feature, as many already do. Such a feature allows employees to buy shares at the lower of two prices: the price at the beginning of the offering period (usually one year) or the price at the end. Research shows that look-back features and higher discounts increase participation in the plans.

Pursuing a Handful of Other Ideas

State and federal governments in the United States interact with the economy in all sorts of ways, not just through taxes. They spend money on economic development. They contract with companies for goods and services. Congress and state legislatures have an opportunity to use this economic muscle to reshape the ownership landscape.

The government aid opportunity. Federal, state, and local governments give out tens of billions of dollars in corporate aid every year. They provide tax credits, incentives, and outright subsidies for certain kinds of actions and investments. States, for example, offer tens of billions in tax breaks or cash grants to encourage companies to relocate (or to stay put if they are already in the state). Many of these subsidies aren't particularly effective—but if a state is going to hand out money, why not condition the aid on sharing ownership with employees? Companies could fund that requirement with contributions of shares to a qualified plan, so they would have no cash outlay. Later, when employees cash in their shares, the money stays in the community instead of lining the pockets of absentee owners. The same logic applies to the many special tax benefits the federal government gives out to companies, often those with powerful political support. Some portion of those subsidies could be conditioned on sharing equity.

The procurement opportunity. Both the federal government and many state governments have set-aside requirements for a given fraction of their contracts: so much must go to companies owned by minorities, women, or disabled veterans. The intent is not just to benefit individual owners but also to encourage the hiring of people in those categories. At the moment, companies owned by an ESOP do not qualify for most of these set-asides, even though many of the individual employee owners might be in qualifying categories. So an opportunity to spread ownership to more members of the target populations is lost.

Adding ESOP-owned businesses to the eligible categories would be one way to encourage employee ownership. By itself, that might diminish the available pool of funds for the companies these programs are aimed at, putting ESOPs in competition with other potential beneficiaries. So perhaps ESOP companies should qualify only if a majority of shares are held by individuals in the target groups. Alternatively, ESOP companies might qualify if the CEO and a majority of the board are in the target groups. In both cases, the company would have to be more than 50 percent owned by the ESOP.

Create outreach programs. One big obstacle to the spread of employee ownership is ignorance. Company owners often don't know about ESOPs or worker cooperatives. They may get misleading information from their advisors. State governments can take the lead in informing and educating business leaders about the possibilities and providing incentives for them to consider employee ownership.

Colorado, for example, has the nonprofit Rocky Mountain Employee Ownership Center and a state office of employee ownership, both of which offer education and basic technical assistance for employee ownership transitions. In 2021 the legislature enacted a 50 percent tax credit to help fund the conversion costs involved in sales to ESOPs, co-ops, or trusts. These costs often discourage sellers from considering employee ownership, so the tax credit may make a significant difference. Halfway through 2021—even prior to the new tax law—20 new employee-owned companies were formed in Colorado with help from the state programs, about twice what would be expected without them.

Several other states have information and assistance centers, though only one other (Massachusetts) enjoys state funding. A number of cities have launched outreach programs as well. Most programs so far have been supported by grant funds and have focused mainly on worker cooperatives, but the nonprofits behind these efforts (notably Project Equity and the Democracy at Work Institute) are working to extend them to ESOPs. Congress can help. Vermont senator Bernie Sanders proposed in 2018 that Congress allocate $300,000 per state program to fund these outreach efforts, with amounts increasing every year for five years. He revived this effort in discussions concerning the Biden administration's $3.5 trillion follow-on proposal to the 2021 infrastructure bill. Meanwhile, the Main Street Employee Ownership Act of 2018 directed the US Small Business Administration (SBA) itself to create an outreach program on employee ownership. With its extensive network of Small Business Development Centers, the SBA is well positioned to do this at minimal cost, but it has so far failed to follow up on the congressional direction. Congress should ensure that the SBA does what the law intended.

Reinforce the S in ESG. ESG, as we noted in Chapter 4, refers to a corporation's environmental, social, and governance goals. More and more shareholders of public companies, including institutional investors, are asking companies to report their progress on these objectives. Both major stock exchanges in the US, as well as many worldwide, have set out guidelines for this kind of reporting.

The goals are often quite specific for the environmental and governance part of ESG. But Pete Stavros of KKR points out that the employment aspect of "S" provides little guidance on the quality or fairness of employment practices. One of these, he argues, should be how much equity a company shares, and with which employees. Compiling such a report would be an easy task for most companies. Current Securities and Exchange Commission rules in the US require equity disclosures only for a company's top five officers. If the SEC required broader disclosures, activist investors could pressure companies to do more on employee equity. That might encourage companies to have something positive to report on.

Preventing regulatory overreach. The US Department of Labor (DOL) oversees how ESOPs are run. That's a vital role—there needs to be active oversight of any policy that involves significant tax benefits, otherwise someone will find ways to abuse it. Where ESOPs are concerned, the DOL can audit a company and even take it to court, as it does in a handful of cases every year. In addition, perhaps 40 to 50 companies end up being investigated each year and paying some settlement fee. Some of these cases involved egregious behavior. Others have turned out to be administrative errors.

Many in the ESOP community believe that the DOL, in a small number of cases each year (about 0.1 percent of all ESOPs), has gone after companies that have done everything right. These actions have discouraged some companies from setting up an ESOP, even though the risk of DOL action is in fact extremely small. The most significant of the DOL's actions have concerned the valuation of stock. Yet the department's regulators have never issued any guidance on how stock should be valued, which leaves it to a matter of judgment and differing opinions. Clear guidance from the DOL, working with the ESOP community, would go a long way toward resolving the problem.

. . . .

Tactical discussions like those in this chapter—how to bring about more employee ownership through this or that method—may seem disconnected from the ambitions of employee ownership advocates. Here we have this grand vision of reshaping capitalism into a better, fairer system, and we're talking about tweaking the tax code? About providing a little more information to company owners or investors? Where's the Grand Plan, the revolutionary program that is more in keeping with our ambitions?

The answer, of course, is that we're talking evolution, not revolution. And evolution is always and everywhere a series of small steps. Most of the proposals here have modest (or no) costs, would garner bipartisan support, and do not require major changes to the tax or securities laws of the US or most other countries. They just need a push.

But small steps build on themselves, and may eventually add up to a kind of tipping point. Imagine a time when most political and business leaders support employee ownership, when workers and consumers seek out companies that share equity broadly, when millions of wage earners enjoy comfortable nest eggs because they are owners, not just hired hands. That would indeed be a kind of revolution, albeit a peaceful and gradual one. It would create the kind of economy that truly serves its citizens, and that the rest of the world could emulate. These modest reforms are steps on the path to that goal.

Takeaways

○ How to spread employee ownership? The good news is that we don't need major changes in tax or other laws. Relatively minor tweaks to existing rules, funding state and local outreach programs, and proving financing support for transactions could all make a big difference at a small cost.

○ The real challenge is to spread the word. Employee ownership needs to be a priority for political discussion, academic research, and activist efforts.

TOMORROW THE WORLD

Wealth is created by ownership.

—GREGORY ROCKSON
Cofounder and CEO, mPharma
Accra, Ghana

OWNERSHIP PATTERNS DIFFER from one country to another. Big Japanese companies often count banks among their major shareholders. Some large European businesses, including IKEA and Bosch, are owned by foundations. Employee ownership is no different: countries around the world take a variety of approaches to get shares into workers' hands. None has yet reached the scope or penetration of US-style ESOPs, which in many ways are the most far-reaching and effective of employee-ownership structures. But the British employee-owned sector is growing rapidly, and many other countries are exploring or developing creative ways to turn wage-earners into owners. This chapter reviews some of the most important ones—along with one big missed opportunity.[1]

Australia

Public-company employee ownership in Australia focuses mostly on stock purchase plans, often with some kind of company incentive. For instance, almost half of the 11,000 employees at Brambles, a supply-chain logistics company, participate in a plan that offers one free share for each share purchased. The average employee puts in about A$3,200 per year, so that can add up to a substantial equity stake over time.[2] Australian tax law allows employers to contribute up to A$1,000 (about US$720 in 2021) per year in shares that are not taxable to employees, provided at least 75 percent of employees are offered the chance to participate in a share matching program. Some companies also allow employees to borrow money to buy the shares.

Small start-up companies (up to 50 employees and less than 10 years old) can offer what's known as an Employee Share Scheme, in which the company grants stock options or discounted shares (up to a 15 percent discount) to employees. The company must grant options or shares to at least 75 percent of the workforce. The shares have full voting rights. Employees can defer taxes until they exercise the options.

Consultants in Australia have also created a trust model for closely held companies that mimics some of the tax benefits ESOPs have in the US, especially the ability to acquire the shares with pretax dollars.

Canada

Until now, employee ownership in Canada has been relatively rare. Canada does not provide tax benefits for employee-owned companies or owners who sell to their employees, and existing broad-based plans—which are few in number—are mostly in private companies whose employees have purchased shares.

But that may be changing. Both the Conservative and Liberal parties have strongly endorsed employee ownership. First, the Liberal Trudeau government proposed a new budget stating:

> Employee ownership trusts encourage employee ownership of a business, and facilitate the transition of privately owned businesses to employees. Both the United States and the United Kingdom support and encourage employee ownership through these types of arrangements. Budget 2021 announces that the government will engage with stakeholders to examine

what barriers exist to the creation of employee ownership trusts in Canada, and how workers and owners of private businesses in Canada could benefit from the use of employee ownership trusts.

Early discussion focused on providing some of the same tax benefits that are available under US ESOP law.

A few months later, the Conservative Party went even further, pushing for major changes in Canadian law to create an employee ownership structure similar to ESOPs in the US and employee ownership trusts in the UK. The Conservatives endorsed providing capital gains deferrals for owners selling to employee ownership trusts as well as government support to help finance the sales. The platform states:

Canadian employees deserve the opportunity to earn more than just a salary for their hard work. They also deserve greater security in retirement. Canada's Conservatives will increase employee ownership of Canadian companies by establishing Employee Ownership Trusts, which provide a tax advantage for company owners to sell to their employees. This will take the form of a reduction in capital gains tax when the owner sells to a trust owned by the employees, enabling ownership to transfer to the people who have partnered in building the business. We will also ensure that BDC [the Business Development Bank of Canada] makes financing available to support these trusts.

At this writing, it seems possible that Canada will join the UK and the US as a leading promoter of employee ownership after a new Parliament is seated in 2022.

China

In the mid-1990s, the NCEO partnered with the Chinese government to hold two major conferences for business, union, and government leaders in China. For several years thereafter, delegations from the State Committee on Economic Restructuring came to the US to visit the NCEO and ESOP companies (preferably companies that were located near Disneyland). In 1997, Chinese premier Jiang Zemin announced that the Chinese government would be strongly encouraging the privatization of most of its economy through employee ownership. Jiang included employee ownership as part of the Communist Party's goal to move to "socialism with Chinese characteristics."

Employee ownership started in the small and medium-sized enterprises that had been primarily owned by township and village governments. In the Chinese context, "small and medium-sized" businesses can be quite large, in many cases with thousands of workers. These enterprises employ 80 percent of the country's nonfarm workforce. The late Gao Shangquan, then vice-minister of the State Commission for Restructuring the Economy, urged that small and medium-sized enterprises be sold to the employees through a system of worker collectives. Such a system was already in place in Shandong Province. There, 250 companies had already been sold to these collectives, which function similarly to employee ownership trusts.

Over the ensuing years, employee ownership became a common phenomenon in China, both through this privatization program and, more recently, in entrepreneurial companies. Most of the recent plans are funded by employees buying stock at market value. Chinese employees have traditionally saved a significant fraction of their income, but interest rates have often been kept artificially low. So buying stock in an employer has offered a potentially more lucrative, though riskier, return.

For all that, the process of building employee ownership in China has proceeded in fits and starts. In 1998, ownership plans were suspended in public companies because of concerns that investment in these companies was too speculative. Indeed, many of the private company plans failed. In 2005, employee ownership was reauthorized for public companies, with broad-based plans offering share purchase arrangements for employees. "Broad-based," however, turned out to refer largely to what researcher Huifen Pan calls *core staff*—people at any level of the company whose skills were deemed essential. About 2 percent or less of the plans are truly broad based; most provide equity opportunities to only about 20 percent of the workforce.[3] There are no good data on closely held companies.

In 2021, China's securities regulator issued draft regulations intended to facilitate more broad-based employee ownership in publicly traded companies. According to this draft, public companies could make up to 10 percent of their shares available to employees, who could then use payroll deductions to buy the shares. Participating employees would be required to hold the shares for 36 months, and no employee could buy more than 1 percent of the company's shares. The draft regulations would establish a trust to hold the shares. There are no special tax incentives for these plans.

The best known example of employee ownership in China is Huawei Technologies, the telecommunications giant that some political leaders have accused of being an arm of the government. Huawei is the largest telecommunications equipment manufacturer in the world and the second-largest manufacturer of smartphones. It has more than 180,000 employees worldwide, mostly in China. A 2020 paper by Colin Hawes, a professor at Australia's University of Technology Sydney, provides the most detailed and reliable analysis of its ownership to date and concludes that Huawei's employee ownership is genuine.[4] Almost all the value of Huawei equity is owned broadly by about 90,000 employees who buy what Americans would call phantom stock rights. Unlike most phantom plans in the US, however, the shares carry a right to interim profit distributions. Employees must redeem the shares when they leave the company; they cannot sell or transfer them to anybody else.

The trade union at the company is designated as the legal person to hold the shares (much like the trustee in a US ESOP). The employee shareholding committee is elected by the employee shareholders, and the elected representatives represent these shareholders at the company's general meetings. The committee has to be made up of nonmanagement employees. At this writing it has 115 members elected on a one-share, one-vote basis. From 2004 to 2016, the company's capital-raising from employee purchases averaged about $50,000 per employee. Huawei's plan has helped it attract talented people and has thus fed its ability to grow.

Huawei is not alone. Another major Chinese firm, Legend Holdings, owner of the Lenovo Group, Digital China, Legend Capital, Raycom Real Estate, and Hony Capital, is 35 percent owned by its employee stock ownership association. The company employs about 30,000 people. In 2021, Gree Electric launched an employee stock ownership plan allowing its 12,000 workers to buy stocks at half price.

Continental Europe

Countries on the continent of Europe encourage employee ownership through a variety of methods.[5]

Public companies. According to a report by the European Federation of Employee Share Ownership, 7.1 million employees in 2020 were shareholders in the 2,723 largest companies in the 32 European countries. Fifty-three percent of public European companies offered some kind of broad-based employee ownership plan, though the average percentage of shares held by nonmanagement employees was only 1.6 percent. The percentage of public companies offering broad-based plans had increased every year since 2006; still, worker participation in these plans was only 18.5 percent, down from 23 percent in 2006. That number is lower than for comparable plans in the US. Part of the reason is globalization: employees in other, often poorer, countries participate less than Europeans do.

Except in France, most European plans are voluntary stock purchase plans. Companies may match employee purchases, provide a discounted price, or both. Some countries provide tax relief for employees who participate in these plans. Broad-based employee ownership plans in Germany, for instance, are almost all stock purchase plans in public companies. Employees can buy shares at a discount of up to 20 percent and get a tax break on the first €1,440 in benefit they receive. If an employee buys €7,200 worth of shares, the €1,440 discount is not taxable. If the company gives you €1,440 in free shares, that too is not taxable.

France has conventional stock-purchase plans as well, but it also has a number of plans for employee profit sharing that can be used to facilitate ownership. One kind of plan is compulsory for companies with 50 or more employees; another kind is voluntary. In either case, the profit share must be invested in a set of dedicated investment funds that every company has to provide; the funds offer a full range of investments, one of which is company shares. (This is much like 401(k) plan rules in the US.) Employees can also use their own savings to invest in these plans. In addition to the profit sharing plans, most large French companies are launching yearly capital offers that are reserved for employee purchase plans. The plans usually provide a 20 percent discount and an added company match; they require employees to hold the shares for five years.

One unusual business is Voestalpine a 50,000-employee Austrian multinational steel manufacturer, one of the most successful steel companies in Europe. Its Austrian employees—somewhat over half the workforce—own close to 15 percent of its stock through a trust. Each year, as spelled out in a collective bargaining agreement, a portion of employees' wage increase is paid in the form of shares (10 percent in the most recent year). Employees also get shares from a profit-sharing bonus, typically amounting to 3 or 4 percent of pay each year. As employee shareholders, they elect a representative to the company governing board. Company contributions to the plan are tax-deductible, and the first €4,500 of what employees receive is exempt from income taxes. Employees cash in their shares when they leave the company. Twenty percent of Voestalpine employees in nine other countries participate in discounted share purchase plans.

Privately held companies and co-ops. About a million employees are in employee ownership plans in European private companies. Two countries, the UK and France, have more than 100 privately held, majority employee-owned companies with 100 or more employees. Just three other countries (Spain, Italy, and the Czech Republic) have 10 or more such enterprises. The continent does have a sizable number of worker cooperatives, nearly all of them with fewer than 100 employees. About 30,000 Italians work in co-ops; 50,000 French; and 90,000 Spaniards plus the employees of Mondragon, to be discussed in a moment. (In Spain, the cooperative model has been encouraged by federal law, especially by allowing unemployed workers to get an advance on their unemployment benefits to start a co-op.) Worker cooperatives can be found to some extent in almost every other country. In the most comprehensive analysis of the research on worker cooperatives and economic performance, Virginie Pérotin of the University of Leeds found that "worker cooperatives are never found to be less productive than conventional firms and may be more productive. The key factor explaining this productivity seems to be members' involvement in governance."[6]

Mondragon. And then there is the Mondragon Corporation, which may be the best known and most widely studied worker co-op in the world.

Mondragon was started in 1956 by Father José María Arizmendiarrieta as a way to deal with the devastating unemployment in Spain's Basque region under the Franco regime. Arizmendiarrieta set up a few small worker cooperatives and a cooperative bank to help fund them. As the co-ops flourished, they helped other co-ops get off the ground; the bank created an entrepreneurship program to provide training in business development. Each co-op became a member of the Mondragon Cooperatives, a governing body with a general assembly in which each employee member had one vote. Over time, Mondragon became one of the great success stories in Spain, with businesses ranging from supermarkets to manufacturing to high tech. The corporation has its own social welfare agency, a university, and a number of business incubators. It has been able to hire exceptionally talented managers who are attracted to its business stability and philosophy. Today it employs about 80,000 people, with international sales accounting for about 70 percent of total revenue. Employees laid off at one company can join another or, with help from an incubator, apply to start their own co-op with financing from the bank.

Mondragon has been much admired by advocates of employee ownership. That has been both a blessing and a curse. Though inspiring, the Mondragon model has proven exceptionally hard to replicate. A European model that is perhaps more relevant to the US is that of the Emilia-Romagna region, in Northern Italy. About a third of the region's GDP is generated by cooperatives. Small enterprises in the manufacturing sector, many but not all worker co-ops, have created or joined flexible manufacturing networks that collaborate at a regional level. (This model inspired The Industrial Commons/Carolina Textile District in North Carolina, described in Chapter 10.) Emilia-Romagna has also organized much of its care sector using multistakeholder social cooperatives, which are the preferred providers for government social-service contracts.

Looking forward. Although Europe trails the US in employee ownership, there is growing interest in the American ESOP model. A 2017 action plan from the European Commission Capital Markets Union said, "Research shows that companies partly or entirely owned by their employees are more profitable, create more jobs and pay more taxes than their competitors without employee ownership."[7] The European Federation of Employee Share Ownership, a nonprofit information organization, has proposed creating a European version of the ESOP and has received endorsements from public officials in various countries.

Slovenia is a pioneer in this area. Thanks to the efforts of local activists, some businesses are piloting a hybrid co-op/ESOP concept much like that proposed by the European Federation, and enabling legislation is under consideration in the nation's Parliament.[8] In the Slovenian model, the trustee is a co-operative legal entity. The system ensures continuous rolling over of individual capital accounts: companies begin buying back some of employees' shares after a few years and reallocating them to other employees. So when new employees join, they automatically start building a capital account based on the annual redistribution of shares. When employees retire or leave, their share accounts are closed to additional contributions, but the balance in their accounts is paid out over time.

EUROPEAN EMPLOYEE OWNERSHIP: THE LARGEST COMPANIES[9]

The top five European companies measured by stock value held by employees are

Roche (Switzerland, 3 percent of shares held by employees)

Adyen (Netherlands, 22 percent)

Vinci (France, 12 percent)

Mondragon (Spain, 91 percent)

Total (France, 6 percent)

The largest companies in which a majority of shares are held by employees are

Mondragon (Spain, 82,000 employees)

John Lewis Partnership (UK, 81,000)

STEF (France, 19,000)

Manutencoop (Italy, 18,000)

Arup Group (UK, 16,000)

Korea

South Korea has long provided modest incentives for employees to buy shares in their companies and for companies to grant them shares or stock options.[10] In 2021, the government added new benefits in an effort to increase participation. As many as 80 percent of Korea's publicly traded companies offer share purchase plans, often with a match of free shares. Employee purchases and/or company contributions to these plans are excluded from taxable income for up to about $1,900 (in 2021). If employees hold the shares six years or more, the gains are exempt from income tax. Purchases can be made in monthly installments. Korea also allows employees to buy shares with money loaned from banks and then to repay the loan in shares if they cannot pay back the amount borrowed.

Shares in all these plans must be placed in an ownership trust operated by the private Korean Securities Finance Corporation (KSFC). The shares are subject to a lock-up period of at least one year if the employee has bought the shares and four years if the shares have been at least partially paid for by the employer. While the number of companies offering the plans is large, as in the US and Europe, the percentage of shares held by employees is small, generally under 2 percent. The KSFC says only about 10 percent of eligible employees participate in the plans.

In 2021, the South Korean video game holding company Krafton, Inc. surprised both current and prospective employees with a gift of up to $89 million in Krafton shares. Krafton is the producer of the enormously popular PlayerUnknown's Battlegrounds (PUBG) video games. Company chairman Byung-Gyu Chang personally gifted his own shares to global employees who weren't eligible for the company's employee ownership plan (which is limited to employees based in South Korea). The shares were available to all current employees and to anybody who joined the company before September 2021.

South Africa, Kenya, and Other African Nations

In the 2019 national elections, South Africa's ruling African National Congress (ANC) party and the main opposition party, the Democratic Alliance, both named broad-based employee ownership as a key goal for the coming years. The ANC manifesto pledged to introduce "legislation for the extension of company ownership to a broad base of workers through an employee ownership scheme and similar arrangements to supplement workers' incomes and build greater partnerships between workers and owners to build these businesses." At this writing, the only changes have been to make it somewhat easier for companies to qualify their employee ownership plans for South Africa's Black Economic Empowerment (BEE) program.

The BEE program gives companies government contracting preferences for sharing ownership with employees South Africa traditionally defined as *black*. Originally that term was defined as most nonwhites of any origin but was recently changed to mean "previously disadvantaged people/populations." Because government contracting has a wide scope, most large companies want to qualify for the BEE program, which they can do by accumulating points for various ways of empowering black South Africans.

Changes in the law in the past few years have given companies more credit for having broad-based employee ownership plans; several hundred companies have set up such plans, possibly covering several hundred thousand employees or more (precise data are not available). The plans are typically employer trusts funded by the company that hold about 5 percent of the shares. Some companies also get financing from the government's economic development agency that is contingent on an employee ownership plan, often a leveraged trust that repays the loan from dividends. (This can be problematic when dividends are inadequate to the purpose.) For instance, in 2021 Coca-Cola Beverages South Africa (CCBSA) announced that it would be increasing the ownership share of both employees and black empowerment investors to a 20 percent stake. This will increase the ownership stake of nearly 8,000 employees from 5 percent to 15 percent. In 2018, the Clicks Group, an 8,000-employee South Africa–based retailer of health and wellness products across Africa, announced that employees would receive a payout of 1.3 billion rand ($110 million) as the first of two installment distributions of their employee stock ownership plan. That amounted to a year's pay for most workers. Clicks stock has quadrupled since the plan was initiated.

Tendani Nelwamondo, the head of the South Africa Employee Ownership Association, told the NCEO in 2021 that although recent steps by the government are encouraging, South Africa needs a more appealing way to finance these plans at the corporate level, tax incentives more like those in the UK and the US, and greater opportunities for employee input at the governance level.

Kenya and Zimbabwe both have programs to encourage or, in Zimbabwe's case, require foreign companies to set up substantial employee ownership programs or face nationalization. The plans typically operate through employer-funded trusts. Only a few companies in each country have been affected by these plans. Meanwhile, a handful of new entrepreneurial companies founded by Silicon Valley veterans offer broad-based stock options to their employees. Examples include mPharma, which provides healthcare services and pharmacy supply-chain management in half a dozen African nations, and Sokowatch, which offers supply-chain and e-commerce capabilities to local sellers of staple goods, also in several African countries.

United Kingdom

In the UK's 2011 Parliamentary elections, leaders of all three major parties at the time pledged to create a *John Lewis economy*. The pledges made front-page news and ultimately led to 2014 legislation creating new rules and benefits for employee ownership trusts—including exemption from capital gains tax for business owners who sell to a trust.

The John Lewis economy refers to the iconic John Lewis Partnership, operator of John Lewis department stores and Waitrose supermarkets. Famous for its customer service as well as for its ownership structure, John Lewis remains one of the most admired companies in the UK. Its payroll peaked a few years ago at about 87,000 employees (Partners, as they are known), dropped to 78,000 as the company was hit hard by the coronavirus pandemic, and has rebounded a little at this writing.

The partnership has been wholly owned by a permanent trust since 1950. Employees do not have a share interest, and the trust cannot be sold. Instead, employees get a share of annual profits. Historically, the share has averaged about 15 percent of pay, but it dropped somewhat post-Brexit and there was no payout in 2020 (for the first time ever) because of the pandemic. Partners also get a variety of benefits, including access to vacation facilities, nearly free dining, time off to work for a charity for up to six months, and tuition support. Employees are considered members of the partnership from the first day of employment.

The partnership operates on democratic principles, sharing power with all Partners. Its first democratic council was set up back in 1919. Today the network of elected councils, committees, and forums enables Partners to participate in decision making, challenge management on company performance, and have a say in how the business is run. More than 3,000 specially elected representatives feed into three governing authorities—the Partnership Council, the Partnership Board, and the Chairman, which together run the company.

Largely because of the John Lewis model, the trust has become the most common form of employee ownership in the UK (see Chapter 10 for a discussion of trusts). Although US owners who sell at least 30 percent of their stock to an ESOP can qualify for a deferral of capital gains taxes, UK owners who sell at least 51 percent to a trust are entirely exempt from such taxes. In 2021, the UK's Employee Ownership Association reported that the country had 730 employee-owned businesses, most of which were using the trust model. Just in the 18 months from January 2020 to June 2021, there were 250 new transitions to employee ownership, a remarkable rate of growth.

The UK also has a public-company plan similar to—but more attractive than—American-style employee stock purchase plans (ESPPs). Called Save as You Earn, the plans allow employees to put aside up to £500 a month over three to five years. At the end of that time, the employee can buy shares at a discount of up to 20 percent. The interest on the savings and any bonus received at the end of the period are tax-free, and no capital gains taxes are due if the proceeds are moved into a retirement plan. Over two million employees in 550 companies participate in these plans—although, oddly enough, the 22 percent average rate of participation is even lower than in US ESPPs.[11] The number of plans and the number of participants have both declined over time.

Another UK plan is the Share Incentive Plan, used by about 800 companies and covering an estimated 3 million employees. These plans allow companies to give up to £3,600 worth of stock to employees in each tax year. Employees normally pay taxes when they take the shares. Plans can also offer a matching component, in which the employees get a certain number of extra shares for each one purchased.

As in the US, there has been considerable research on the impact of employee ownership in the UK.[12] The largest review of the literature found that employee ownership improves the economic performance of firms, increases the ability of companies to deal with economic and business crises, and increases employee engagement. A report in June 2021 found that 40,000 jobs had been created or sustained by employee ownership trusts in the 576 companies that had set them up by then.[13]

A UK TRUST

Aardman, a UK film animation company and creator of the Academy Award–winning *Wallace & Gromit* films, became an employee-owned trust in 2018. The company employs about 140 people. In a press release, former owners Peter Lord and David Sproxton said, "This approach, the creation of an employee trust, is the best solution we have found for keeping Aardman doing what it does best, keeping the teams in place and providing continuity for our highly creative culture . . . those that create value in the company will continue to benefit directly from the value they create."[14] The company had been courted by major studios, but Lord and Sproxton, who are staying on, said they wanted to keep it independent.

Eastern Europe and Russia: The Failure of Employee Ownership in Privatization

Perhaps the biggest lost opportunities to broaden employee ownership were the misguided attempts in Russia and Eastern Europe to use it in restructuring the newly privatized sector of the economy in the 1990s.

Starting in 1988, the Russian Federation launched a privatization program for its vast network of state-owned enterprises. The program, completed in 1994, transferred shares to employees of any enterprise with more than 200 employees at little or no cost. The Russian economy was in such dire circumstances that just transferring shares at an average of less than $100 per employee could move 100 percent of the ownership into employee hands. Employees did own a majority of the shares in most privatized companies by 1992, but that proportion fell to 40 percent just two years later and close to zero several years after that. The 1988 Law on Cooperatives also allowed employees to form their own collective enterprises without paying prohibitive taxes for the privilege, as had been required before. A number of small employee-owned companies were created, but they too did not last, largely because of the country's difficult economic situation.

So what happened? At a conference in 1993, Corey Rosen and others met with the officials in charge of the transformation. The officials made it clear that the goal of transferring ownership to employees had never been to have employees own the stock over the long term. It was simply a way to get shares out into the marketplace, where they could be purchased by fund managers, private equity firms, other companies (possibly non-Russian), and other investors. These investors, it was thought, would bring market discipline and capitalist expertise to Russia's new economy. To make that happen, employees could sell their shares freely. In fact they often had no choice, because their employers were not paying them wages, often for months at a time.[15]

So the vision for a new capitalism was realized at only a small number of companies. Instead, the same managers who had run the companies before usually purchased enough shares to consolidate their control. They often diluted employees' ownership by issuing new shares as well, sometimes exchanging these shares for debt held by banks. The workers made a small profit on the sales—the equivalent of a paycheck or two—but they lost ownership. Over time, the economy drifted more and more toward the kind of crony capitalism that characterizes today's Russian economy.

Other former Soviet Bloc countries also saw employee ownership as a possible way forward. The list included Poland, Hungary, Lithuania, Estonia, Ukraine, and what was then Czechoslovakia. At this writing, however, only Poland and Hungary hold out hope for the future.

In the 1990s in Poland, employees were allowed to buy their companies, and they often did so when the companies might otherwise close. By 1995, there were about 300,000 employee owners in several hundred Polish firms that had been privatized by selling shares to employees. The companies showed moderate economic improvement since privatization, doing somewhat better than the rest of the economy on most, but not all, measures. There were no restrictions on employees selling shares, however, and about a third of the employees who bought shares sold them within just the first few years.[16] Today, only a few employee-owned companies remain.

The idea did not go away, however. In 2017, the deputy prime minister and minister of development and finance in Poland, Mateusz Jakub Morawiecki, wrote a laudatory introduction to a Polish translation of *Equity: Why Employee Ownership Is Good for Business*, a book the present authors and Martin Staubus published with Harvard Business School Press in 2005. Morawiecki, who became Prime Minister later that year, wrote, "We should focus on creating mechanisms that will enable Polish people to make a profit out of capital rather than their own work alone. On the one hand, this capital will increase national savings by gradually leveling out Poland's negative investment balance; on the other hand, it will help the economy, companies, and people grow."

The next year, Corey Rosen met with government officials in Poland to discuss how to create a new law that would institutionalize employee ownership through a trust-based model that combined various funding options including employee share purchases and financing by the company. A proposal from Polish employee ownership advocates is still "in the realm of rhetoric," Kris Ludwiniak, an attorney and long-time promoter of employee ownership in Poland told us recently, but "we have been promised that it will be considered." Ludwiniak said that earlier efforts on employee ownership failed in Poland for much the same reason they did in Russia. He continued,

> The idea fails when it happens as part of a harsh version of stern budget medicine because workers need money and quickly sell their shares. In many, top management and opportunistic investors turn the employee ownership idea into a management buyout partly aided by the fact that trade unions were manipulated by top management and the Communist Party in some cases. Finally, civil society norms of fair play had been depleted by communist rule, making it difficult to create the kinds of institutional structures where employee ownership can co-exist with other investors as it does in a Southwest Airlines or a Procter & Gamble.

Hungary also relied on employee purchases but used a trust-based model. Starting in 1992, employees could buy shares, often along with management, as part of the privatization process. Employees received modestly preferential terms for the purchase, including favorable credit terms to borrow money to buy shares. The shares were then held in trust until the loans were repaid, at which point employees could sell. Employees ended up buying a controlling interest in about 125 companies, some with more than 1,000 employees. That came to 14 percent of private assets.[17] Most of these are no longer employee owned, though employees still own 75 percent of the famous ceramics firm Herend.

But interest in employee ownership rebounded in recent years. In 2015, a new law created a Hungarian ESOP. Under the law, employers can set up an ownership trust and transfer shares to employees on a nondiscriminatory basis. As in the UK's employee ownership trusts, employees get the right to dividends on the shares. The company gets a 23.5 percent reduction in taxes attributable to the contributions, and the employee is taxed on the earnings at less than half the rate other compensation is taxed.

There are no data as yet on how common the plans are, but one Hungarian attorney said they were "springing up like mushrooms."[18]

. . . .

So employee ownership has gained some traction in countries outside the US, and interest in the idea has been growing. In addition to the countries mentioned here, there are activists in Japan, India, and many other countries who are advocating for the idea. Our colleague Christopher Mackin has argued persuasively that sovereign wealth funds—investment funds owned by governments from China to Norway to Abu Dhabi—should invest in employee-owned companies around the world. "If they continue to rely on traditional investment practices," writes Mackin, "they will become increasingly vulnerable to charges that they are opportunistically extracting value across borders. It is time for them to explore a different path that shares value with corporate managers, engineers and workers within the nation-states where these funds invest."[19]

Still, there's a long way to go. A major barrier has been that legislatures and companies have had a hard time accepting the idea that ownership should be a benefit of employment, not a piece of property that employees can buy and sell. That buy-and-sell model has been tried over and over again, with limited success everywhere but China. Trust-based, company-funded models create long-term ownership interests that have proven to be good for employees, good for companies, and good for a country's economy.

But the economic difficulties outlined in this book aren't going away. Virtually every nation faces the same challenges as the US in finding a way to share the benefits of economic growth broadly, rather than concentrating the gains among the wealthy or the well connected. Few options are as economically sound and politically viable as employee ownership. It is an idea that has been embraced by the right and the left in the UK, Canada, the US, France, Germany, Spain, Poland, Hungary, and South Africa as well as the ruling party in China. No other economic reform we can think of boasts that kind of record.

Takeaways

○ Many countries around the world are experimenting with employee ownership. So far, most have focused too heavily on employees buying stock.

○ More inclusive models for employee ownership have gained a foothold in many countries, including China, and are growing faster in the UK than in the US. There is reason to think this momentum may continue.

CONCLUSION
How You Can Make a Difference

*If you don't know where you are going, you might
wind up someplace else.*

—YOGI BERRA

IMAGINE A SOCIETY in which ownership of capital isn't the privilege of the few but an opportunity for the many.

Impossible? We hope we have convinced you that it's very much possible. Employee ownership is a practical antidote to the sad fact that capitalism leaves so many behind. A society with broader ownership of capital would be one where more people could buy a new home, afford a secure retirement, repay their student debt, send their kids to college, start a new business, or just be able to sleep at night knowing that the next financial emergency won't put them out on the street. Creating that society requires neither a political revolution nor a major overhaul of our tax and regulatory systems. It doesn't involve a vast new outlay of government money. All it takes are some simple steps that build on what has already been created.

But there's a long way to go. For all its success, the reality of employee ownership is still unfamiliar to many people. Even the concept isn't well understood. Wall Street and the rest of the business world, for the most part, continue on their merry way, ignoring the problems they are creating. Liberals and conservatives in the political arena repeat the tangled debates of the past while ignoring a powerful option that most could agree on.

So the opportunity now is to get more people learning about these new forms of ownership, talking about them, experimenting with them, publicizing them, and implementing policies designed to encourage them. The opportunity is to put employee ownership on the agendas of businesspeople, investors, professors, policy mavens, political leaders, and citizens everywhere.

First (and Second) Steps

Some of the immediate possibilities are right there for the taking:

Company owners. Perhaps you own and run a successful business, one that will outlast you. At some point you're going to want to plan for its future. You can search out a corporate or private-equity buyer, pocket the proceeds, and walk away, leaving your creation and your employees to the mercy of financial managers. Or you can look into selling the company to the employees through an ESOP. If that's the route you choose, you'll get a fair price and some tax advantages. You'll also get the satisfying feeling that you have rewarded the people who helped build the business—and that you have done your part to create a more equitable form of free enterprise. By the way, if your attorneys and accountants scoff at the idea, find some attorneys and accountants who are more knowledgeable.

Professional investors. Or suppose you're a professional in the world of finance. If you work in private equity, take a page from Pete Stavros's book, described in Chapter 9. Stavros, a senior leader at KKR, may be a visionary, but you don't have to be a visionary to learn from him. Share equity in a meaningful way with a company's employees and you begin to transform a workplace. Follow it up with a participative style of management, a style in which people come to understand the economics of the business and learn to act as partners, and suddenly you have a different kind of company on your hands.[1] People are on the same side, working together instead of at cross purposes. They come up with ideas for innovations. They go the extra mile to take care of customers. As Stavros has found, the payoffs are numerous—better financial results, a more rewarding workplace, the feeling that you're making a difference in the world.

Ordinary investors. Other investors can learn the same lesson. The environmental, social, and governance (ESG) movement, for instance, is fine as far as it goes—but let's look hard at the workplace as well as at the environment and the boardroom. No company should get a gold star for its ESG efforts unless it is committed to broad-based equity sharing and building an employee-centered workplace. Socially minded investors can push for greater disclosure of employee-ownership measures. They can preferentially put their money in companies that take equity sharing seriously.

Board members. Does your company share equity with its employees? Does it plan to do so when the current owner is ready to retire? Start investigating the options now—and encourage the CEO and other executives to look into both ownership and participative management styles. Learning the economics of the business prepares employees to be owners and, when ownership is a reality, helps them think and act like the owners they are.

Business attorneys, accountants, and other experts. Learn about employee ownership! Read this book! Too many of your colleagues and competitors know very little—or what they think they know is wrong. You owe it to your clients to educate yourself about the benefits of sharing equity, and about the possibilities of sale to employees through an ESOP, trust, or co-op. Ignorance and misinformation among the experts are two of the biggest obstacles to the spread of employee ownership.

Political leaders. Politicians and government officials at every level have a host of opportunities for transforming the ownership landscape, which we addressed in Chapter 11. They include measures like these:

○ Tweak the tax law so that every seller of a company gets a tax benefit from selling the business to its employees. This wouldn't cost much—the taxes are just deferred, not eliminated.

○ Provide financing guarantees for sales of companies to their employees. Again, the cost would be minimal. Research shows that employee-owned companies have an extremely low default rate.

○ Create more state outreach programs, as Colorado and Massachusetts have done with public funds and many other states have done with private funds. These can make a huge difference in educating people about employee ownership. They typically cost just a few hundred thousand dollars a year.

○ Put stiffer limits on what public companies can deduct for executive equity distributions unless their companies share ownership broadly. This change would either have no fiscal impact or, more likely, a positive one. It might even pay for the other programs suggested here.

○ Allow 100 percent ESOPs to qualify for set-aside programs if the companies benefit target groups, including women, minorities, and veterans. Governments and large companies set aside billions of dollars every year for these preferences.

○ Offer grants and impact-investment capital for platform cooperatives. The gig economy badly needs reform, but a collection of gig workers won't find it easy to start their own co-op. Government grants or loans could help get the platform started, with the requirement that everyone who works for a minimum number of hours in a year becomes a member of the cooperative.

○ Fund worker cooperatives. Start-ups and co-op conversions usually find that capital sources aligned with their values are scarce. There are already some grant programs to help them get started, but there's a need for more. Co-ops usually remain small, but they can still make a contribution, especially in traditionally low-wage sectors such as home care and cleaning.

Modest measures, right? And cheap. But never underestimate the importance of seemingly minor changes. One simple incentive—the existing tax deferral for sales of C corporations to ESOPs or co-ops, known as the 1042 rollover—has encouraged the creation of thousands of employee-owned companies. A whole series of similar initiatives, each one seemingly small, would help put employee ownership on everybody's mental map.

HOW CHANGE HAPPENS

In Chapter 7 we told the story of Allied Plywood owner Ed Sanders, who took his idea for a change in ESOP tax policy to Corey Rosen. His idea eventually became law. Later, Rosen and others raised the same idea with staffers at Her Majesty's Treasury in the UK; it became law there too. Now, as we indicated in Chapter 12, it may become law in Canada. All of those efforts resulted in an important spur to employee ownership, and all were spearheaded by just a few committed individuals.

A more remarkable story comes from Dick Peterson, Larry Dunn, and Bill Kirton, three retired friends in the Denver area, who in 2010 read about employee ownership and decided they wanted to do something about it. Dick had been a successful businessman. Larry was an IT guy. Bill was a retired Methodist minister. They talked to people at the NCEO and decided they would launch the Rocky Mountain Employee Ownership Center. It was an all-volunteer effort.

After a few years, they got the center launched, eventually landing some donations and grant funds. The center hired full-time staff and started an outreach program. Meanwhile, Dick and others had been setting up meetings with legislators and the governor's office, urging the state to play a more active role. Jared Polis, who became governor in 2019, liked the idea of employee ownership; as an entrepreneur, he had given his employees stock options. Under Polis's leadership, the state set up an employee ownership office and provided some funds for the ownership center. Then, in 2021, the legislature passed a law providing funding for companies to convert to employee ownership and for the state's own employee ownership outreach effort, an effort that quickly led to a number of new conversions. Colorado today is a leader in the field.

The Citizen's Role

To some, employee ownership seems like a peculiar sort of reform. It has never had much grass-roots support. Nobody marches in the streets to demand it. Nobody floods political leaders with e-mails and phone calls. Rather, a handful of committed individuals have been responsible for its success to date. In this respect it's sort of like the earned income tax credit, a wonky idea that garnered bipartisan support and has done much to mitigate economic insecurity among low-income workers.

At any rate, the future may be different. Think, for example, of the campaigns to curb cigarette smoking or drunk driving—campaigns that, after years of hard work on the part of citizen advocates, complemented by grass-roots activism by organizations such as Mothers Against Drunk Driving and the Campaign for Tobacco-Free Kids, finally caught the eye of the public and its political leaders. If you're old enough, think about how common smoking used to be and how rare it is now by comparison. Think about how having "one for the road" was accepted practice when people were about to leave a bar or a party and the concept of a designated driver was unknown. (If you're not old enough to remember those days, count yourself lucky.)

So good ideas do sometimes make their way—slowly, to be sure—to the forefront of a society's priorities. That suggests a different kind of opportunity, one that everyone who reads this book can take part in. It is to insert discussions about ownership—and employee ownership in particular—into everyday conversations.

For example: the next time you see an article about economic insecurity, consider writing a letter to the editor or even an op-ed about employee ownership. Or maybe contact the NCEO to get the names of employee-owned companies in your area, and then suggest that the local paper or locally oriented website write about these interesting businesses. If you belong to a trade association, ask for a seminar or webinar on the topic. If you're a member of your local Chamber of Commerce or Rotary Club, line up a speaker. (The NCEO can help you find a good one.)

Really, the possibilities are endless. Write about the idea on your social media sites. Raise it with friends. Point out the employee-owned companies that you patronize. If you are an academic, get in touch with the Institute for the Study of Employee Ownership and Profit Sharing at Rutgers University's School of Management and Labor Relations or the Beyster Institute at the Rady School of Management, University of California, San Diego; consider teaching a class or undertaking research in this area. If you are a high-school teacher, add employee ownership to your curriculum or suggest that your colleagues do. If you are a student, undertake a research project on the subject.

Also, keep an eye out for the organizations that are building grassroots support for employee ownership, including state-level advocacy centers, the groups we have already mentioned, and new national organizations such as Ownership America. Here's the current list of national and international groups; you can find information about all of them easily on the web.

THE UNITED STATES

The National Center for Employee Ownership (NCEO)

The ESOP Association (which also has state and regional chapters)

Employee-Owned S Corporations of America (ESCA)

The Employee Ownership Expansion Network (EoX)

Ownership America

Certified EO

Project Equity

The Democracy at Work Institute (DAWI)

Fifty by Fifty (a project of the Democracy Collaborative)

OTHER COUNTRIES

The Esop Centre (UK)

The Employee Ownership Association (EOA) (UK)

The European Federation of Employee Shareholders (EFES) (based in Belgium)

The ESOP Association (Canada)

The Korea Securities Finance Corporation

The South African Employee Ownership Association (SAEOA)

Meanwhile, you can help people cut through some fruitless debates. Redistribution of wealth or income, for instance, is necessary in any capitalist economy, but only up to a point. Advocates and opponents typically acknowledge that, and then proceed to bludgeon each other over exactly where that point should be. Until the issue is resolved, you might point out, we can do some *pre*distribution simply by broadening the ownership of capital. That's a solution that can get liberals and conservatives on the same side.

Many other arguments about the economy—reining in Wall Street, curbing the role of private equity, encouraging union organizing, and so on—are also being thrashed out in the political arena. But the debates can be softened, or even bypassed, if employee ownership is on the table. If every private equity firm behaved like Pete Stavros's division of KKR, wouldn't the industry enjoy greater support in Congress and among the public than it does today? If large public companies made a point of broad-based equity sharing, wouldn't they earn more of the public's trust than they have at present? If unions figured out how to support employee ownership—and took a collaborative approach to their efforts rather than a purely oppositional one—would they face quite the uphill battle that they do now? We need to change all these conversations. We need to bring the good idea of employee ownership forward to the point where it's *always* part of the discussion.

One final word for people outside the United States, the UK, and (we hope) Canada. We bet that there have been employee-ownership efforts in your country that haven't produced results. The reason, usually, is that advocates had the right idea but the wrong tools. You can't just give employees stock—most will sell it at the first opportunity. Nor can you expect large numbers of employees to buy significant numbers of shares, even with a discount. Instead, you need something like the American ESOP or the UK's trusts: an entity that is funded by the company, and that holds stock on behalf of employees. Governments can provide tax incentives for these arrangements in return for meeting basic rules of fairness, perhaps similar to those governing ESOPs in the US. Any other approach will leave countries in the same rut they found themselves in before. So if this book has inspired you, contact your representatives, your associations, your pundits, your business leaders, and your unions—and then make the case.

As a reform, employee ownership is hardly a panacea. It can't cure poverty or lack of opportunity all by itself. It doesn't help people who don't have a job, or who work for organizations (such as government agencies) that don't have owners. What it does do is help millions and millions of people find greater economic security and a deeper sense of purpose when they go to work. It builds a society in which more companies act responsibly, with long-term prosperity and the well-being of their employees in mind. It helps create a kind of capitalism that really does work for the many and not just for the few.

Those, we believe, are no small matters.

AFTERWORD

BY MICHAEL QUARREY,
Vice President, Web Industries

I AM AN OWNER OF WEB INDUSTRIES. I did not found the company; I did not inherit my interest from my family; and I did not invest my own money in Web's shares. Like 600 of my colleagues, I earned my ownership stake gradually over 24 years of service. And like 50 other Web employee owners, 75 percent of them nonexecutive, my ownership stake is now worth more than a million dollars. Web employees' ESOP accounts are worth, on average, over ten times the typical 401(k) balance for equivalent years of service.

Web is a highly successful manufacturing business, serving the world's leading industrial, aerospace, and medical device companies. We've survived financial crises. We survived the pandemic. Through innovation and the personal involvement of hundreds of owners, we have beaten the stock market by more than 100 percent over the past two decades.

Web is not alone. We are one of several thousand companies that appear quite normal on the outside but are quietly revolutionizing the economy. These companies hold the promise that we all can create broad prosperity, restore dignity to work, and renew the American dream.

We Americans live in a time of environmental, economic, political, and social crisis. Too often our leaders are stuck in their narrow ideological corners, promoting old ideas that won't really solve our problems. They have a scarcity-based view of our future, as if there won't be enough for everyone, reinforcing fears that fuel our divisions.

We are losing trust in institutions like learning and science, religion and faith, and equal justice under the law. More and more we are separated by class, by race, by region. Something about the country we love is fading away.

But I have hope in a brighter future. My company, like the many companies profiled in this book, is not getting stuck in this destructive cycle of fear and greed and selfishness and blame-someone-else.

What Web is doing, what the companies Corey Rosen and John Case chronicle in *Ownership* are doing, is reinventing capitalism for the people. We are demonstrating a new model of prosperity and equality that can galvanize citizens around a shared vision of a better world.

We are at the dawn of this new world, a world with a fair share for everyone. A world where every voice matters. A world where differences are celebrated for their creativity. A world where all people flourish. A world where, together, we apply our gifts in work filled with meaning and purpose. A world that draws out our greatest potential. A world where relationships matter.

Can you imagine it? This new world, waiting to be born? It is a world that can be, that will be, if we are bold enough to lead the way.

Employee ownership is not just about Web Industries being more competitive, although it is that. Employee ownership is about a world where every company shares ownership, and where every company is more creative and productive. When every workplace taps into the power of ownership, what a world that will be.

And employee ownership is not just about making Web's employees wealthy, although it is that. Employee ownership is about a world where everyone is an owner and employees at all companies share in the vast wealth of the global economy. When everyone has an ownership stake, when poverty and injustice are visible only in history's rearview mirror, what a world that will be.

And employee ownership is not just about putting people ahead of profits at Web Industries, although it is that also. Employee ownership is about a world where relationships are honored everywhere. When women and men of all colors and creeds, all orientations and abilities, when every person has the dignity conferred by ownership, and every voice is heard, and every person matters, oh, what a world that will be!

Rosen and Case give us a roadmap to this new world. They provide a practical guide to the policies and practices that will accelerate the ownership revolution. It is a peaceful revolution, a gradual revolution, where ordinary employees secure financing to purchase their companies at fair market value from willing sellers.

The story of human civilization is one of great progress. Despite U-turns and setbacks, despite wars and wickedness and despotism, the long arc of history does indeed bend toward justice, and love, and compassion.

And employee ownership is one way we can pull and bend that arc. Everything my colleagues and I are doing to make Web a great example of employee ownership is part of a larger phenomenon, part of a greater movement. It matters, not just to us, but to the whole world, and to all the people who will follow us down through the ages.

You, too, can join this movement. You can buy from employee-owned companies. You can seek out and find a job with an employee-owned company. You can vote for representatives who support policies promoting more employee ownership.

Do not be troubled by the old ways that are dying around us. We have caught the wave of the future. Let us ride it with purpose to a new world. Let us raise up our standards and our stories and lead the way.

And let us celebrate, let us celebrate that we are part of something larger than ourselves: a better world waiting to be born.

May it be so.

DISCUSSION GUIDE

This guide offers a way to think about both the questions raised by this book and the world beyond it. We hope it serves as a useful jumping-off point for thinking more about the issues raised here, whether on your own or in a book group, a discussion with employees, a classroom, or other setting.

Chapter 1: The Ownership Crazy Quilt

People have very different views about what it means to say capitalism is working or not. What do you think defines how well capitalism is working? Is there a necessary tradeoff between economic growth and economic fairness?

The first chapter compares Walmart and Publix. Both are very successful companies with loyal shoppers. What would Walmart look like if it were employee owned? And what would Publix look like if Walmart bought it? Who would win, who would lose, and who should public policy support?

Chapter 2: Wall Street: Faceless Ownership

Are publicly traded companies still needed in the modern economy? If they did not exist, what kinds of problems might be created for business?

Do you hold stock in a public company? Do you think of yourself as an owner? If not, why not?

Imagine you are a CEO of a public company and need to make a decision about a long-term investment. You think it would help the company compete down the road, but profits will be reduced in the short term. What should you do—and what can you do?

Chapter 3: Private Equity: Concentrated Ownership

What is private equity? How does it affect the companies it buys?

Imagine that the owner of a closely held company is approached by a private equity firm to buy the owner out. The private equity firm offers a really good price, but the owner is concerned about what will happen to the company and the employees. How do you think most owners would respond and why?

We raised a lot of concerns in the chapter about the impact of private equity buyouts. What arguments can be made for them?

Chapter 4: The Limits of (Conventional) Reform

There are a number of proposals for making the economy more fair. Which ones make the most sense to you?

Consider the proposals that are raised in this chapter. Think about which of these are politically practical and which are not. What does this tell you about the politics of reform?

Chapter 5: Ownership in Today's Economy

Capitalism gets its name because the providers of capital own and control companies. What is the difference between what we think of as capital today and what we thought of as capital a century or two ago? Is the provider of a great idea contributing capital, for instance?

Given the different kinds of capital you have thought about, what should the rights of each kind be?

Chapter 6: A Different Kind of Company

How do employee-owned companies differ from those that are conventionally owned? Do some of these differences affect what companies can do?

People have different expectations about what they would want as employee owners. What do you think are reasonable expectations? Can people expect too much?

Employee ownership appeals to all sides of the political spectrum. Why is that?

Chapter 7: Why Isn't There More Employee Ownership?

Productivity has gone up much faster than wages, as Louis Kelso anticipated. That was never true before—why has it been true in the last few decades?

Classical economics tells us that if something makes a company more competitive, then the market will favor companies that adopt that practice. So why doesn't every company become employee owned?

Imagine you are an advisor to a company looking to sell. Why might you tell them an ESOP is not a good idea?

Chapter 8: Opportunity #1: Employee Ownership on Wall Street

If the company you work for offered you the chance to buy shares at a discount, would you? Would your coworkers? Why or why not?

Some companies offer their own stock in a 401(k) plan. Should you buy it?

Chapter 9: Opportunity #2: Private Equity and Impact Investing

KKR and a few other private equity firms are now sharing a small but financially meaningful percentage of the ownership with all employees. Do you think this will move the needle forward very much on rethinking ownership? Why or why not?

Impact investors have largely ignored employee ownership. Why do you think that is?

Chapter 10: Opportunity #3:
Trusts, Co-ops, and the Gig Economy

Worker cooperatives attract a lot of attention from academics and the media; sometimes it seems that there are more studies of co-ops than there are co-ops. What makes this kind of ownership so intriguing? Should we be making more of an effort to encourage it?

Platform cooperatives seem like a great way to transform gig work. What are the barriers to making this happen more and how can they be addressed?

Chapter 11: Opportunity #4:
Policies and Programs for Spreading
Employee Ownership

The policy proposals discussed in this chapter are fairly modest. Are they enough, or do we need to be more ambitious? What would that look like?

Imagine you are meeting with a state legislator or member of Congress and pitching employee ownership. They say the idea seems fine, but you can tell it is not going to be a priority. What could you say or do to persuade them otherwise?

Chapter 12: Tomorrow the World

Employee ownership is best established in modern industrial economies. Would it work in other economies, and if so what would it look like?

Outside the US and UK, employee ownership still usually relies on employees buying stock. Why do you think countries don't adopt the UK or US model?

Conclusion: How You Can Make a Difference

After reading this book, are you interested in trying to move this idea forward? What would you do?

NOTES

Preface

1   See, for example, Public Policy Polling, "National Survey Results," June 27–28, 2015, accessed December 15, 2021, *https://www.nceo.org/assets/pdf/articles /PPP_results_employee_ownership.pdf.* Sixty-eight percent of respondents in this poll said they "support the concept of companies being owned by their employees." Seventy percent said they considered "employee ownership of their company to be All American like baseball, hot dogs, and apple pie."

Introduction

1   See Board of Governors of the Federal Reserve System, *Report on the Economic Well-Being of U.S. Households in* 2017 (May 2018), 2, *https://www .federalreserve.gov/publications/files/2017-report-economic-well-being-us -households-201805.pdf;* and United States Government Accountability Office, "Retirement Security: Most Households Approaching Retirement Have Low Savings" (May 2015), 7, *https://www.gao.gov/products/gao-15-419.*

2   United States Bureau of Labor Statistics, "Occupational and Wage Statistics, May 2020, 35-3031 Waiters and Waitresses," accessed October 4, 2021, *https:// www.bls.gov/oes/current/oes353031.htm;* and "Occupational and Wage Statistics, May 2020, 47-0000 Construction and Extraction Occupations," accessed October 4, 2021, *https://www.bls.gov/oes/current/oes470000.htm.*

3   James Manyika, Jan Mischke, Jacques Bughin, Jonathan Woetzel, Mekala Krishnan, and Samuel Cudre, "A New Look at the Declining Labor Share of Income in the United States," McKinsey & Company, May 22, 2019, *https:// www.mckinsey.com/featured-insights/employment-and-growth/a-new-look-at -the-declining-labor-share-of-income-in-the-united-states.* See also University of Groningen and University of California, Davis, "Share of Labour Compensation in GDP at Current National Prices for United States [LABSHPUSA156N-RUG]," FRED, Federal Reserve Bank of St. Louis, February 3, 2022, *https://fred .stlouisfed.org/series/LABSHPUSA156NRUG.*

4   Board of Governors of the Federal Reserve System, "Distribution of Household Wealth in the U.S. Since 1989," December 17, 2021, *https://www.federalreserve .gov/releases/z1/dataviz/dfa/distribute/chart/#quarter:127;series:Corporate% 20equities%20and%20mutual%20fund%20shares;demographic:income ;population:1,3,5,7,9,11;units:shares.*

5   "Stock ownership is highly affected by race and ethnicity, which also are highly correlated to income and wealth. Some 61% of white, non-Hispanic families owned stocks in 2019, only 34% of Blacks and 24% of Hispanics did. Measured by value, 24% of white, non-Hispanic family assets were in stocks, compared to 13% for Blacks and 10% for Hispanics." Tim Smart, "Who Owns Stocks in America? Mostly, It's the Wealthy and White," *U.S.News*, March 15, 2021, *https://www.usnews.com/news/national-news/articles/2021-03-15 /who-owns-stocks-in-america-mostly-its-the-wealthy-and-white.*

6   Elise Gould, "State of Working America: Wages 2019," Economic Policy Institute, February 20, 2020, *https://www.epi.org/publication/swa-wages-2019/.*

7   "Compound Annual Growth Rate (Annualized Return)," Money Chimp, accessed October 4, 2021, *http://www.moneychimp.com/features/market _cagr.htm.*

8   Isabel V. Sawhill and Edward Rodrigue, "Wealth, Inheritance and Social Mobility," Brookings Social Mobility Memos, January 30, 2015, *https://www .brookings.edu/blog/social-mobility-memos/2015/01/30/wealth-inheritance -and-social-mobility/.* Other estimates place the proportion as high as 60 percent. See Facundo Alvaredo, Bertrand Garbinti, and Thomas Piketty, "On the Share of Inheritance in Aggregate Wealth: Europe and the USA, 1900–2010," *Economica* 84, no. 344 (April 2017): 239–60, *https://doi.org/10.1111/ecca .12233.* For the summary figures, see Christopher Ingraham, "People Like the Estate Tax a Whole Lot More When They Learn How Wealth Is Distributed," *Washington Post*, February 6, 2019, *https://www.washingtonpost.com/us-policy /2019/02/06/people-like-estate-tax-whole-lot-more-when-they-learn-how -wealth-is-distributed/.*

9   Ruth Igielnik, "70% of Americans Say U.S. Economic System Unfairly Favors the Powerful," Pew Research Center, January 9, 2020, *https://www.pewresearch .org/fact-tank/2020/01/09/70-of-americans-say-u-s-economic-system-unfairly -favors-the-powerful/.* Remarkably, the percentage saying "unfair" varied little by income level.

Part I: What's Wrong with What We Have?

Chapter 1

1   See Ibis World, Supermarkets & Grocery Stores Industry in the US - Market Research Report, December 29, 2021, *https://www.ibisworld.com/united-states /market-research-reports/supermarkets-grocery-stores-industry/.*

2   David Montgomery, Rick Rojas, and Giulia McDonnell Nieto del Rio, "Texans Needed Food and Comfort after a Brutal Storm. As Usual, They Found It at H-E-B," *New York Times*, February 22, 2021, *https://www.nytimes.com/2021 /02/22/us/texas-heb-winter-storm.html.*

3   H-E-B itself is 15 percent owned by a profit-sharing plan that holds company stock on behalf of employees.

4   See "Billion-Dollar Dynasties: These Are the Richest Families in America," *Forbes*, December 17, 2020, *https://www.forbes.com/sites/kerryadolan /2020/12/17/billion-dollar-dynasties-these-are-the-richest-families-in -america/?sh=4b49b48c772c.*

5   Kevin Phillips, *Wealth and Democracy* (New York: Broadway Books, 2002).

6   Christopher Tkaczyk, "My Five Days of 'Bleeding Green,'" *Fortune*, March 3, 2016, *https://fortune.com/longform/publix-best-companies/.*

Chapter 2

1   Some leaders of public companies—Jeff Bezos of Amazon is the most commonly cited example—ignore the incentives and the pressures from Wall Street and do focus on the growth of their companies over a period of years. Another iconoclast was the late Ken Iverson, the storied leader of a steel company called Nucor. In a talk to Wall Street analysts, he said the following: "Many of you, with your short-term view of corporations, remind me of a guy on drugs. You want that quick fix, that high you get from a big spike in earnings. So you push us to take on more debt, capitalize start-up costs and interest, and slow down depreciation and write-offs. All you're thinking about is the short term. You don't want to think about the pain of withdrawal that our company will face later on if we do what you want. Well, Nucor isn't going to respond to that kind of thinking. We never have and we never will." Iverson is quoted in James O'Toole, *The Enlightened Capitalists: Cautionary Tales of Business Pioneers Who Tried to Do Well by Doing Good* (New York: HarperBusiness, 2019), 269. Bezos, Iverson, and a handful of others are the exceptions to the rule.

2   Many people have pointed out the holes in the logic. See, for example, Joseph L. Bower and Lynn S. Paine, "The Error at the Heart of Corporate Leadership," *Harvard Business Review*, May-June 2017, *https://hbr.org/2017/05/the-error -at-the-heart-of-corporate-leadership?ab=seriesnav-spotlight.* Bower and Paine observe that the shareholders don't really own a corporation and that the board has a fiduciary duty to the organization itself, not to its alleged owners. See also Lynn Stout, *The Shareholder Value Myth: How Putting Shareholders First Harms Investors, Corporations, and the Public* (San Francisco: Berrett-Koehler, 2012) and David Ciepley, "Wayward Leviathans: How America's Corporations Lost Their Public Purpose," Hedgehog Review, Spring 2019, *https:// hedgehogreview.com/issues/animals-and-us/articles/wayward-leviathans.*

3   Lawrence Mishel and Jori Kandra, "CEO Pay Has Skyrocketed 1,322% since 1978," *Economic Policy Institute*, August 10, 2021, *https://www.epi.org/pub-lication/ceo-pay-in-2020/.* For one insider's retrospective account of how the CEO compensation proposal was put together, see the blog by Robert

Reich, secretary of labor under Bill Clinton: "Personal History: Why CEO Pay Exploded," November 2, 2021, *https://robertreich.substack.com/p/why-ceo-pay -exploded?fbclid=IwAR2lN_0-nchWgcNwCK3RCl3FFDf54gQPqP42dhme _0CyifQeSjtPI8URtQc.*

4   BusinessWire, "Age and Tenure in the C-Suite: Korn Ferry Study Reveals Trends by Title and Industry," January 21, 2021, *https://www.businesswire.com /news/home/20200121005146/en/.*

5   For details and examples, see Karen Berman and Joe Knight, with John Case, *Financial Intelligence: A Manager's Guide to Knowing What the Numbers Really Mean* (Boston: Harvard Business Review Press, 2013), Chapter 8.

6   A study led by Heitor Almeida of the University of Illinois found that buybacks were more common when companies would have missed their earnings targets without the buyback. See Heitor Almeida, Vyacheslav Fos, and Mathias Kronlund, "The Real Effects of Share Repurchases," *Journal of Financial Economics*, June 19, 2015, *http://dx.doi.org/10.2139/ssrn.2276156.*

7   William Lazonick, Mustafa Erdem Sakinç, and Matt Hopkins," Why Stock Buybacks Are Dangerous for the Economy," *Harvard Business Review*, January 7, 2020, *https://hbr.org/2020/01/why-stock-buybacks-are-dangerous-for-the -economy.*

8   See Edward Yardeni, Joe Abbott, and Mali Quintana, *Corporate Finance Briefing: S&P 500 Buybacks & Dividends*, Yardeni Research, October 1, 2021, *https:// www.yardeni.com/pub/buybackdiv.pdf.* The reporter was Michael Steinberger, "What Is the Stock Market Even For Anymore?" *The New York Times*, May 26, 2020, *https://www.nytimes.com/interactive/2020/05/26/magazine/stock -market-coronavirus-pandemic.html.*

9   Matt Egan, "Stock Buybacks Exploded after the Tax Cuts. Now They're Slowing Down," CNN Business, August 22, 2019, *https://www.cnn.com/2019/08/22 /investing/stock-buybacks-drop-tax-cuts.*

10 Kyle Arnold, "American Airlines Spent $12 Billion on Stock Buybacks during Flush Times. Now It Says It Needs a Bailout," *The Dallas Morning News*, March 18, 2020, *https://www.dallasnews.com/business/airlines/2020/03/18 /american-airlines-spent-12-billion-on-stock-buybacks-during-flush-times -now-it-says-it-needs-a-bailout/.*

11 This story was well chronicled by the trade website Fierce Pharma. See, for example, Carly Helfand, "Ex-Valeant Skipper Pearson Claims He's Owed $30M-plus in Unpaid Severance, Consulting Fees," March 28, 2017, *https:// www.fiercepharma.com/pharma/former-valeant-skipper-pearson-sues-over -withheld-stock-award-consulting-fees.* See also Bethany McLean, "Wall Street's Drug Problem," *Vanity Fair*, Summer 2016, *https://archive.vanityfair.com/article/2016/6/wall-streets-drug-problem* and the report from the US Senate's Special Committee on Aging, "Sudden Price Spikes in Off-Patent Prescription Drugs:

The Monopoly Business Model That Harms Patients, Taxpayers, and the U.S. Health Care System," December 2016, *https://www.aging.senate.gov/imo/media /doc/Drug%20Pricing%20Report.pdf.*

12   Large stocks have averaged about twice the rate of return for bonds since the 1920s and, of course, yield much better returns over time than bank savings accounts. Real estate investment has offered better returns than stocks in some recent years, but is unavailable to most investors outside of their home.

13   Dominic Barton, James Manyika, and Sarah Keohane Williamson, "Finally, Evidence That Managing for the Long Term Pays Off," *Harvard Business Review*, February 7, 2017, *https://hbr.org/2017/02/finally-proof-that-managing -for-the-long-term-pays-off.*

14   William N. Goetzmann, Dasol Kim, Alok Kumar, and Qin Wang, "Weather-Induced Mood, Institutional Investors, and Stock Returns," *The Review of Financial Studies* 28, no. 1 (January 2015): 73–111, *https://doi.org/10.1093/rfs /hhu063.*

15   Michael J. Cooper, Huseyin Gulen, and P. Raghavendra Rau, "Performance for Pay? The Relation between CEO Incentive Compensation and Future Stock Price Performance," November 1, 2016, *https://dx.doi.org/10.2139/ssrn. 1572085.* The classic book making this argument is Lucien Bebchuk and Jesse Fried, *Pay without Performance: The Unfulfilled Promise of Executive Compensation* (Boston: Harvard University Press, 2004).

16   Dan Catchpole, "The Forces behind Boeing's Long Descent," *Fortune*, January 20, 2020, *https://fortune.com/longform/ boeing-737-max-crisis-shareholder-first-culture/.*

17   Lawrence Mishel and Jori Kandra, "CEO Compensation Surged 14% in 2019 to $21.3 Million," Economic Policy Institute, August 18, 2020, *https://www.epi .org/publication/ceo-compensation-surged-14-in-2019-to-21-3-million-ceos -now-earn-320-times-as-much-as-a-typical-worker.* The CEO figures are what the EPI calls *realized* compensation, which is what CEOs actually received in salary, stock, and stock options.

18   Jonathan Stempel, "No Prison Terms for Gulf Spill as Final Defendant Gets Probation," *Reuters*, April 6, 2016, *https://www.reuters.com/article/us-bp-spill -sentencing/no-prison-terms-for-gulf-spill-as-final-defendant-gets-probation -idUSKCN0X3241.*

Chapter 3

1   Gretchen Morgenson and Emmanuelle Saliba, "Private Equity Firms Now Control Many Hospitals, ERs and Nursing Homes. Is It Good for Health Care?" NBC News report, May 13, 2020, *https://www.nbcnews.com/health /health-care/private-equity-firms-now-control-many-hospitals-ers-nursing -homes-n1203161.*

2   See Jakob Wilhelmus and William Lee, "Companies Rush to Go Private,"
    Milken Institute, August 2018, *https://milkeninstitute.org/sites/default/files
    /reports-pdf/WP-083018-Companies-Rush-to-Go-Private-FINAL2_2.pdf.*

3   EY, "PE Pulse: Quarterly Insights and Intelligence on PE Trends, Q4 2020," 4,
    accessed February 22, 2022, *ey-pe-pulse-2020-q4-interactive-pdf.pdf.* Data
    on 401(k) plans is from Investment Company Institute, News and Resources,
    March 24, 2021, *https://www.ici.org/faqs/faq/401k/faqs_401k#:~:text
    =As%20of%20March%2031%2C%202021,and%20public%2Dsector%20
    employers)%2C.*

4   EY, "Economic Contribution of the US Private Equity Sector in 2018," prepared
    for the American Investment Council, October 2019, *https://thisisprivateequity
    .com/wp-content/uploads/2019/10/EY-AIC-PE-economic-contribution-report
    -10-16-2019.pdf.*

5   It's like buying a house. If you put down $100,000 and borrow $300,000 for a
    $400,000 house—and then if you resell it for $500,000—you make close to a 100
    percent profit on your investment. If you had to put down all $400,000 for the
    initial purchase, you'd make only 25 percent.

6   The 2017 tax reforms capped interest deductions at 30 percent of EBITDA,
    which is one measure of a company's profitability. The rules governing this cap
    changed during the pandemic and may change again in the future.

7   Brian Ayash and Mahdi Rastad, "Leveraged Buyouts and Financial Distress,"
    July 20, 2019, SSRN, July 20, 2019, *https://dx.doi.org/10.2139/ssrn.3423290.*

8   Eileen Appelbaum and Rosemary Batt, *Private Equity at Work* (New York:
    Russell Sage Foundation, 2014). This chapter draws on several of the examples
    developed by Appelbaum and Batt.

9   Sabrina Willmer, "Private Equity Piles on Debt to Pull Cash from Health
    Firms," Bloomberg News, March 24, 2021, *https://www.bloomberg.com/news
    /articles/2021-03-24/private-equity-piles-on-debt-to-pull-cash-from-health
    -care-firms?sref=zr8EZugD.*

10 Dan Primack, "How Workers Suffered from Shopko's Bankruptcy while Sun
    Capital Made Money," Axios: Economy & Business, June 11, 2019, *https://
    www.axios.com/shopko-bankruptcy-sun-capital-547b97ba-901c-4201
    -92cc-6d3168357fa3.html.*

11 This divorce of risk from the consequences of failure is known to economists
    as *moral hazard.* PE creates a "classic moral hazard situation," say Appelbaum
    and Batt (p. 53).

12 Steven J. Davis, John Haltiwanger, Kyle Handley, Ben Lipsius, Josh Lerner,
    and Javier Miranda, "The Economic Effects of Private Equity Buyouts," SSRN,
    July 12, 2021, *http://dx.doi.org/10.2139/ssrn.3465723.*

13 Jonathan B. Cohn, Nicole Nestoriak, and Malcolm Wardlaw, "Private Equity
    Buyouts and Workplace Safety," *The Review of Financial Studies* 34, no. 10

(February 13, 2021), *https://doi.org/10.1093/rfs/hhab001*. An *establishment*, in business-research vernacular, is a single facility—a store, a factory, an office, a warehouse. Any one company may operate many different establishments. The primary topic of this article is workplace injury rates; the authors found a decrease in injury rates following PE buyouts.

14   "Everything Is Private Equity Now," *Bloomberg BusinessWeek*, October 3, 2019, *https://www.bloomberg.com/news/features/2019-10-03/how-private-equity -works-and-took-over-everything?sref=zr8EZugD*.

15   Quoted in Appelbaum and Batt, *Private Equity at Work*, 68.

16   This is a process known as *greenmail*, now outlawed in many states (including Ohio).

17   Brian Alexander, *Glass House: The 1% and the Shattering of the All-American Town* (New York: St. Martin's Press, 2017).

Part II: How Can We Change Things?

1   Steven Johnson, *Where Good Ideas Come From: The Natural History of Innovation* (New York: Riverhead Books, 2010), 11.

Chapter 4

1   See the summary of "Pax World" in *The Sustainable Business Case Book* (online only), accessed October 7, 2021, *https://saylordotorg.github.io/text_the -sustainable-business-case-book/s16-02-pax-world.html*.

2   Harry Matyjaszek, "CSR Is a Thing of the Past: Why More Businesses Need to Invest in ESG," Energy Live News, July 28, 2020, *https://www.energylivenews .com/2020/07/28/csr-is-a-thing-of-the-past-why-businesses-need-to -invest-in-esg/*.

3   Tim Quinson and Mathieu Benhamou, "Banks Always Backed Fossil Fuel Over Green Projects—Until This Year," *Bloomberg News*, May 19, 2021, *https:// www.bloomberg.com/graphics/2021-wall-street-banks-ranked-green-projects -fossil-fuels/*.

4   Peter S. Goodman, "Stakeholder Capitalism Gets a Report Card. It's Not Good." *The New York Times*, Updated December 2, 2020, *https://www.nytimes .com/2020/09/22/business/business-roudtable-stakeholder-capitalism.html*.

5   Reynolds American Inc., "Reynolds American Parent BAT Named Third-Highest Rated ESG Performer in Global Ranking," press release, March 24, 2021, *https://www.prnewswire.com/news-releases/reynolds-american-parent -bat-named-third-highest-rated-esg-performer-in-global-ranking-301255055 .html*.

6   Lynn S. Paine, "CEOs Say Their Aim Is Inclusive Prosperity. Do They Mean It?" *Harvard Business Review*, August 22, 2019, *https://hbr.org/2019/08/ceos -say-their-aim-is-inclusive-prosperity-do-they-mean-it*.

7   US Department of Labor, "US Department of Labor Releases Statement on Enforcement of Its Final Rules on ESG Investments, Proxy Voting by Employee Benefit Plans," press release, March 10, 2021, *https://www.dol.gov /newsroom/releases/ebsa/ebsa20210310.*

8   Sarah Stranahan and Marjorie Kelly, "Ownership Design for a Sustainable Economy," The Democracy Collaborative/Fifty By Fifty, January 2020, *Ownership-design-for-sustainable-economy-FINAL-CX.pdf.*

Chapter 5

1   Joseph Parilla and Sifan Liu, "Examining the Local Value of Economic Development Incentives: Evidence from Four US Cities," Brookings Institution, March 2018, *https://www.brookings.edu/research/examining-the-local-value -of-economic-development-incentives/.*

2   Bruce Berman, "$21 Trillion in U.S. Intangible Assets Is 84% of S&P 500 Value: IP Rights and Reputation Included," Aon and Ponemon Institute, *2019 Intangible Assets Financial Statement Impact Comparison Report,* June 6, 2019, *https://ipcloseup.com/2019/06/04/21-trillion-in-u-s-intangible-asset-value-is -84-of-sp-500-value-ip-rights-and-reputation-included/.*

3   Ron Miller, "Salesforce Confirms It's Laying Off around 1,000 People in Spite of Monster Quarter," TechCrunch, August 27, 2020, *https://techcrunch .com/2020/08/27/salesforce-confirms-its-laying-off-around-1000-people-in -spite-of-monster-q.*

4   James O'Toole, *The Enlightened Capitalists: Cautionary Tales of Business Pioneers Who Tried to Do Well by Doing Good* (New York: HarperBusiness, 2019).

5   O'Toole, *Enlightened Capitalists,* 436.

Part III: Reinventing Capitalism for the 21st Century

Chapter 6

1   National Center for Employee Ownership, "Employee Ownership by the Numbers," December 2021, *https://www.nceo.org/articles/ employee-ownership-by-the-numbers.*

2   Nancy Wiefek and Nate Nicholson, "Measuring the Impact of Ownership Structure on Resiliency in Crisis," National Center for Employee Ownership, December 2021, *https://esca.us/wp-content/uploads/2022/01/ESCA-Report- FINAL.pdf.*

3   National Center for Employee Ownership (NCEO), "Employee Ownership and Economic Well-Being," accessed July 22, 2021, *https://www.ownershipeconomy .org.*

4   The study adjusted its data to account for changes in industry growth rates. For a review of the major studies on employee ownership and corporate performance,

see the National Center for Employee Ownership, "Key Studies on Employee Ownership and Corporate Performance," February 2022, *https://www.nceo.org /article/key-studies-employee-ownership-and-corporate-performance*.

5   Joseph Blasi, Douglas Kruse, and Dan Weltmann, "Firm Survival and Performance in Privately Held ESOP Companies," in *Sharing Ownership, Profits, and Decision-Making in the 21st Century*, Vol. 14 (Emerald Group Publishing Limited, Bingley, 2013), 109–124, *https://doi.org/10.1108/S0885-3339 (2013)0000014006*.

6   Corey Rosen, "The Impact of Employee Ownership and ESOPs on Layoffs and the Costs of Unemployment to the Federal Government," NCEO website, July 2015, *https://www.nceo.org/observations-employee-ownership/c/impact -employee-ownership-esops-layoffs-costs-unemployment-federal-government*.

7   Joseph Blasi and Douglas Kruse, "Employee-Owned Firms in the COVID-19 Pandemic: How Majority-Owned ESOP and Other Companies Have Responded to the Covid-19 Health and Economic Crises," Employee Ownership Foundation and Rutgers School of Management and Labor Relations, June 2021, *https://employeeownershipfoundation.org/sites/eof-master/files /2020-10/EOF_COVID_2020.pdf*.

8   NCEO, "Employee Ownership and Economic Well-Being."

9   Peter A. Kardas, Adria L. Scharf, and Jim Keogh, *Wealth and Income Consequences of Employee Ownership: A Comparative Study of Washington State* (Oakland, CA: National Center for Employee Ownership, 1998).

10   National Center for Employee Ownership, "After Establishing an ESOP: How Do Employer 401(k) Contributions Change?" *The Employee Ownership Report*, March–April 2020, 3, *https://www.nceo.org/system/files/newsletters /NCEOnews_marchapril2020_0.pdf*.

11   A tip of the hat to *Washington Post* editor Steven Pearlstein, whose fine book *Can American Capitalism Survive?* (New York: St. Martin's Press, 2018) contains a list similar to this one (and includes this particular difference about debt and balance sheets).

12   Jenna McGregor, "Chobani Is Going Public. Its 'Anti-CEO' Founder Won't Be the Only Employee Who Could See a Big Payday," *Forbes*, November 19, 2021, *https://www.forbes.com/sites/jenamcgregor/2021/11/19/chobani-is -going-public-its-anti-ceo-founder-wont-be-the-only-employee-with-a-big -payday/?sh=7fb70bc21c78*.

13   So-called qualified profit-sharing plans operate much like an ESOP or 401(k). The rules for eligibility are the same as for ESOPs, as are (mostly) the allocation rules. Employees get their money when they leave the company and can roll it over tax-free into an individual retirement account (IRA). Most companies invest the funds in a diverse portfolio, but a profit-sharing plan can invest in company stock; an NCEO study found that about 4,000 of these plans hold

20 percent or more of their assets in company stock. These plans lack some of the advantages of an ESOP, but they are less expensive to set up and operate.

14 The poll was performed for Employee Owned S Corporations of America (ESCA), an organization promoting the interests of companies organized as S corporations and having an employee stock ownership plan (ESOP). Results of the survey can be found at *https://www.nceo.org/assets/pdf/articles/PPP _results_employee_ownership.pdf* (accessed October 29, 2021).

15 "Understanding Support for ESOPs: Charts on Public Polling Data on Employee Ownership, 2018," data from National Opinion Research Center, based on the 2018 General Social Survey. The questions were designed and the results analyzed by Douglas Kruse and Joseph Blasi at the Institute for the Study of Employee Ownership and Profit Sharing, Rutgers University School of Management and Labor Relations. The Employee Ownership Foundation provided funding to the National Opinion Research Center at the University of Chicago for the General Social Survey employee ownership questions. Summary results can be found at *https://cleo.rutgers.edu/wp-content/uploads/2019 /12/Understanding-Support-for-ESOPs-Charts-on-Public-Polling-Data-on -Employee-Ownership.pdf* (accessed October 29, 2021).

16 See "We Believe in America," Republican Platform (2012), p. 7, *https://www .presidency.ucsb.edu/documents/2012-republican-party-platform*. The 2016 platform contained similar language.

Chapter 7

1 We tell Kelso's story in considerably greater detail in our earlier book, *Equity: Why Employee Ownership Is Good for Business*, written with Martin Staubus (Boston: Harvard Business School Press, 2005). We borrow some of that book's language here.

2 The term *predistribution* was coined by Yale University political scientist Jacob Hacker. So far it has gained more political currency in the UK than in the US.

3 Appraisers must follow certain rules in evaluating a company: assessing its financial results, comparing its results to others in the industry, and so on. A so-called *strategic buyer*, often a larger corporation or a private equity firm, may see unrealized value in the business's technology, location, market position, and the like. It's not so different from real estate. The tax appraiser will evaluate your house according to its size, condition, and location—factors that an individual buyer would consider. A developer who has big plans for your neighborhood may find it worthwhile to pay well over the appraised value.

4 "The Grapes of Rath," *Wall Street Journal*, November 14, 1983, 1.

5 Joel Palmer, "Twenty Years after Its Last Day, Rath Packing Co. Still Holds a Place in the Heart of Waterloo," Waterloo *Courier*, December 26, 2004, *https://*

*wcfcourier.com/news/top_story/twenty-years-after-its-last-day-rath
-packing-co-still-holds-a-special-place-in/article_7fb95a93-3c82-5e1c-8836
-e023d7616d4f.html.*

6   Ella Jennings, "What Happened to Weirton Steel, Part 3: As Goes the Mill...,"
West Virginia Public Radio, July 15, 2019, *https://www.wvpublic.org/news
/2019-07-15/what-happened-to-weirton-part-3-as-goes-the-mill.*

7   This experience is also discussed at greater length in *Equity.* For another
definitive account, see the unpublished article by Christopher Mackin,
"United It Was Not," accessed November 11, 2021, *https://web.archive.org
/web/20200902082138/https://employeeownedamerica.com/2018/11/27
/united-it-was-not/.*

8   "Avis Group Holdings, Inc. – Company Profile, Information, Business
Description, History, Background Information on Avis Group Holdings, Inc."
website of Reference for Business, accessed June 30, 2021, *https://www
.referenceforbusiness.com/history2/7/Avis-Group-Holdings-Inc.html.*

Chapter 8

1   Owen Young was John Case's grandfather. As far as we know, this was his only
public pronouncement on employee ownership.

2   Joseph R. Blasi, Richard B. Freeman, and Douglas L. Kruse, *The Citizen's Share:
Putting Ownership Back into Democracy* (New Haven, CT: Yale University
Press, 2013).

3   For a summary of GSS data, see the Rutgers School of Management and Labor
Relations news release "72% of Republicans and 74% of Democrats Agree on
This: They Prefer to Work for an Employee-Owned Company," May 24, 2019,
*https://www.businesswire.com/news/home/20190524005008/en/72-Of
-Republicans-and-74-of-Democrats-Agree-on-This-They-Prefer-to-Work-for
-an-Employee-Owned-Company.*

4   Sarah Holden, Jack VanDerhei, and Steven Bass, "401(k) Plan Asset Allocation,
Account Balances, and Loan Activity in 2018," Employee Benefit Research
Institute, March 4, 2021, *https://www.ebri.org/retirement/content/401(k)-plan
-asset-allocation-account-balances-and-loan-activity-in-2018.*

5   Christopher Mackin points out another wrinkle: "A legally permissible 'stock
lock' feature that pegged the [stock's] value to a high average stock price
achieved during the 1996–2000 time period meant that when the company's
fortunes declined, employees were not able to exit the stock in any of their three
retirement plans in a timely manner." Mackin, unpublished memo to the Secretary of Commerce, April 10, 2014. For more details of the case, see US District
Court for the Southern District of Texas, "In Re Enron Corp. Securities, Deriva-
tive & ERISA, 284 F. Supp. 2d 511 (S.D. Tex. 2003)," accessed November 4, 2021,
https://law.justia.com/cases/federal/district-courts/FSupp2/284/511/2534153/.

Enron wasn't the first or only major implosion of a 401(k) plan with company stock, just the most dramatic. By 2007, 53 cases had resulted in approximately $1.47 billion in judgments and settlements affecting about 1.3 million participants. See Corey Rosen, *ESOP and 401(k) Plan Employer Stock Litigation Review 1990–2021* (NCEO, 2021).

6   About three million of these participants have left their companies and will be getting a distribution of their benefits in the next few years.

7   See "Employee Ownership by the Numbers," NCEO, December 2021, *https:// www.nceo.org/articles/employee-ownership-by-the-numbers*.

8   These figures are based on analysis of Form 5500 filings, which companies must file annually with the Department of Labor. Data availability lags by one to two years, so the figures cited here are the most recent available at time of writing.

9   Ilona Babenko and Rik Sen, "Money Left on the Table: An Analysis of Participation in Employee Stock Purchase Plans," *Review of Financial Studies* 27 (April 23, 2015): 3658–3698, *http://dx.doi.org/10.2139/ssrn.2166012*.

10   Joseph Blasi, "Tech Companies Are Shutting Employees Out of the Stock Market's Boom," *Fortune*, April 12, 2017, *https://fortune.com/2017/04/12/tech -stock-market/*.

11   Readers interested in a more detailed review of the research can find it at the NCEO's website in an article written by Corey Rosen, "Research on Employee Ownership, Corporate Performance, and Employee Compensation," October 11, 2018, *https://www.nceo.org/articles/research-employee-ownership-corporate -performance*.

12   Fidan Ana Kurtulus and Douglas L. Kruse, *How Did Employee Ownership Firms Weather the Last Two Recessions? Employee Ownership, Employment Stability, and Firm Survival in the United States: 1999–2011* (Kalamazoo, MI: W.E. Upjohn Institute for Employment Research, 2017), *https://doi.org/10 .17848/9780880995276*.

13   E. Han Kim, and Paige Ouimet, "Employee Capitalism or Corporate Socialism? Broad-Based Employee Stock Ownership," AFA 2010 Atlanta Meetings Paper, updated September 20, 2012, *http://dx.doi.org/10.2139/ssrn.1107974*.

14   Yael V. Hochberg and Laura Lindsey, "Incentives, Targeting, and Firm Performance: An Analysis of Non-executive Stock Options," *Review of Financial Studies*, 23, no. 11 (November 2010): 4148–4186, *https://academic.oup.com/rfs /article/23/11/4148/1609512?login=true*.

15   ProPublica, "The Executive Pay Cap That Backfired," February 12, 2016, *https://www.propublica.org/article/the-executive-pay-cap-that-backfired*.

16   Ellerman has written widely on this subject. For a summary of his views and some references, see "The Philosophy of Employee Ownership," Ownership

America, October 2020, *https://ownershipamerica.org/2020/10/the-philosophy -of-employee-ownership/*.

17 See Zeynep Ton, "The Case for Good Jobs," *Harvard Business Review*, November 30, 2017, *https://hbr.org/2017/11/the-case-for-good-jobs*; Dennis Campbell, John Case, and Bill Fotsch, "More Than a Paycheck," *Harvard Business Review*, January–February 2018, *https://hbr.org/2018/01/more-than-a-paycheck*.

Chapter 9

1 Bryan Burrough and John Helyar, *Barbarians at the Gate: The Fall of RJR Nabisco,* 20th anniversary ed. (New York: HarperBusiness, 2008).

2 Melissa Karsh, "In New Twist, Private Equity Shares Its Windfall With Hourly Employees," *Bloomberg News*, August 16, 2021, *https://www.bloomberg.com/ news/articles/2021-08-16/kkr-hands-500-million-to-ingersoll-rand-workers -after-162-gain?sref=zr8EZugD*.

3 National Center for Employee Ownership, "Default Rates on ESOP Loans, 2009-2013," March 8, 2017, *https://www.nceo.org/articles/default-rates-esop -loans-2009-2013*.

4 Sabrina Willmer, "Buyout Funds Want to Save the Planet," *Bloomberg Business Week* November 8, 2021, online title "Buyout Giants Rebrand as Forces for Good While Seeking Profits," November 4, 2021, *https://www.bloomberg.com /news/articles/2021-11-04/private-equity-funds-embrace-esg-for-good-while -seeking-profits?sref=zr8EZugD*.

5 TaylorGuitarNews, "Taylor Transitions to 100% Employee Ownership Through an ESOP," blog, Taylor Guitars, January 11, 2021, *https://blog.taylorguitars.com /taylor-transitions-to-100-employee-ownership-through-an-esop*.

6 Taylor had to get a private ruling from the IRS approving this. Most ESOP companies with international employees provide some other form of employee ownership in order to avoid any potential legal issues, but ESOP companies can do what Taylor did if the plan is set up correctly. The largest USAID contractor, Chemonics, has an ESOP for its employees in over 70 countries.

7 In the United States, pension funds are required by law to maximize the value of plan assets for participants. In 2020, the Department of Labor issued regulations that allowed pension funds to take social goals into account, but only if they could demonstrate that doing so made for better investment choices. Pension funds might rely on the low-default-rate data on ESOP loans to justify receiving lower rates for their money, but this has not yet been tested.

Chapter 10

1 The company's divisions currently include American Ductile Iron Pipe, American Flow Control, American SpiralWeld Pipe, and American Steel Pipe.

2 "The American Story," American website, accessed November 5, 2021, *https://american-usa.com/about/story*. See also Reference for Business, "American Cast Iron Pipe Company - Company Profile, Information, Business Description, History, Background Information on American Cast Iron Pipe Company," Reference for Business, accessed October 2021, *https://www.referenceforbusiness.com/history2/69/American-Cast-Iron-Pipe-Company.html*.

3 An ESOP trustee, charged by law with running the plan for the benefit of the participants, must consider generous acquisition offers. If the trustee judges an offer to be in the best interests of participants, the offer generally goes to a vote of the workforce. New Belgium Brewing, for years an ESOP-owned company, was acquired in 2019 by a unit of Japan's Kirin Holdings Company through this process.

4 The authors thank Melissa Hoover of the Democracy at Work Institute for her contributions and insightful comments on this section.

5 Margaret Lund, *Cooperative Equity and Ownership: An Introduction* (Madison, WI: University of Wisconsin Center for Cooperatives, April 2013), 8, *https://resources.uwcc.wisc.edu/Finance/Cooperative%20Equity%20and%20Ownership.pdf*.

6 Alexis Butler, Shevanthi Daniel-Rabkin, Kyle Funk, Melissa Hoover, Tina Lee, Lauren Lowery, Julian McKinley, and Zen Trenholm, *Economic Recovery and Employee Ownership* (The Democracy at Work Institute and the National League of Cities, 2021), 25, *https://www.nlc.org/wp-content/uploads/2021/08/DAWI-Employee-Ownership-Report.pdf*.

7 Typically, ESOPs must include every employee who works at least one year full time. In limited cases they can exclude employees of separate lines of business; they can also exclude members of collective bargaining units, provided the union involved can bargain over the issue of inclusion.

8 "C-W Interview: Blake Jones," Community-Wealth.org, January 2013, *https://community-wealth.org/content/blake-jones*.

9 David Weil, "Understanding the Present and Future of Work in the Fissured Workplace Context," *RSF: The Russell Sage Foundation Journal of the Social Sciences* 5, no. 5 (2019): 147–165. See also I. Mitic, "Gig Economy Statistics: The New Normal in the Workplace," Fortunly, Feb. 17, 2022, *https://fortunly.com/statistics/gig-economy-statistics/*.

Chapter 11

1 Two of these laws were later repealed. But still.

2 Many of the proposals in this section are adapted from a paper that the authors helped develop for Ownership America, a grassroots organization focused on developing political support for employee ownership. The white paper, available on the organization's website, is titled "Turning Employees

into Owners: Rebuilding the American Dream." See *https://secureservercdn .net/192.169.220.85/11l.986.myftpupload.com/wp-content/uploads/2021/11 /WhitePaper-TurningEmployeesIntoOwners.pdf* for the full text (accessed November 9, 2021). A slightly different version of the paper appeared as John Case and Michael Quarrey, "Turning Employees into Owners: An Analysis of Policy Initiatives for Rebuilding the American Dream," *Journal of Participation and Employee Ownership* 2, no. 3 (2019): 202–211, *https://www.proquest .com/docview/2447265440.*

3   US Department of the Treasury, "State Small Business Credit Initiative: Capital Program Policy Guidelines," November 10, 2021, *https://home.treasury .gov/system/files/256/SSBCI-Capital-Program-Policy-Guidelines-November -2021.pdf.*

4   Richard C. May, Robert C. Hockett, and Christopher Mackin, "Encouraging Inclusive Growth: The Employee Equity Loan Act," *Challenge* 62, no. 6 (2019): 377–397, *https://www.tandfonline.com/doi/abs/10.1080/05775132.2019.1668645.*

5   Deloitte, "US Divestitures Quarterly Update: 2019 Year in Review," accessed August 9, 2021, *https://www2.deloitte.com/content/dam/Deloitte/xa/Documents /corporate-finance/us-dcf-divestiture-update-2019-year-in-review.pdf.*

6   The reason takes us into the weeds of tax-related lawmaking. In 1996, Congress decided to change tax law for S corporations so that nontaxable entities could be owners, provided they paid the highest level of ordinary income tax rates on any income attributable to their share of ownership. That included an ESOP trust. The very next year, however, Congress decided that to tax the ESOP trust and then to tax employees when they left the trust with their shares was taxing the income twice. So ESOPs were exempted from this requirement. That stimulated the growth of 100 percent ESOP companies that pay no tax because they are structured as S corporations. Congress never considered whether to extend the tax deferral provision to sales of S corporations to ESOPs.

7   There would need to be a clawback provision if the new ESOP fails to retain a minimum level of ownership for a period of years; the current tax law for deferrals of gains in sales to ESOPs for closely held companies already has such a provision.

8   At first, some companies used the cheap loans to fund 401(k) matches they were already funding anyway. So the effect on ownership in those cases was minimal and the cost significant. Congress tightened the rules in 1989 to prevent that kind of abuse, but the whole thing was abandoned amid the budget cuts of the early 1990s.

Chapter 12

1   The NCEO regularly gathers data about other countries' experiences with employee ownership from news reports, documents, interviews, and

organizations based in those countries. Unless otherwise cited, the data in this chapter reflect this effort and are the responsibility of the NCEO.

2   Employee Ownership Australia, " Sharing In Success – How Participation in the Brambles Global MyShare Employee Share Plan Grew 5% during a Pandemic," April 29, 2021, *https://employeeownership.com.au/sharing-in -success-brambles-interview/.*

3   Huifen Pan, "Core-Staff-Based ESOPs : A New Concept of Employee Share Ownership in China" (doctoral paper, Université de Lorraine, 2021), *https:// hal.univ-lorraine.fr/tel-03193245/document.*

4   Colin Hawes, "Why Is Huawei's Ownership So Strange? A Case Study of the Chinese Corporate and Socio-political Ecosystem," *Journal of Corporate Law Studies* 21, no. 1 (2021): 1–38, *https://www.tandfonline.com/doi/full/10.1080 /14735970.2020.1809161.* Hawes is an associate professor in the law faculty at the University of Technology Sydney and a research associate at the UTS Australia-China Relations Institute.

5   All of the data and descriptions in the section on continental Europe except for Mondragon come from Marc Mathieu, *Annual Economic Survey of Employee Share Ownership in European Countries* (European Federation of Employee Share Ownership, 2020), 47, 49. *http://www.efesonline.org/Annual%20 Economic%20Survey/2020/Survey%202020.pdf.*

6   Virginie Pérotin, "The Performance of Workers' Cooperatives," in Patrizia Battilani and Harm G. Schröter, eds., *The Cooperative Business Movement, 1950 to the Present* (Cambridge, UK: Cambridge University Press, 2012), 214.

7   European Federation of Employee Share Ownership, *Employee Share Ownership: The European Policy,* May 2019, 5, *http://www.efesonline.org/LIBRARY /2018/Employee%20Share%20Ownership%20--%20The%20European %20Policy.pdf.*

8   David Ellerman and Tej Gonza. 2020. "A Generic ESOP Employee Share Plan for Europe," *European Federation of Employee Share Ownership,* May 22, 2020, *http://www.efesonline.org/LIBRARY/2020/A%20Generic%20ESOP% 20Employee%20Share%20Plan%20for%20Europe.pdf.*

9   Marc Mathieu, *Annual Economic Survey of Employee Share Ownership in European Countries* (European Federation of Employee Share Ownership, 2020), 47, 49, *http://www.efesonline.org/Annual%20Economic%20Survey/2020 /Survey%202020.pdf.*

10   Material on Korea is based on conversations between Corey Rosen and Choi Hyun-Min of the KSFC on November 16, 2021.

11   ProShare, "SAYE and SIP Report 2019," The Chartered Governance Institute, October 2020 *https://www.proshare.org/assets/files/proshare-saye-sip-report -2019-final-pdf.pdf.*

12 Joseph Lampel, Aneesh Banerjee, and Ajay Bhalla, "The Ownership Effect Inquiry: What Does the Evidence Tell Us?," Alliance Manchester Business School and Cass Business School, paper published online, June 2017, *http://theownershipeffect.co.uk/wp-content/uploads/Global_literature_review_The _Ownership_Effect_Inquiry-What_does_the_evidence_tell_us_June_2017.pdf*.

13 Devreaux Gravell, Lisa Hayward, Alexandra Nelson, Michael Playford, and Alex Schaafsma, "Employee-Ownership Trusts: Issues with Lending to Employee-Owned Companies," Birketts, November 2, 2021, *https://www.birketts.co.uk /insights/legal-updates/lending-to-employee-owned-companies*.

14 Employee Ownership Association, "EOA Congratulates Aardman on Securing Its Future through Employee Ownership," EOA, November 10, 2018, *https:// employeeownership.co.uk/news/eoa-congratulates-aardman-on-securing-its -future-through-employee-ownership/*.

15 This discussion is based primarily on Joseph Blasi, Maya Kroumova, and Douglas Kruse, *Kremlin Capitalism* (Ithaca, NY: Cornell University Press, 1997) and the experience of Corey Rosen in meeting with Russian officials and employee ownership advocates during the 1990s.

16 See the review by Dariusz Zalewski of *Employee-Owned Companies in Poland*, edited by Maria Jarosz, *Polish Sociological Review*, No. 112, (1995): 393–396, *https://www.jstor.org/stable/41274597*.

17 Béla Galgóczi and János Hovorka, "Employee Ownership in Hungary: The Role of Employers' and Workers' Organizations," (working paper, International Labour Office, Geneva, Switzerland, March 1998), 2–3, *https://www.ilo.org /wcmsp5/groups/public/---ed_emp/---emp_ent/documents/publication /wcms_126688.pdf*.

18 István Csővári, "ESOP—The Latest Craze," *Taxative* (blog), Jalsovszky Law Firm, May 19, 2017, *https://jalsovszky.com/blog/en/esop--the-latest-craze*.

19 Christopher Mackin, "Sovereign Wealth Funds Must Choose a Different Path," *Financial Times*, April 7, 2019, *https://christophermackin.org/sovereign-wealth -funds-must-choose-a-different-path-financial-times/*.

Conclusion

1 For a step-by-step guide as to how to do this, see Bill Fotsch with John Case, *Partners on the Payroll* (Pensacola, Florida: Indigo River Publishing, 2022).

ACKNOWLEDGMENTS

This book grows out of a decades-long friendship and a shared passion for helping to create a more equitable and effective economy and society. Over these years, we have had the privilege of visiting with and learning from countless employee owners, from CEOs to shop-floor workers, about how they have transformed their workplaces to create a more secure economic future for themselves, their families, and their communities—workplaces that treat people with dignity and respect. Many of these companies have become the outstanding performers in their industries, admired by customers and competitors alike. This book exists because of the work they have done.

The employee ownership community is one that is exceptionally open and sharing. People are proud of what they have done and want others to know. They want the idea to grow. We hope this book can help.

Many individuals have played an important role in making our work possible, far too many to acknowledge individually. Special thanks are due to the members of the National Center for Employee Ownership, whose support and involvement have helped the organization grow from one room in Corey's basement to a staff of 17. Among the many leaders in the employee ownership community, we need to give special thanks to Jack Stack, CEO of SRC Holdings and creator of the Great Game of Business; Michael Quarrey, vice-president of Web Industries, who contributed the Afterword to the book; and Joseph Blasi, whose tireless support for employee-ownership research has made so much difference to scholars and to the entire community. All are good friends and extraordinary thinkers who have helped create new models of employee involvement and engagement. We also owe a great deal of thanks to the members of the Lake Quinsigamond group, including Gellert Dornay,

Christopher Mackin, Steve Ringlee, and the late Jared Kaplan, for a series of provocative discussions that fed into this book and ultimately led to the creation of Ownership America with Jack Moriarty as executive director.

This book would not have been possible without the guidance and support of Steve Piersanti, the founder and former CEO of Berrett-Koehler, itself an employee-owned company. Steve not only championed this book, but he and the whole team at Berrett-Koehler provided a level of feedback, guidance, and support that match what most publishers give only to their star writers. We learned a great deal in the process and have been enriched by the experience. Thanks, too, to our agent, James Levine, who supported the project from the beginning and helped connect us with Berrett-Koehler.

Corey adds: On a personal level, I want to thank Loren Rodgers, who took over as director of the NCEO ten years ago and has guided its substantial growth since then, and Scott Rodrick, our publications director (and much more), whose 27 years at the NCEO have transformed the organization and who has helped me become a much better writer. I continue to work for the NCEO, and it has been a great comfort to see it in such good hands. Of course, I want to thank my co-author, John Case, who first suggested this book, and whose ability to express the ideas included here far surpasses anything I could have done on my own. John, I have learned a great deal from you, but most of all I have cherished the opportunity to share time and ideas with you. And finally, I want to thank my wife, Carol Hepsley, the most decent, caring person I know, who has made my life so much richer and whose wisdom and advice have made me (I hope) a better person.

John adds: I have learned so much about employee ownership from so many people. Corey, I believe, knows more about the subject than anyone else on the planet; he has the additional (and rare) gift of being able to explain even its complexities clearly and simply. I have deeply treasured our friendship and our collaborations. George Gendron gave me the freedom to write about employee-owned companies during my time at *Inc.* magazine. Cecil Ursprung, CEO of Reflexite when it was one of the nation's leading employee-owned companies, offered me the opportunity to spend time at Reflexite and write about it; in retrospect, that was a turning point in my thinking about business, and he has remained a friend ever since. Bill Fotsch, an open-book management expert with whom I worked for many years, helped me see how essential it is—in employee-owned companies and others—that employees understand a company's fundamental economics. I also have learned a great deal from David Ellerman, who has done much to lay the philosophical foundation for employee ownership.

I want to thank my sons, Brendan Case and Liam Malloy, early readers of portions of the manuscript, who saved me from making some errors in the drafting. And I owe untold thanks, as always, to my wife, Quaker Case, whose expertise lies elsewhere, but without whom I would probably never have written one published word.

I dedicated my share of our previous book to the three grandchildren I had at the time, adding "may they live and work in a more equitable world." Since then the flock has expanded by two, and I hope that the younger ones—Brenna and Fenella—get that chance as well.

INDEX

A

Aardman, 183
accountability, 34–36
accountants, 104, 191
accounting rules, 115, 117
activist investors, 27, 40–41
adjacent possible, 6, 54
Adler, Mortimer, *The Capitalist Manifesto* (with Kelso), 98, 109
advisors, 104, 121, 190, 191
advocacy methods, 108, 194–197
agricultural co-ops, 71
airlines, 105–106, 118
Alexander, Brian, *Glass House*, 50
Allied Plywood, 100, 193
Alvarado, José Juan, 83
American Airlines, 30
American Cast Iron Pipe Company (now American), 140–141
Amsted Industries, 81
Anchor Hocking, 50–51
Appelbaum, Eileen, *Private Equity at Work* (with Batt), 44, 46
Apple, 32–33
Arizmendiarrieta, José María, 176
attorneys, 191
Australia, 169–170
Austria, 175
automation, 98, 109
automobile industry, 15
Avis, 106–107

B

B Lab, 64–65
Babenko, Ilona, 116
Bain Capital, 46

banking industry, 60, 115
bankruptcies, 43, 50–51, 85, 104–107
Barbarians at the Gate (book, film), 126
BAT (formerly British American Tobacco), 60–61
Batt, Rosemary, *Private Equity at Work* (with Appelbaum), 44, 46
benefit corporations, 64–65
Benioff, Mark, 61
Berkshire Hathaway, 104
bipartisan support, 92, 158
Black Economic Empowerment (BEE, South Africa), 179–180
Blasi, Joseph, 112, 116
board of directors, 26–27, 41, 191, 209n2
Boeing, 33–34
Bolen, Mike, 88
bonds, 17
British Petroleum (BP) Deepwater Horizon, 35
Buffett, Warren, 37, 103–104
business brokers, 104
business operations
    behavior reforms, 55–57
    and owners' interests, 3, 4, 85
Business Roundtable, 59–60

C

C corporations, 161, 192–193
California Polytechnic State University study, 43, 85
campaigns for employee ownership, 194–195
Campbell, Dennis, 122
Canada, 170–171

capital availability, 68, 72
capital gains taxation, 36, 71, 100, 130,
    162, 182
Capital Safety, 137
capitalism
    "enlightened," 76
    evolution of, 67–71, 166–167
    participation in, 3–4, 98–99
    and redistribution, 62–63
    reforms, 55–57, 196–197
    and risk, 72–73
Capitalist Manifesto, The (Kelso and
    Adler), 98, 109
Cardin, Ben, 92
Carolina Textile District (CTD), 155, 177
carried interest, 48, 56, 158
Case, John, Equity: Why Employee
    Ownership Is Good for Business (with
    Rosen and Staubus), 185
Cerberus Capital Management, 14, 50
Chang Byung-Gyu, 179
Certified EO, 195
C.H.I. Overhead Doors, 127
childcare providers, 153
China, 171–174
Chobani, 90
citizen engagement, 194–197
Citizen's Share, The (Blasi, Freeman,
    and Kruse), 112
Clayton, Dubilier & Rice, 15, 43
cleaning companies, 153
Clicks Group, 180
Coca-Cola Beverages South Africa
    (CCBSA), 180
Cohn, Jonathan, 47
Colorado state government, 164–165,
    193–194
communities
    and businesses, 3, 20, 50–51
    ESOP benefits, 136–137
    see also Lancaster, Ohio; Weirton,
        West Virginia

companies
    accountability in, 34–36
    buyouts and divestitures, 19, 47,
        128–132, 159–162
    as investment assets, 19–21, 41–42
    ownership models, 16–17, 89–91
    troubled, 104–106
    under private equity ownership,
        42–45, 46–48
    see also employee-owned
        companies; specific companies
company owners
    and ESOP decision, 102–104,
        112–113, 128–132, 190
    see also entrepreneurs; family-owned
        businesses
company performance
    of employee-owned companies,
        84–85, 118–119, 183
    and executive compensation,
        32–33
    and spending priorities, 33–34
    under long-term vs. short-term
        management, 31–32
compensation
    at employee-owned companies, 86
    of executives, 27–28, 32–33, 34,
        119–120, 162
    of private equity firms, 42–45
consulting and management fees, 44
Consumers Union, 70
Cooper, Michael, 33
Cooperative Home Care Associates
    (CHCA), 148–149
cooperatives (co-ops), 17, 91
    see also agricultural co-ops;
        platform co-ops; secondary
        co-ops; worker co-ops
Corbett, Jack, 57
corporate social responsibility (CSR),
    58, 59
cost-cutting strategies, 28–29, 31

customer influence, 70
Czech Republic, 175

D

Davey Tree Expert Company, 81, 84
Davis, Steven, 46–47
day traders, 25
debt
    and dividend recapitalization, 44
    ESOP financing, 132, 134–136,
        159–161, 191–192
    in private equity acquisitions, 43
Deepwater Horizon oil spill, 35
Democracy at Work Institute, 145, 154,
    165, 196
Democracy Collaborative, 65, 145
Department of Labor (DOL), 166
deskilling, 69
dividend recapitalization, 44
Dr. Bronner's, 75, 76
Drivers Cooperative, The, 139, 153
Dunn, Larry, 193

E

Eagen, John, 140
Eastern Airlines, 105
Economic Policy Institute, 34
economy
    and investors' interests, 19–20
    see also United States (US)
      economy
Ellerman, David, 121
Emilia-Romagna worker co-ops, 177
Employee Equity Investment Act
    (EEIA), 160–161
employee-owned companies
    characteristics, 85–88
    employee attitudes at, 78, 83–84
    examples, 79–81
    leadership comments about,
      88–89
    in networks, 155

performance of, 84–85
    see also companies; *specific*
      companies
Employee-Owned S Corporations of
    America (ESCA), 195
employee ownership
    in B corporations, 65
    citizen support for, 194–197
    government programs for, 163–166
    as income security, 82–83
    investor support for, 190–191
    models, 89–91, 112–117
    non-US countries, 169–187
    planning for, 190, 197
    political and public support for,
      91–93, 108, 117–118, 158
    tax incentives for, 162–163
    see also equity sharing; ESOPs;
      ESPPs; *specific countries*; trusts
Employee Ownership Association
    (UK), 182
Employee Ownership Expansion
    Network (EoX), 195
employee ownership trusts, 140–143,
    170–171, 181–182
Employee Retirement Income Security
    Act (ERISA), 99–100
employee stock ownership plans
    (ESOPs) *see* ESOPs
employee stock purchase plans *see* ESPPs
employees
    barriers to ownership, 101–102, 116,
      117, 136, 184, 186
    job satisfaction, 21–22, 78
    and risk, 20, 73–74
    value creation of, 72, 123
    see also wage earners
Enron, 113–114
entrepreneurs
    and outside financing, 16, 20
    and risk, 73
    visionary, 75–76

EOT Advisors, 143
equity
    social, 128
    synthetic, 90
equity sharing, 101–102, 119, 120–121,
    136–137, 192, 196
    see also employee ownership
ERISA (Employee Retirement Income
    Security Act, 1974), 99–100
ESG (environmental, social, and
    governance) movement, 59, 60–62,
    64, 132, 133, 165–166
ESOP Association (Canada), 196
ESOP Association (US), 195
Esop Centre (UK), 196
ESOPs (employee stock ownership plans)
    and company performance, 36–37,
        118–119
    conversions to, 122–124, 159–161
    early experiences, 104–107, 114–115
    feasibility factors, 102–104, 121–122
    government programs for, 163–166
    in impact funds, 133–137
    invention of, 98–101
    legal mechanisms, 96–97
    in private equity sales, 128–132
    taxation of, 161–162
    trends, 81–82, 102, 108, 112, 118, 177
    vs. trusts, 142–143, 151
    see also equity sharing
ESPPs (employee stock purchase
    plans), 91, 115–116, 162–163
European countries, 174–178, 181–187
European Federation of Employee
    Share Ownership, 174, 177
Evergreen Cooperatives, 136
executives
    accountability of, 35
    compensation, 27–28, 32–33, 34,
        122, 162
    incentives of, 26, 119–120
    and share price management, 28–30

F
Facebook (now Meta), 90
family-owned businesses, 14, 17–18,
    34, 72
Federal Reserve studies, 1, 2
feudal enterprises, 68
Fifty By Fifty, 196
financial engineering, 43–44
financial literacy training, 127
first-loss capital, 135–136
food and beverage companies, 15
Forman, Erik, 139, 153
Fortune, "100 Best Companies to Work
    For," 22
founders see entrepreneurs
401(k) retirement plans
    in ESOP companies, 86, 97, 115
    vs. ESOPs, 101
    trends, 47, 113–114
France, 175–176
franchise co-ops, 153
Fund for Employee Ownership, 136

G
GameStop, 32
Gao Shangquan, 172
Gardner Denver, 127
General Social Surveys, 85, 92, 112
Germany, 174
gig companies, 151, 152
gig workers, 71, 151–152, 192
Gillibrand, Kirsten, 92
Gleason Corporation, 126
going retail, 47
governments
    corporate aid, 163–164
    as economic stakeholders, 69
    and employee ownership, 107–108,
        191–193
    loan guarantee programs, 160–161
    overreach, 166
    procurement policies, 158, 164, 171

and reforms, 57
  see also legislation; political leaders
Grassley, Charles, 92
Gree Electric, 174

H

H-E-B, 13–14
Harley-Davidson, 128
Harry & David, 43, 44
Hawes, Colin, 173
healthcare companies, 39–40, 44
Healthcare of Ontario Pension Plan,
  134–135
HealthTrust, 107
Hemstreet, Molly, 155
Hertz, 43, 44
Hochberg, Yael V., 119
Hoover, Melissa, 154
Huawei Technologies, 173
Hungary, 186–187
Hypertherm, 88

I

Icahn, Carl, 27, 50
impact investing, 133–137
income inequality, 34, 117
incomes
  distribution, 62–63, 196
  wage earners vs. owners, 1–3, 98
Industrial Commons, The, 155, 177
Ingersoll Rand, 127
intellectual capital, 72
investments
  company ownership as, 19–21
  options, 16–17
  socially responsible, 57–62
  see also impact investing; private
    equity firms; stock market
investors
  activist, 27
  and business reforms, 57–62, 121
  in evolution of capitalism, 67–71

impact investors, 134–137
  as influencers, 190–191
  interests of, 3
  Small Business Investment
    Companies, 159–160
  see also private equity firms;
    shareholders; Stavros, Pete
IRA retirement funds, 47
Italy, 175–176, 177
Iverson, Ken, 209n1

J

JAB Holding Company, 15, 18
Jasper Holdings, 83
Jenkins, George, 21
Jiang Zemin, 171–172
job losses and layoffs, 46–47, 73–74,
  85–86, 119
John Lewis economy, 181
John Lewis Partnership, 140, 178,
  181–182
Johnson, Luke, 49
Johnson, Steven, 54
joint ventures, 132
Jones, Blake, 149, 150

K

Kachua Impact Fund, 150–151
Kelso, Louis O., 95, 97–100, 108, 109
Kelso & Company, 107
Kendeda Fund, 136
Kennett, Larry, 88
Kenya, 181
Kim, E. Han, 119
Kirton, Bill, 193
KKR, 125–126, 127–128, 137
knowledge workers, 70
Korean Securities Finance Corporation
  (KSFC), 179
Krafton, Inc., 179
Kruse, Douglas, 112, 118
Kurtulus, Fidan Ana, 118

L

labor markets, 70–71
   see also employees; gig workers;
     wage earners
Lancaster, Ohio, 50–51
layoffs and job losses, 73–74, 85–86, 119
Lazonick, William, 29
Legend Holdings, 174
legislation
   and business behavior, 55–57
   equity-sharing reform, 120–121
   ESOPs, 99–101, 112–113, 114–115
   of gig workers, 71
   procurement, 158, 171
leveraged buyouts (LBOs), 41
limited liability, 68
Lindsey, Laura, 119
liquidity events, 19
Litehouse Inc., 93–94
loans and loan guarantees, 159–161, 191
Long, Huey, 99
Long, Russell, 99–101, 108, 157
long-term enterprises (LTEs), 37, 123
long-term vs. short-term thinking,
   28–29, 31–32, 33–34, 36, 86–88
Lord, Peter, 183
Ludwiniak, Kris, 185–186
Lund, Margaret, 144
Lustig, Kurt, 134

M

Mackin, Christopher, 187
Main Street Employee Ownership Act
   (2018), 165
management and consulting fees, 44
Manos Home Care, 89
Mars, Inc., 18
Martin, Roger L., 23, 37, 122–124
McCarthy Building Companies, 79,
   81, 88
media companies, 15
media coverage of ESOPs, 104–106

memberships
   in co-ops, 145–146, 147–148, 150
   in ESOPs, 220n7
Meta (formerly Facebook), 90
Metis Construction, 142
mezzanine debt, 134, 159, 162
Michael, Chris, 143
Mondragon Corporation, 144,
   176–177, 178
Monomoy Capital Partners, 50
moral hazards, 212n11
Morawiecki, Mateusz Jakub, 185
mPharma, 169, 181

N

Namasté Solar, 149–150
National Defense Authorization
   Act, 158
National Steel Corporation, 105
NCEO (National Center for Employee
   Ownership), 114, 115, 116–117, 132,
   171, 195
Nelwamondo, Tendani, 180
network organizations, 155
nonprofits, 16, 155
Nuttall, Graeme, 141

O

"100 Best Companies to Work For"
   (*Fortune*), 22
Oneida Group, 50–51
O'Toole, James, *The Enlightened
   Capitalists*, 76
Ouimet, Paige, 119
outreach programs, 164–165, 192
ownership
   broadly shared, 3–4, 82–83
   and business reform, 63
   complex landscape of, 13–15
   and economic security, 1–3, 74
   models, 10, 16–17
   and risk, 72–74

and value creation, 71–72
see also employee ownership;
investors; private equity firms;
shareholders
Ownership America, 195
Ownership Works, 128

P

Paine, Lynn S., 61
Pan, Huifen, 172
partnerships, 16–17, 71
Pax World Fund, 58
Pearson, Michael J., 30–31
pension funds, 61–62, 121, 134–135
Pension Protection Act (2001), 114
Pérotin, Virginie, 176
Perri, Mike, 84
Peterson, Dick, 193
Pew Research, 4
Phillips, Kevin, 20
plan fiduciaries, 62
platform co-ops, 152–157, 192
Platform Cooperativism Consortium,
153–154
Poland, 185–186
Polis, Jared, 193
political leaders
on employee ownership, 91–93,
107–108, 170–171, 191–193
on regulation reforms, 56
Polyguard, 83, 84
Portman, Rob, 92
Powell, Peggy, 148–149
predistribution of wealth, 102
Prewitt, Nancy, 84
Primack, Dan, 45
principal-agent problem, 28
Prior, Kelly, 93–94
private companies
employee ownership of, 89–90
ESOPs in, 112–113, 114
interests of, 26

private equity firms
business model, 40–45
effects of, 46–47
and equity sharing, 190–191
in ESOP deals, 107, 128–132
interests of, 10, 49, 72, 104
investors in, 47
KKR model, 126–128, 131
trends, 21, 39–40, 48, 85
privatization, 122–124
procurement policies, 158, 164, 171
productivity vs. wages trends, 109–110
professional services, 71
profit-sharing plans, 175, 181
Project Equity, 145, 165, 195
public companies
characteristics, 36
employee stock ownership in,
90–91, 111–112, 113, 114–115
and ESOP decision, 103–104,
121–122
executives, 26–28, 119–120
privatization through ESOP, 122–124
Publix Super Markets, 14, 21–22
pump-and-dump scams, 32
Purdue Pharmaceuticals, 35

R

R. J. Reynolds, 126
Rath, Kevin, 89
Rath Packing Company, 104–105
Reagan, Ronald, 92
Recology, 1, 81
redistribution programs, 62–63
reforms
advocates, 37, 53, 108
ESOPs as, 102
through investor pressure, 57–60
through legislation, 55–57, 120–121
through ownership, 63
through redistribution, 62–63
see also ESG movement

Reich, Robert, 20
Republican Party, 92
retirement plans, 86, 97, 123
    see also 401(k) retirement plans
retirement security, 1–2, 83
risk
    and ESOP companies, 97
    and ownership, 72–74
Roark, Bill, 89
Rocky Mountain Employee Ownership
    Center, 164–165, 193
Romney, Mitt, 46
Rosen, Corey, 20, 100, 106, 184,
    185, 193
Russia, 183–184

S

S corporations, 161
Sackler family, 35
Salesforce, 61, 74
Samuelson, Paul, 109
Sanders, Bernie, 165
Sanders, Ed, 100, 193
Save as You Earn (UK), 182
SBICs (Small Business Investment
    Companies), 159–160
Scheiblehner, Matthias, 142
Scholz, Trebor, 153
Scot Forge, 83
secondary co-ops, 152
Securities and Exchange Commission
    (SEC), 166
Sen, Rik, 116
Seyle, Mike, 141
Shaheen, Jennifer, 158
Share Incentive Plan (UK), 182–183
shared capitalism, 92
shareholders
    dominant, 121–122
    in principal-agent problem, 28
    rights and interests, 10, 23–24,
        35, 72

shares
    price management of, 28–30, 32
    tradeability of, 16–17, 20, 36
    at WATG, 142–143
Sharpe, Jason, 150
Shell, Jon, 134, 135
Shopko, 44–45
short-term thinking see long-term vs.
    short-term thinking
Slovenia, 177
Small Business Administration (SBA), 165
Small Business Investment Companies
    (SBICs), 159–160
Social Capital Partners (SCP), 134–135
socialism, 63
Sokowatch, 181
South Africa, 179–180
South African Employee Ownership
    Association (SAEOA), 196
South Korea, 178–179
Southwest Airlines, 118
sovereign wealth funds, 187
Spain, 175–177
Sproxton, David, 183
SRC Holdings Corp (formerly
    Springfield ReManufacturing Center
    Corporation), 79
Stack, Jack, 80
stakeholder capitalism, 59, 59–60
Stanford, Leland, 111–112
Starbucks, 90, 116–117, 118
startup companies, 71, 73, 90, 146–147
    see also entrepreneurs
State Small Business Credit Initiative
    (SSBCI), 160
Stavros, Pete, 125–128, 131, 137, 165–166
Stewart, Donald, 100
stock
    buybacks, 29–30, 33–34
    in employee ownership models,
        89–91, 101–102, 111–114, 116–117,
        162–163, 169–170

as executive compensation, 27–28,
32–33, 119–120, 162
returns, 2
see also ESOPs (employee stock
ownership plans); ESPPs
(employee stock purchase
plans)
stock bonus plans, 99
stock market
as absentee ownership, 121
investors, 23–26
performance, 31
scams, 32
stock options, 90, 116–117, 118
Stocksy United, 152–153
Sun Capital Partners, 44–45
supermarket companies, 13–15
Surpin, Rick, 148–149
synergistic prices, 162
synthetic equity, 90
Szlembarski, Leo, 83

T

taking price, 31
taxes
and ESOP legislation, 100–101,
114–115, 131, 161–162, 191
and executive compensation, 162
as market mitigation, 36, 48, 56
and share price management, 28
trusts and worker co-ops vs.
ESOPs, 151
see also capital gains taxation
Taylor, Bob, 134
Taylor Guitars, 133–135
technology and job security, 98
technology companies, 33, 116–117
1042 rollover, 101, 193
textile industry, 155
The Drivers Cooperative, 153
The Industrial Commons, 155, 177
Tkaczyk, Christopher, 22

Tobin tax, 36
Today show, 106
TOMS, 75, 76
Ton, Zeynep, 122
Torch Technologies, 89
tradeable shares, 16–17, 20, 36
trucking industry, 105, 107
trusts, 96, 140–143, 151, 170–171,
181–182
Tuberville, Tommy, 158
2 and 20 method, 42
Tyson, Luther, 57

U

Uber, 152
Ulukaya, Hamdi, 90
unions
in buyouts, 104, 106
as employee ownership advocates,
196–197
influence of, 70, 110, 122, 173, 186
in worker co-ops, 149
United Airlines, 105–106
United Food and Commercial Workers
Union, 104
United Kingdom (UK), 140, 175,
181–183
United States (US) economy, 74, 108,
109–110, 196
US Federation of Worker Cooperatives,
91, 145

V

Valeant, 30–31
value (financial)
creation, 71–72, 152
in private equity ownership, 41–42
and strategic buyers, 130
synergies, 162
values (social), 149–150, 155
venture capitalists (VCs), 19
Voestalpine, 175

W

W. L. Gore & Associates, 81
wage concessions, 104–106, 107, 184
wage earners
    economic security of, 1–2, 109–110
    see also employees
wages trends, 2, 109–110
Wall Street
    business culture, 26–27, 31
    see also stock market
Wall Street Journal, 104, 106
Walmart, 21, 60
warrants, 131–132
Warren, Elizabeth, 56, 158
WATG, 141–142, 142–143
wealth
    distribution, 62–63, 102, 196
    inherited, 4
    ownership and, 2, 47, 63, 82–83

Web Industries, 84
Wegmans, 13
Weirton, West Virginia, 105
Wesray Capital Corp., 106
Wheeler-Flint, Rosanne, 84
WinCo Foods, 14, 83
worker co-ops
    characteristics, 17, 91, 145–148, 151
    in continental Europe, 175–177
    examples, 148–151
    funding and support for, 144–145,
        160, 192
workforces
    evolution of, 69, 109–110
    see also gig workers
workplace improvements, 126–127

Z

Zimbabwe, 181

ABOUT THE AUTHORS

 **Corey Rosen** is the founder and an active staff member of the National Center for Employee Ownership (NCEO), a nonprofit organization that is the nation's primary source of information on employee ownership. One of the world's leading experts on the subject, he has spoken with government leaders, business owners, employee groups, and academic leaders around the globe.

Corey started his career teaching political science at Ripon College in 1973, after earning his PhD from Cornell University. In 1975 he was awarded an American Political Science Association Congressional Fellowship and went to work for the Senate Small Business Committee, where he later became a full-time professional staff member. While there, he read about employee ownership and became involved in drafting successful legislation to encourage employee stock ownership plans (ESOPs). ESOPs seemed like that rare idea that could appeal to all political sides and link the self-interests of business owners to economic fairness.

As Corey learned more about the idea, he became convinced that it could help create a more equitable economy, one in which people could build a secure retirement while working for companies that valued their input and treated them with dignity and respect. But at that time few people had even heard of employee ownership, and even fewer knew whether it could work or, if it could, what made it work best. So he started the NCEO to conduct academic-level research on the subject and to provide reliable, objective information to the public, the business world, and legislators. Launched with no funds in a small room in his basement, the NCEO has grown to 17 staff members and has earned a worldwide reputation. It is funded almost entirely by the information services it provides.

Corey has written numerous books on employee ownership for the NCEO and for outside publishers, including *Equity: Why Employee Ownership Is Good for Business* (Harvard Business School Press, 2005), written with John Case and Martin Staubus. He previously served as a director at the Great Place to Work Institute (creators of the "100 Best Companies to Work for in America" list) and is currently on seven ESOP company boards. In 2009, he was awarded the Txemi Cantera International Social Economy Award, given annually in Spain. He lives with his wife and dogs in San Rafael, California.

The NCEO's website is *www.nceo.org*.

 **John Case** is a veteran observer and analyst of the business world and a nationally known writer on business and economics. He is author or coauthor of six previous books and collaborator on several others, and he has written for a wide variety of periodicals.

John's interest in alternative ownership structures goes back to the early days of his career, when he helped to found and edit a magazine called *Working Papers for a New Society*. Like most little magazines, that venture didn't last long—but John then found work covering the entrepreneurial revolution for *Inc.* magazine. During his 13 years at *Inc.* he wrote numerous feature stories on entrepreneurship and business management, including at employee-owned companies. He also developed and wrote a nationally syndicated weekly newspaper column entitled *The Inc. Report*, published for three years in the *Boston Globe* and elsewhere. His book *From the Ground Up: The Resurgence of American Entrepreneurship* was published by Simon & Schuster in 1992.

Later, John focused his work on the phenomenon of open-book management, writing extensively in *Inc.* and elsewhere, editing a newsletter, and publishing two books on the subject. From 1998 through 2000 he was executive editor at Harvard Business School Publishing and editor of *Harvard Management Update*, a subscription-only newsletter. He is coauthor, with Corey Rosen and Martin Staubus, of the book *Equity: Why Employee Ownership Is Good for Business* (Harvard Business School Press, 2005), and collaborator, with Karen Berman and Joe Knight, on the bestselling book *Financial Intelligence: A Manager's Guide to Knowing What the Numbers Really Mean* (Harvard Business Review Press, 2013).

In recent years John has contributed occasionally to *Inc.*, *Harvard Business Review*, the *New Republic*, and other magazines and has served as a consulting writer for a variety of clients, including Bain & Company, Southwest Airlines, the Business Literacy Institute, and Open-Book Coaching. He served a three-year term on the board of the NCEO, for which he developed the popular booklet *Employee Ownership: Building a Better American Economy*. In 2018 he launched the online publication *Employee-Owned America*, now part of the organization Ownership America.

Now mostly retired, John lives with his wife in Jamestown, Rhode Island.

Berrett–Koehler
Publishers

Berrett-Koehler is an independent publisher dedicated to an ambitious mission: *Connecting people and ideas to create a world that works for all.*

Our publications span many formats, including print, digital, audio, and video. We also offer online resources, training, and gatherings. And we will continue expanding our products and services to advance our mission.

We believe that the solutions to the world's problems will come from all of us, working at all levels: in our society, in our organizations, and in our own lives. Our publications and resources offer pathways to creating a more just, equitable, and sustainable society. They help people make their organizations more humane, democratic, diverse, and effective (and we don't think there's any contradiction there). And they guide people in creating positive change in their own lives and aligning their personal practices with their aspirations for a better world.

And we strive to practice what we preach through what we call "The BK Way." At the core of this approach is *stewardship,* a deep sense of responsibility to administer the company for the benefit of all of our stakeholder groups, including authors, customers, employees, investors, service providers, sales partners, and the communities and environment around us. Everything we do is built around stewardship and our other core values of *quality, partnership, inclusion,* and *sustainability.*

This is why Berrett-Koehler is the first book publishing company to be both a B Corporation (a rigorous certification) and a benefit corporation (a for-profit legal status), which together require us to adhere to the highest standards for corporate, social, and environmental performance. And it is why we have instituted many pioneering practices (which you can learn about at www.bkconnection.com), including the Berrett-Koehler Constitution, the Bill of Rights and Responsibilities for BK Authors, and our unique Author Days.

We are grateful to our readers, authors, and other friends who are supporting our mission. We ask you to share with us examples of how BK publications and resources are making a difference in your lives, organizations, and communities at www.bkconnection.com/impact.

Dear reader,

Thank you for picking up this book and welcome to the worldwide BK community! You're joining a special group of people who have come together to create positive change in their lives, organizations, and communities.

What's BK all about?

Our mission is to connect people and ideas to create a world that works for all.

Why? Our communities, organizations, and lives get bogged down by old paradigms of self-interest, exclusion, hierarchy, and privilege. But we believe that can change. That's why we seek the leading experts on these challenges—and share their actionable ideas with you.

A welcome gift

To help you get started, we'd like to offer you a **free copy** of one of our bestselling ebooks:

www.bkconnection.com/welcome

When you claim your **free ebook**, you'll also be subscribed to our blog.

Our freshest insights

Access the best new tools and ideas for leaders at all levels on our blog at ideas.bkconnection.com.

Sincerely,

Your friends at Berrett-Koehler

Certified

Corporation